"One of the greatest advantages of my professional career has been using Monty's teachings, thereby creating harmonious partnerships between my horses and myself. My love for horses came from within; my knowledge came through schools and universities; but my horsemanship was truly awakened during the four years I spent with Monty as his pupil."

—Satish Seemar
Trainer at Sheikh Mohammed bin Rashid Al Maktoum's
Zabeel Racing Stables, Dubai, UAE

"What intrigues me, whether I am watching Monty Roberts work or using his method of Join-Up myself, is that the horses are relaxed and happy when they leave the arena. There is trust and respect; there is no winner and no loser. Monty's methods leave the horse his dignity. These concepts cause happiness to reach your soul. We must help Monty leave the world better for horses and for people. This book shows the way."

—Brigitte von Rechenberg
DVM, University of Zurich,
Dipl. European College of Veterinary Surgeons

"I discovered the work of Monty Roberts in late 1988. I encouraged him to travel to England to demonstrate his concepts to Her Majesty, the Queen. I have observed his work for more than a decade now, and I view with pride my decision to assist in bringing his discoveries to the world. This book should be read by every person who appreciates the animal kingdom."

—Col. Sir John Miller
Crown Equerry to Her Majesty Queen Elizabeth II

"It was a great personal experience to observe Monty Roberts train a previously untouched wild horse to accept a saddle and rider in just two days."

—Richard E. Fagan
Wild Horse & Burro Program Manager
U.S. Bureau of Land Management

"I began to compete with Monty Roberts in the late 1940s. You could never count your money until Monty had finished competing. His junior years were jammed with championships. His time in the show ring as a professional was filled with some of the best horses in the world. We should all be grateful to Monty for the gift of From My Hands to Yours, because with it he gives us the heart and soul of his principles."

—Bobby Ingersoll
World Champion cow-horse, cutting horse and
snaffle-bit futurity winning trainer and competitor

To Liz

Monty

ALSO BY MONTY ROBERTS

The Man Who Listens to Horses

Shy Boy: The Horse That Came In from the Wild

Horse Sense for People

From My Hands to Yours

Lessons from a Lifetime of Training
Championship Horses

Monty Roberts

illustrations by Jean Abernethy

2002 / MONTY AND PAT ROBERTS, INC. / SOLVANG, CALIFORNIA

This book is designed to provide information on how to train horses using Monty Roberts' methodology, concepts and practices. It should be purchased with the understanding that at no time is the author responsible for the implementation of his concepts, methodology and practices. The hands that hold the reins are entirely responsible for the actions of the horse. Should readers not fully understand the implications of this book or be in a position to carry out these techniques, they should seek the advice of professionals.

The author urges the reader to watch videos and become familiar with the information available concerning the training of horses without pain and restraint. The author further advises that before you start to use these methods, you should attend a clinic or course to better understand the concepts.

Every effort has been made to make this manual as complete and accurate as possible. The author is not responsible for others' interpretation of the methods, or any ensuing results.

This book is intended to be educational. The author, Monty and Pat Roberts, Inc., and publishers shall have neither liability nor responsibility to any person, horse, or entity with respect to any loss or damage caused or alleged to have been caused directly, or indirectly, by the information contained in this book.

Drawings copyright © 2002 by Jean Abernethy

Flag Is Up Farms®, Monty Roberts®, Join-Up® and Dually™
are service marks, trademarks, and/or trade dress of Monty and Pat Roberts, Inc.

Book design and typography: Studio E Books,
Santa Barbara, CA   www.studio-e-books.com

Photos: Jean Abernethy, Ben Allen, Caroline Baldock, Laura Davis, Bus Jackson,
Jane Fallaw, Milne, Dennis Murphy, Frank Nolting, Michael Schwartz, Lavoy Shepherd,
Harpreet Singh, Lucille Stewart, Thaggis, Anna Twinney, Werbung Studio, Bremen, Germany,
Sasha Wöehler and Monty and Pat Roberts, Inc. archives.

Published by Monty and Pat Roberts, Inc.
Post Office Box 1700
Solvang, CA 93464

10 9 8 7 6 5 4 3 2 1
10 09 08 07 06 05 04 03 02

LIBRARY OF CONGRESS CATALOGING-IN-PUBLICATION DATA
Roberts, Monty, 1935–
  From my hands to yours : lessons from a lifetime of training championship
horses / Monty Roberts ; illustrations by Jean Abernethy.
    p. cm.
Includes bibliographical references (p.   ).
  ISBN 1-929256-56-6 (hardcover)
  1. Horses—Training. 2. Human-animal communication. I. Title.
  SF287 .R62 2002
                2002010931

I dedicate this book to Pat Roberts with love.
I do this mindful that, but not because, she has
put up with me for forty-six years. The fact that Pat
has been the mother to our children, foster children,
and my partner in business throughout our adult lives
is only incidental to the assistance that she has
been to me where this book is concerned.
Without Pat, it simply would not exist.

A VERY SPECIAL ACKNOWLEDGMENT

While it is true that this book would not exist if it
weren't for my wife, Pat, it is also true that there
probably wouldn't have been a reason
for the book if it hadn't been for
Her Majesty, Queen Elizabeth II of England.
The ongoing interest and support of
Her Majesty has opened doors for my
work that would otherwise never have
been opened in my lifetime.
I will be eternally grateful for
the generous recognition
of Her Majesty.

Acknowledgments

Jean Abernethy and Caroline Baldock are to be commended for their outstanding support and collaboration during the long process of writing this book. Jean worked tirelessly to make sure I had every diagram perfectly illustrated, enabling you to better understand the "Language of Equus" and use this knowledge for the benefit of your horses.

I wish to thank Caroline Robbins of Trafalgar Square Publishing for the final editing of *From My Hands to Yours*. It is with her assistance and excellent input that the book came alive and began to flow, so that you have, in the context, a better understanding of my concepts and experiences with horses.

Our daughter, Debbie, took time out of her busy life to read my manuscripts. I appreciate her husband, Tom Loucks, and my grandsons, Matthew and Adam, for sharing their mom during this time. Also, I would like to thank Mindy Gatchell for her assistance as well.

I owe Crawford Hall and Anna Twinney a great debt of gratitude. As a team, they work hard to teach the principles of Join-Up to the students who come from all over the world to study at my International Learning Center.

Without their capable assistance, I could not travel to demonstrate my work, which enables me to teach thousands of those who have the desire to learn but who cannot come to California. Jane Turnbull, my literary agent, thank you for your encouragement in all my endeavors.

My good friends and fellow horsemen, Dr. Robert Miller and Richard Shrake, I thank you for sharing your knowledge with me. You have my admiration and respect for what you have contributed to the benefit of all horses. Sheila Varian, I thank you for the opportunity to experience the greatest Arabian stock horse, Ronteza. I could never neglect acknowledging the horsemen from whom I have gained immensely from their shared experiences. Among them is my late friend Greg Ward, the late Jimmy Williams, and even the old master himself, Don Dodge. Thank you for your generosity. And to Sister Agnes Patricia, my humble thanks for the path you provided me with your insight.

M.R.

Contents

Preface

This book contains the heart of my training methodology. It is the book I have spent my life putting together in practice. I have started over 12,000 horses in my career. Each horse is an individual and each has for me significantly added to my knowledge. They have been my universities.

Writing about horsemanship is not easy. Many people who are interested in perfecting their horsemanship are uncomfortable with the process of reading, of absorbing the written word, thus learning horsemanship from a book is fraught with shortcomings. Most equestrians learn their horsemanship "hands on." They are observers of behavior and architects of harmony. Good students watch for a moment of perfection, retain it in memory and then seek to recreate it. Each horse reacts to man in a different way. Therefore, every Join-Up I do is unique. With these facts in mind, we must realize that there can never be one book that addresses, let alone solves, all problems.

Learning should be an ever-changing and never-ending process. To keep an open mind is essential. During the writing of this book, I discovered several procedures new to me that appear to have value while training horses. My students will often hear me offer the following quotation: "My way is the best way—for me today." I will go on to tell them, "If you show me a better way, it will be my way tomorrow."

Introduction

"A good horse trainer can get a horse to do what he wants him to do. A great trainer can get a horse to want to do it."

The concept of choice is the heart of my training system. Man should have the freedom to choose and so should the horse. The trainer who embraces these concepts will reap the rewards that come with exemplary communication. This is true whether it is with your horse or in human relationships. It is difficult to get it right with your horse until you get it right with yourself. If an attitude of partnership is employed, the potential for success increases. Only through willingness can true harmony be found, which should be the aim of every dedicated horseman.

People often say to me, "I've got a really stupid horse." Horses are not stupid. My answer is, "That is impossible! Horses have survived for approximately 50 million years and, if stupid, would surely have become extinct."

My aim is to give you, the reader, through the written word the essential elements of my work. It is my hope that through this effort I will bring a better understanding of man's communication with horses. My method does not rely on pain or restraint. I believe that a horse should never be forced to do anything. A horse using the freedom of choice becomes the centerpiece of my work and the result is optimal learning.

I communicate with a horse in what I call the "Language of Equus." It is a silent language and is predictable, discernible and effective. It is my intent to fully describe this language within the pages of this book. Through the channels of communication I can understand the horse and the horse comes to understand me. The elements of this language are really quite simple, but simplicity becomes its greatest strength.

"Join-Up" is the process of communicating with the horse to create an environment of cooperation. I will fully explore all of the elements of this procedure. I intend to break down the essential elements of Join-Up to educate you not only of its importance, but how to do it. The reader should fully understand that the execution of the principles of Join-Up is likely to produce a partnership with the horse, virtually eliminating the creation of remedial problems.

It is important for all horsemen to know that remedial problems are, in almost every instance, the product of training error. If I were to write the perfect book and every reader did a perfect job of executing the principles, there would be no need to discuss recommended procedures for dealing with remedial problems. It is a given that I will not write the perfect book and no reader will understandably work without mistakes. With that knowledge in mind, I will include on these pages practices that I have discovered to be effective in dealing with man-made problems.

Since the horse is a flight animal, he reacts and responds rather than initiates. This fact dictates that the presence of what we perceive as a remedial problem is caused by us and our shortcomings. If the horseman conducts his training each day with these facts clearly understood, it is likely that he will reduce the potential for creating negative behavior.

I give you my recommendations for dealing with remedial horses that display undesirable behavior such as bucking, biting, kicking, rearing, and much more. I will attempt always to educate you in the use of tactics that will produce results without violence. My goal is to create work that can be done safely and in comfort. I often tell my students that if they are unable to smile while working with a remedial horse, it is likely that they need to improve their methods.

As knowing horsemen, we need to understand that our equine students can only have two goals in life. One is to reproduce and the other is to survive. Equine negative behavior stems from fear and not from meanness. The horseman who understands this and acts appropriately is far more likely to succeed than is the trainer who acts harshly, misunderstanding his student.

I am a true supporter of the horse I am working with. I want my reader to become a strong fan of the species. I believe that it is virtually impossible for an adversary to teach its opponent anything. I have also decided to pass on to the reader elements of equine conformation. My life has been strongly linked to assessing equine conformation, and I feel it is an important factor in creating a successful career with horses (see Chapter 12).

While I have dealt with horses in many disciplines, I am certainly less than an expert in many activities that the horse industry embraces. I will try to provide you with information that will be appropriate for the widest possible number of disciplines. My life has been most actively led in the Western disciplines and in the world of Thoroughbred racing, but I have trained and competed in show jumping, polo, rodeo, Quarter Horse racing, and many gymkhana activities. I have dealt with mules and donkeys, along with horses, in packing and mountain riding, and also racing. Advice to the leisure rider has been a part of my career since the mid-forties, when I began to act as a riding instructor in my parents' operation.

In Chapter 1, Chapter 2 and at the end of Chapter 4, you will find a dictionary of the Language of Equus. It is illustrated to educate the reader in the signs and signals that I use to communicate with horses.

Greatest Strength

Break him, the tough guy said.

He's got to know who's boss.

Tie him up, pull him down, put some sense in his head.

He might get hurt, but that's the risk, it's only the horse's loss.

Is he mean, or simply filled with fear?

Tradition would say it doesn't matter.

Break his will to fight...you hear?

Or your body he will batter.

I've come to learn it isn't so,

This traditional belief.

Communicate, and let him know.

Violence will only get you grief.

Create a path, and watch him learn

To partner with *our* kind.

Be fair, and his trust you'll earn.

Be gentle, and a friend you'll find.

Training is not a battle that a man is obliged to win.

Learning should be looked upon as a way of having fun.

Leave your horse his dignity, and view him with a grin.

Now your horse will see it through, 'til every job is done.

The greatest strength a man can achieve

Is gentleness—I know.

Cause your horse in you to believe,

And your inner strength will grow.

Monty Roberts, 2002

From My Hands to Yours

Chapter 1

The Nature
of Equus

Survival of the Fittest

My concepts and training methods are all based on an understanding of the nature of equus. I have spent a lifetime studying horses in the wild, and also in domestic surroundings. Understanding the nature of the horse is primary to becoming a "trauma-free" trainer and to the use of Join-Up, the technique of starting horses that I explain in detail in Chapter 4. These ideas work because they are rooted in the natural instincts of the horse. To master these concepts and to achieve clear communication, man is required to learn the horse's language.

As with humans, the relationship between horse and man takes time to develop. As relationships are formed, it is critical to stay true to the instincts of equus. Horses are individuals. They have different personalities, abilities and levels of sensitivity, much like people do. With this in mind, you should realize that you cannot simply apply traditional methods to all horses. Until you learn to communicate in their language, you are not likely to effectively deal with their individual needs. When you do, I have found that horses will work as willingly with man as they do with one another.

There is a great deal of evidence that over the millennia horses have been much abused by people. Yet amazingly, they continue their efforts to be our partners. Now with the use of their own language, we can read their responses and establish a true working partnership.

Many people say to me, "It was not until I saw your work that I realized that I already use many of your methods." They speculate that their horses were their teachers. Some people who achieve high levels of success with horses are so in tune with them that they seem instinctual in using a reciprocal and understandable body language. I believe that it is likely that their awareness is so deep in the subconscious that they have no idea why they are so effective with horses. People who provide for their horse a comfort zone, leadership and

> *"I did not create my training concepts. I only discovered what nature already had in place."*
>
> —*Monty Roberts*

clear parameters within which the horse can operate at his optimal level, are likely to be effective trainers.

Prey–Predator and Flight–Fight

It is important to remember that the horse is a "prey" animal, his defense being to flee. Man is inherently predatory or "predatorial" as I say, using fight as a defense. Under pressure, these natural tendencies will come into play and man will force the horse as a first response, while the horse will only want to escape from danger. Aggressive acts by the horse, such as kicking and biting, most likely occur when he feels cornered and without any option to flee. This natural response to flee is the basis for my technique of Join-Up.

If you describe responses as "flight–fight," then the horse is at the flight end of the flight–fight spectrum. He is committed to survival and procreation; fighting is for him a last resort. Man, however, is at the fight end of the flight–fight spectrum. It is in man's nature to fight when faced with perceived opposition or resistance. If you think you are going to successfully fight with your horse over anything, you are making a terrible mistake. To work effectively with a horse, his true nature must be understood and the trainer must also retrain his own responses to match those of the horse. So often it is the thoughtless act from a human or the loss of patience that can push a horse metaphorically "over the edge" and cause him to move into survival mode. It is that thoughtlessness, that moment of panic or fear, which I am seeking to replace with knowledge, understanding and calm to create a more harmonious partnership.

1.1 The horse tries to outrun his predators.

1.2 The horse will only defend himself as a last resort.

Observing Wild Horses

It was my good fortune to experience circumstances that allowed me to work with mustangs. In 1948, I made my first trip to Nevada to help in the capture of horses to be brought to Salinas, California, for a wild horse race. During the search, gather and capture time, I began to witness communication between these horses seldom seen in the domestically raised animal. I suppose that their existence in the wilderness instills a deeper understanding of the need for safety within the family group.

The presence of predators seems to enhance the instincts of this flight animal. Horses have existed for 50 million years, primarily because of nature's gift of a focused sense of survival.

It was early in that work when I came to realize that the communication system of the horse was essentially a silent, nonverbal body language. It is a system of gestures much like signing

1.3 Every effort is made to rid himself of a predator.

for the deaf. That was a revelation for me, and I recall that for many months I tested and retested this premise. I continue to work today, attempting to understand more of the many gestures that are critical to the language of the horse. In the years that followed, I spent a lot of time with mustangs, and I believe it is fair to say that they were my best teachers. Frequent contact brought forth a greater understanding of their conversational skills.

Out there in the desert, with only a rough notion of what man could achieve, I caused a mustang to Join-Up with me. Within 24 hours or so, I had him following, thus achieving my first goal. Four or five hours later I could touch him, even put a halter on and eventually lead him.

It was during those sessions that my mind absorbed the realization that training through force for years was indeed an error in judgment. It became obvious that violence was not necessary and apparent that it was not nearly as effective.

By taking away the horse's choice, we threaten his survival. There is no more dangerous "button to press" than that one. My concepts do not "press any buttons" of the horse; after all the horse is capable of conscious thought and of influencing an outcome. These concepts provide a path through the natural

survival instincts to communication and trust, and a methodology allowing understanding of the nature of the horse and thus a route to success.

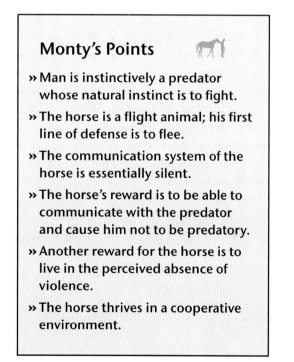

Monty's Points

» Man is instinctively a predator whose natural instinct is to fight.

» The horse is a flight animal; his first line of defense is to flee.

» The communication system of the horse is essentially silent.

» The horse's reward is to be able to communicate with the predator and cause him not to be predatory.

» Another reward for the horse is to live in the perceived absence of violence.

» The horse thrives in a cooperative environment.

Communication and Body Language

Body language is a primal form of communication, and together with basic sound signals, has guided animate life and protected it for millions of years. The horse owes his survival to his efficient communication system that is, as we have already discussed, almost entirely a language of gestures. This language provides the herd with a communication system that allows them to successfully cohabit with predators. Sounds are seldom used by horses, but when they are it is generally for determining location.

Thanks to the years I have spent watching and working with horses of all kinds, I have been able to put together as definitive a meaning as possible to these equine gestures. I have found a way to interpret their body language and to use my body to reply. What I have discovered, I have called the Language of Equus (see chapters 2 and 4). It is predictable, discernible and effective. This means that I can usually tell you before the horse expresses himself what he is about to do. It means that the casual observer can actually see an overt gesture. It is not mystical. It further identifies the language as one that effectively transfers and receives information.

The dictionary definition of communication is "an act or instance of transmitting information." Horses living in a herd have to communicate to survive. Domestic horses tend to be vociferous; however, in the wild it is important to be as silent as possible in order not to attract attention—not to attract predators.

When brought into domestic environments, I have seen mustangs panic at the sound of domestic horses whinnying. I have seen them run to the corner of their enclosure, huddle tightly together and lower their heads to about knee level. I believe they are concerned that the domestic horses will alert the predators, which the mustangs believe are certain to arrive. I have experimented by removing all but one mustang from the enclosure, noting that the remaining individual will fail to call to his removed friends. This simply does not happen with domestic horses.

Domestic horses use sound mainly to signal where they are and to be sure that they have a location on their friends. Horses will learn how to react to certain human sounds like "whoa" and "trot," but this is habituation rather than communication.

Surprisingly, the human communicates using as much as 80 percent body language. Although we base many of our communication systems on the spoken word, body language is the most powerful conveyor of our emotions and intent. Certainly intonation, volume and demeanor of the speaker are virtually as important as the words he utters.

Horses' highly developed sense of smell and eyesight play an important part in their communication and, therefore, their survival. There in the desert, I could watch this communication and the sophisticated social structure it created. I came to realize that if I could learn to use my body, gestures and posture effectively, I also could communicate with them and they would accept me into their society. My communication with the horse is just like "signing" with the deaf; it is a body language.

Horses' social order gives the herd organization to the lead mare. The alpha mare is the power with which to reckon. If a young horse misbehaves, then he may be punished by the matriarch, who, with the use of her language, sends him out of the herd where his survival may be questionable. The isolated horse is at risk. The matriarch, with a different set of gestures, will invite the offender back into the herd only after an appropriate sentence has been served. The elderly or infirm horse, unable to sustain the pace of the family, is consequently isolated and soon harvested by

Eyes on eyes and shoulders square sends the adolescent away.

Ears on:
"I am paying you respect."

SIDE VIEW

Head down:
"Should you like to discuss this, I will let you be the chairman of the meeting."

Licking and chewing. A foal will snap its mouth open and shut, a gesture of submission.

1.4 Equine gestures.

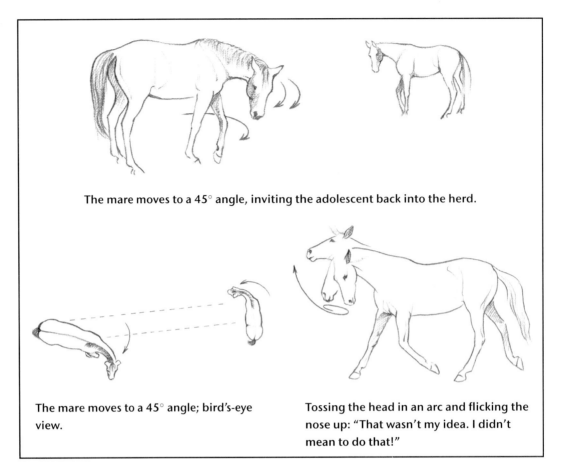

The mare moves to a 45° angle, inviting the adolescent back into the herd.

The mare moves to a 45° angle; bird's-eye view.

Tossing the head in an arc and flicking the nose up: "That wasn't my idea. I didn't mean to do that!"

1.5 Equine gestures (continued).

predators. The horse knows that isolation is not a healthy state in which to remain. (See figures 1.4 and 1.5 for an overview of some equine gestures.)

During Join-Up, when I send the horse away from me in the round pen, I am saying, "I am giving you an opportunity to choose for yourself. Flee, if that is what you feel is best for you." I want the horse to be free to choose his own course, because in that state of mind learning will occur. I patiently wait for the requested gestures of renegotiation. When the horse exercises his option to come to me rather than to go away, I welcome him as strongly as I can in the Language of Equus. I reinforce his choice so that we can work together in har-mony. It is my hope that we can go forward from that point in the certain knowledge that we mean no harm to one another.

The Leadership Void

As the horse is a herd animal, he also relies on good leadership for survival. As I touched on earlier, the alpha mare is essentially in charge of the social order of the family group. She makes the rules, keeping the other mares in line and disciplining the adolescents. She also decides the direction of travel, where to eat, sleep and drink, and is therefore the number-one decision-maker in the family. If you assumed that the breeding stallion was in charge of the daily family decisions, you are mistaken.

I realize that Hollywood has done much to engender that premise. It simply is not a fact. The leading male is in charge of causing pregnancies and keeping other males from stealing his mares. There is little else on which he makes decisions.

When the wild horses take flight, they remain mindful of the power of the family group. They will do their level best not to fractionalize. If some are separated off, they will go to work at once to return to the main group. While wild horses are flight animals, they are first herd animals and they survive in great part because they follow a social order.

Leadership is critically important in the family structure. Each individual has his own purpose and place. As we begin to influence the behavior of our horses by training, it is obligatory for us to become leaders. It is important that each horse we work with looks to us for direction and advice when taking on a challenge. I do not mean to imply that this should be dictatorial. I much prefer to think of it as a partnership in which the horse volunteers to engage with us for a purpose. When we fail to provide leadership, we send mixed messages to the horse that are apt to encourage negative behavior. It is true that many remedial horse problems happen because of the infliction of pain and the assertion of dominance, but about as many problems occur because of the lack of leadership.

Let me give you an example of how important leadership becomes when we domesticate a horse. Someone is leading a healthy, two-year-old Thoroughbred colt across an open barnyard. The colt is well fed and feeling quite good. He has pent-up energy from a night in a box stall and decides to dash sideways away from his handler, then rear and strike out with his front feet. Should the handler allow this behavior to continue, it is very likely that there will be an escalation of this activity. It is also quite likely the horse will get loose, dragging a lead and running dangerously. Injuries can occur to the horse while he is running loose. Many people have been hurt and even killed attempting to catch loose horses in similar circumstances. This sort of behavior can become a habit.

We, as "behavior-shaping" horsemen, must work to become competent at creating partnerships with our horses. These are agreements, so to speak, that reward acceptable behavior and establish parameters of discipline for unacceptable behavior. We must be quick to assess the situation and to hold to the guidelines of these partnerships. The handler of the horse in the scenario I have created must immediately take charge and school the horse quickly before the obstreperous behavior gets worse. There is no room for the shrinking-violet mentality when dealing with a horse, and particularly a two-year-old colt. Our human in this scenario should have been properly equipped to control the horse quickly, and should possess the knowledge and ability to accomplish it or not assume the task of handling such an animal.

Horses will tend to communicate their life's experiences. It becomes our responsibility to learn their language and work at observing their gestures. Horses have a strong propensity to reflect previous treatment. The remedial horses I work with will virtually always demonstrate the nature of the abuse they have suffered, which is not always the same story I hear from their owners or handlers. When a horse throws his head up at any sign of a hand approaching, there is every reason to believe that he has been hit around the head. Equally, if pain has been administered on his body, he will seek to protect himself by wincing and jumping away. The environment where abuse is committed is often logged in the horse's brain. A particular situation may remind a horse of an instance of abuse. The horse may be fine out in the field, but put in a box stall, reminding him of a situation in which he was beaten, he may become at once traumatized and defensive. Great care must be taken in dealing with this type of horse. He may be dangerous although he does not want to be.

A round enclosure is an excellent place to observe a horse, how he interacts with us and how he is affected by our movements. It is crucial to be aware of his extreme sensitivity to movement. Sharp, jerky movements are effective in sending the horse away from you. Looking a horse in the eye when you want to catch him will simply tell him to go away, so do not be surprised when he turns away from you. A horse is highly sensitive to your eye movements. I can slow a horse down from a canter to a walk in the round pen simply by moving my eyes along his neck to his hindquarters (see p. 90). He is not likely to respond to my smile or a frown because these facial expressions are outside the Language of Equus.

If you want a horse to be comfortable around you, move smoothly. You should move as if in heavy oil. These subtleties are easier to learn through experience than they are to describe with the written word. "Intuition tells us, and research confirms, that nonverbal communication is a major force in our lives. In fact, it has been estimated that nearly two-thirds of the meaning in any social situation is derived from nonverbal cues" (Birdwhistell, 1955. Judee K. Burgoon, David B. Buller and W. Gill Woodall, *Nonverbal Communication, The Unspoken Dialogue*. McGraw-Hill, 1996).

Monty's Points

» Body language is a form of communication.

» Horses owe their survival to this silent form of communication.

» A horse's language is predictable, discernible and effective.

» Domestic horses tend to be vociferous.

» Mustangs may panic when they hear domestic horses whinnying, thinking the noise may attract predators.

» Humans use as much as 80 percent body language in communicating.

» The alpha mare brings order to the herd.

» Leadership from the horseman is important.

» Prompt response is critical.

» Proper equipment is essential.

» Mistakes can be dangerous.

» Education is all-important.

» Success is more about knowledge than muscle.

» Horses tend to communicate their life's experiences.

» A round enclosure is an excellent place to observe horses.

Chapter 2

The Language
of the Horse

The Language of Equus

I have identified over 170 gestures of communication between human and horse. As I said earlier, while horses do make sounds, they are not central to their language. As prey animals, there is the need to communicate silently. The natural survival-of-the-fittest facets built into equus over millions of years dictate that the silent horse is far more likely to evade the predator than the noisy one. Carnivores have very little reason to fear negative consequences from the sounds they make; big cats are often quite vocal.

Deer are normally nearly mute. Deer, antelope and almost all of the grazers find it to be quite important to remain stealthy, both from a visual and audible point of view. Yes, we may hear a stallion teasing a mare with guttural sounds, and we experience the odd lost foal whinnying in an attempt to discover his mother's whereabouts. However, my work has taught me that sounds mean very little in the general scheme of the horse's communication.

Sound is, however, important for many animals. When the meadow lark sings, the sound is most likely an identification ritual and not communication. Sea mammals primarily rely on sending out vibrations that can be recognized, traveling surprising distances in the ocean.

Humans have a multidimensional brain that works on many levels. The greater the complexities, the greater the need for a precise language. By comparison, the one-cell amoebas need only reproduce. Animal behaviorists have now discovered that the great apes, orangutans and chimpanzees do not communicate primarily by sound. They make sounds to identify themselves like the birds and the mare and foal, but their main discourse is through gestures.

There are two factors that make communication with humans more complex than between or with animals. Ego and greed. Ego and greed cloud perfect interaction, introducing a potential hidden agenda that horses simply do not have. The human communication system can be hugely distorted by these factors, and what is a simple request may have an undisclosed purpose.

As I have mentioned earlier, for the horse, the only purposes for a language are survival and procreation. A horse only has these two goals in life. He needs to know what is safe and what is not. He needs to know who you are and your intent.

Horses know that humans are predators. People say that I act like the alpha mare. No horse has ever thought that I was the lead mare! They know that I have two arms, two legs, and that I eat meat. Millions of years has taught them how to handle that kind of animal. They are obliged to use those instincts. Horses know that as a predator I have the potential to attack them. An untrained horse may, when I approach him—arms out, eyes on eyes, shoulders square—read my gestures and body language as predatory and stop what he is doing, pay attention and then probably flee.

In the Language of Equus, gestures and body language work together and in synchronization. They must flow to be meaningful. It is critical to remember that your body is communicating whether you realize it or not. It is your obligation to decide how the horse perceives your gestures. Develop a sensitivity to each move you make, each gesture, each flick of your eyes. The horse is watching you.

Gestures are central to the communication of the horse. Many of these gestures are known and have been easily recognized for centuries. Even from a mile or so away, horsemen will recognize the sight of a stallion circling his herd, his tail held high, and his neck arched and animated. His ears are forward as he trots with a high step in his gait. This is unquestionably the alpha male expressing his control of his harem. Later that day, we might see this horse walking the circumference of his family group, occasionally looking outward and pinning his ears flat to his neck. Because ears flat back denote anger and/or aggression, horsemen will at once realize that there is probably another male somewhere out there and he is not happy about it.

Should the intruder make his way closer to the harem, we might witness a gesture not often seen in our daily horse world. It is one that would appear menacing to most observers. Generally confined to a stallion, and virtually

always a threatened stallion, he might well flatten his ears to his neck, lower his head to within six or eight inches of the ground, stretch his neck to its fullest length and point his nose directly toward his adversary. He will then often march with knees slightly bent to lower his forequarters, resembling a large cat stalking its prey. The invader will at once recognize this to be the ultimate admonition to leave at once. (See figure 2.2.)

A mare will use a muted version of this gesture to banish an obstreperous adolescent from the herd. However, when I have seen this, I never felt the same cold chills travel my spine as I did when I witnessed a stallion displaying this gesture.

A pair of forward ears shows interest in something in front of the horse. Forward ears with the head high denote interest in something ahead and at a distance. Forward ears with the head held low might mean an interest in something up close and near the ground.

The head held in a normal position with a "split ear"—one forward and one back—shows an interest in something in front, while at the same time a concern about something slightly to the rear. The ears are, without question, a window to the interest of a horse. Their ears go where the eyes go, and vice-versa (fig. 2.3).

If you are well away from a family group of horses in the wild and viewing them through binoculars, you can often gain insight into their communication patterns. If you can observe horses who are unaware of your presence, you might find them to have their ears hanging low, pointing east and west, that is, each ear pointing outward from the horse's head. This horse is probably at rest, and relatively confident that there is no danger close by. One can usually note that the lips of this horse will most often be relaxed and hanging away from the teeth. It is not uncommon to find this horse resting one hind leg. When all three of these gestures are present simulta-

RESPONSE		ACTION
Go away a lot (flee).		Walking forward, eyes on eyes, shoulders square, fingers open, arms out.
Ear locked on: "I'm paying you respect."		Asking for conversation: arms out, eyes on eyes, fingers open; keeping the pressure on.
Making the circle smaller: "I feel safe close to you."		Arms out, eyes on eyes, throwing the line. Keep the pressure on to complete the conversation.
Licking and chewing.		Arms out, eyes on eyes, walking forward, throwing line. "I am asking for more conversation."
Dropping the head: "I'll let you be the chairman of the meeting."		Bring arm down and across the body; eyes still on the horse's eyes. You may slow down.
The horse considers his options: "Should I join his herd? Is he a worthy leader?"		Going passive, eyes down, shoulder at 45°: "Would you like to come in and Join-Up with me?"
"It feels good to be near you. You seem safe."		"You are welcome to Join-Up with me."
"I can't see where you're touching me; I guess I'll trust you."		"Thank you" (reward).

2.1 A dialog in Equus.

neously, the horse is unquestionably confident that he is safe.

If you scan the surroundings at this point, you are not likely to find remarkable circumstances. It would not be normal to see movement anywhere on the landscape. It is probable that the entire surrounding environment will be tranquil. However, it is also probable that you will find one horse standing as a look-out generally in an elevated area. This animal will have ears and eyes that are scanning the surroundings, and a neck and head that are upright and mobile. Horses rely heavily on sound, but the olfactory system of this guard horse will also be hard at work picking up any smells emanating from a potentially dangerous predator. With eyes constantly at work, the guard horse will seldom remain static very long. To witness the guard horse resting a leg or relaxing the lips would be rare indeed.

As you view the family group, you may see tails moving on horses that seem to be otherwise relaxed and content. The tail that waves slowly to brush the side of the horse is likely to be no more than a fly deterrent. The same phenomenon, however, that lazily moves the tail to clear the flies away is hooked to the brain to

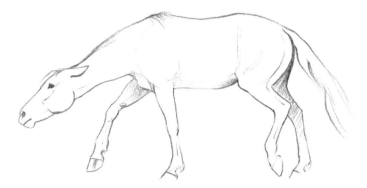

2.2 A stallion "snaking," a gesture that means "Go away now."

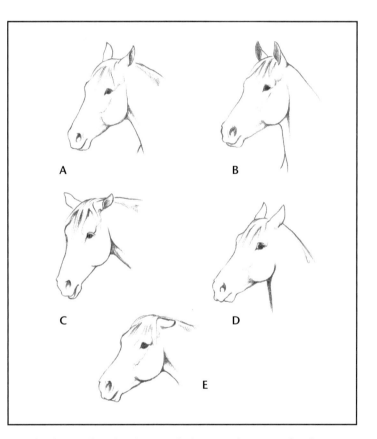

2.3 (A) A horse showing interest in front and concern for the rear. (B) A horse with forward ears shows interest in something front, and at a distance. (C) A horse relaxed and at rest. (D) Ears back shows interest in something behind the horse. (E) Ears back and flat displays anger and/or aggression.

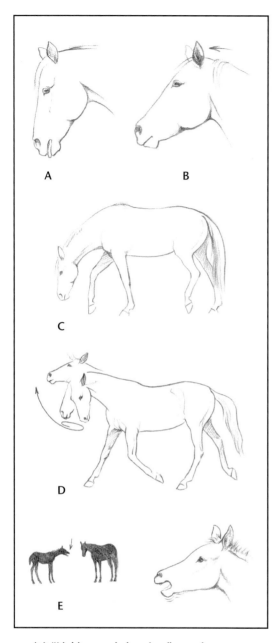

2.4 (A) "Licking and chewing" can show contentment. (B) Ear locked on means the horse is listening to the object the ear is pointing toward. (C) Head down: "I'll let you be the chairman of the meeting." (D) A head toss sometimes means "I didn't mean to do that." (E) "Snapping" in a young horse means "I respect you, so don't harm me."

show discontent or aggravation. This tail movement is of interest to us as horsemen because a boot heel or a spur in the side will often evoke a tail switch. If this occurs during a time of physical exercise, it is usually conveying an attitude of aggravation. Most trainers would consider a "switch-tail" horse to be less than desirable because the tail movements imply that the horse is not happy with requests from a rider.

I have been surprised since the publication of my first book to find out that many good trainers have long understood that "licking and chewing" is a gesture of contentment, and an expression of being agreeable. "Licking and chewing" is one of the four gestures I identify in Join-Up. When I first discovered it, I thought that it was something relatively unknown to the rest of the world of horsemanship. In fact, I have found that 10 to 15 percent of the top trainers with whom I am acquainted were aware of this phenomenon. It is true, however, that very few have ever mentioned it in writings.

Advance and Retreat—Eyes on Eyes

As said before, the horse only has two goals in life, to reproduce and to survive. All his responses are controlled by one of these factors. In order for the horse to survive in the wild, it is essential that he has an understanding of the language of the predators. It is not unusual to see prey and predator drinking from the same water hole. With an understanding of each other's body language, they can communicate and, therefore, there are large periods of time when they coexist harmoniously.

I cannot impress enough upon the student of my work the importance of eye contact. The predator identifies its victim before the chase commences and it does this by first establishing eye contact. During the process of Join-Up and at all other times when dealing with the horse, it is imperative to be aware of where you and the horse are looking. First, you should learn to control eye focus. In order for the gesture to be effective, it must be constant. The eyes of a horseman, like those of an artist, are tools indeed. Our eyes convey our intent, emotion, determination, frustration, and failure. Eyes also convey ambivalence, commitment, fear and trust. Horses see what you are saying with your eyes and respond appropriately. Eyes, accordingly, can be softly focused and gentle, or focused and piercing. You must know not only what they are looking at, but why and how they are looking.

"Eyes on eyes" should immediately put the prey animal on notice that his life is in danger. The horse will virtually always recognize this gesture and begin to make appropriate maneuvers. The determined predator will advance— eyes on eyes, shoulders square and taut muscles—displaying the intent to attack. This should initiate a full-flight response from the horse, who has as his flight distance between a quarter and three-eighths of a mile. This alert and healthy horse will, after that distance, curve his flight path to observe. The horse is fully aware that if he continues to exert extreme effort to run in a straight line for an excessive distance, he is apt to place his life in jeopardy through exhaustion. A subsequent predator could easily make a meal out of the significantly stressed flight animal. In addition, it is critical to conserve energy and not to run mindlessly into the jaws of another predator.

2.5 A predator identifies his victim before the chase commences by establishing eye contact.

2.6 Eyes on eyes: the lion's piercing gaze is locked on his prey.

2.7 The horse flees in an attempt to outrun the predator.

As a human being wanting to communicate with a horse, you can use these concepts to reason with a horse and eventually cause a partnership to result. Consider the scenario of the young man in high school who spots an attractive female classmate. He follows her around for days, offering to carry her books, and waits for her after school. He is obviously infatuated and asks if he may walk her home. After about a month or so, if she shows no interest in him and rebuffs his attempts to be friendly, he might finally give up. She will quickly notice that he's not there and find herself looking for him without realizing why. The young woman suddenly concludes that she subconsciously approved of the attention. Missing his presence, she will begin to advance toward him as he is now retreating from her. I call this the "advance-and-retreat" stage of this phenomenon. He advances and she retreats; he retreats and she advances. This is also what horses do. This is their nature and to a degree, ours, too. It is odd that as brilliant human beings we have not come to understand this phenomenon better, as it would help us in our daily lives.

In the early stages of executing Join-Up, I identify myself to the horse as a predator. Then, as the horse realizes that nothing painful has happened, he begins to reassess the situation. Using his acquired senses, he understands that I could be a useful friend, certainly not predator. Advance and retreat is the process I use to establish our conversation, that if put into words, would sound something like this:

"Don't go away a little, go away a lot. Consider your options. Come and Join-Up with me and I will protect you, or stay out there on your own. But you can trust me. There is an environment near to me and it is perfectly safe."

2.8 After a distance between a quarter and three-eighths of a mile, the horse will turn to observe his predator.

By rubbing the horse on the forehead when he comes in to Join-Up, I am going into an area he cannot see. As I take my hand away, I am confirming to the horse that my intention is friendly. I am not a predator, as was first perceived. I am rewarding the horse in the way the horse understands. I am not causing him pain. Therefore, I earn his trust.

Several factors should be outlined before you launch into the "dictionary" of the Language of Equus in this section and at the end of Chapter 4. I intend to define only the portion of the language of the horse that pertains to interspecies language exchange. Since survival is the only available area of communication, this significantly limits the size of the dictionary.

As you become familiar with the parameters by which you can communicate with horses, be clearly aware that they do not share our concerns for the mundane things in life that seem to preoccupy people, such as what we will eat tonight, the stock market, or the latest style of hair. As discussed earlier, their language with humans is limited to an intense desire to survive.

I am confident that I possess as much knowledge of the Language of Equus as the

Wright Brothers did about the science of manned flight, but it is my belief that I am but scratching the surface of this phenomenon and that within a few decades it will progress significantly.

Equine Vision

It is very important for the student of my methods to know about the primary elements of the horse's vision. The eyesight of the horse and the information the horse receives through his eyes are directly connected to the knowledge of his language and responses to his environment. Much of the language of the horse is learned; it is not all instinctual.

I received two horses at Flag Is Up Farms to be started. One was born, and still is, completely deaf; the other was born blind. The blind horse was rescued and subsequently had eye surgery to remove cataracts. From that time on, he had limited vision, the depth and range of which were difficult for us to judge. The deaf horse responded to Join-Up in an average time, reading all the signs and responding to me normally. The blind horse had very little information about his own natural language and was unable to understand what my gestures meant, having spent the early part of his life blind.

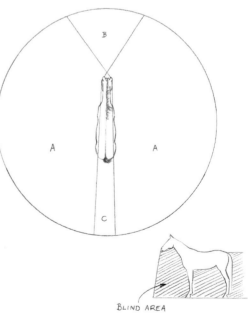

2.9 Equine field of vision: (A) 285° monocular vision; (B) 65° binocular vision; (C) 10° blind.

Chapter 2 / The Language of the Horse

Because of this experiment, I had proof that not only is their language silent, but it is mostly learned. First, the experiment showed that the natural language of the horse is silent. Second, it proved that very little of it is instinctual, as most is passed on, mare to foal, and between herd members.

Man and other predators have forward vision with their eyes set on the front of the head with a restricted arc of vision, but binocular. The horse's eyes are among the largest of any land mammal and because they protrude from the side of the face, they have a very wide field of vision, 350 degrees. About 65 degrees of the 350-degree field of vision are binocular and the remaining degrees are monocular, so there is no depth of focus in approximately 285 degrees of their vision. A shadow could be a hole in the ground which accounts for horses often jumping over shadows.

The structure of the eye gives the horse about 50 percent magnification. Where we see a small plastic bag in the hedge, the horse sees a massive white object, which is moving and possibly dangerous. As I have mentioned, the horse has developed an instinctual reaction to danger, which is to flee. Only when he senses he is at a safe distance will he then take a second look, reassessing the situation. This is why it is so

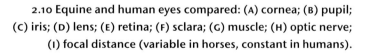

2.10 Equine and human eyes compared: (A) cornea; (B) pupil; (C) iris; (D) lens; (E) retina; (F) sclara; (G) muscle; (H) optic nerve; (I) focal distance (variable in horses, constant in humans).

important not to get angry with a horse when he responds adversely to something we perceive as harmless and small.

2.11 Equine blind spots.

Each eye of the horse individually records information which does not necessarily translate to the other brain hemisphere. Unlike the human, the horse has a limited ability to cross-reference information taken in through each eye. This is why a horse accustomed to being mounted on the nearside may take fright when mounted on the offside. Correct handling of a horse should consider this aspect of his physiology. A horse handled more on the nearside will often be less desensitized on the offside.

Scientists maintain that the horse does have two narrow blind spots. One is immediately behind him in an arc of about 5 degrees, and the other is on the forehead and up to 6 feet (approx. 2 meters) in front of him and beneath his nose. If the horse is attacked from behind, he can defend that approach with his hind feet. Therefore, caution should always be taken when approaching a horse from behind, as it is possible you will be viewed as an intruder into an area difficult for the horse to fully assess.

The flight animal's eyesight is highly evolved to identify moving objects. Obviously, this is linked to survival. He will often be alarmed by shapes or moving objects for which he has no previous reference. Even static objects can cause alarm if seen to resemble a predator. When working around a horse, I always attempt to move smoothly and with consistent speed so as not to be associated with the aggressive movements of a predator.

Night Vision

A horses' night vision is better than a human's. This is primarily because the eye is almost entirely cornea. No light goes through the white of the eye. The horse has very little white and sometimes exhibits none at all. The pupil is set horizontally going from one side of the eye to the other. There is also a membrane at the back of the eye, the tapetum lucidum, which reflects light and the image back through the eye creating more light absorption. This has the effect of magnifying the amount of light on the retina. Because of a horizontal pupil and a large cornea, the horse has the advantage of having more light to work with for identification in the dark. It is important to remember that when riding in the dark, the approaching bright lights of a car are magnified in the horse's vision, which can cause considerable confusion to the horse.

Focus

A horse does not focus as we do by contracting and dilating the pupil. His eyeball is not circular. When light enters through the pupil and falls on the upper part of the retina, it allows him to focus close up. When it falls on the lower part of the retina, he can focus at a distance. This is why a horse moves his head, raising it to see far, and lowering it to make out objects nearby. He does not have the advantage of sharp focus that we do, which may explain the hesitation when faced with some object similar to one he is familiar with, yet not easily identifiable.

It is often helpful to allow a horse to lower his nose to an object on the ground to examine it in detail. When a horse approaches a jump, he may slightly raise his head to focus on the obstacle. As he approaches takeoff, he loses sight of the jump and has to rely on his memory to judge his distance. He may at this point try to lower his head to refocus on the obstacle. A ground line (a jump pole placed on the ground several feet in front of the jump) is very helpful, giving the horse an indication of where he should take off. Certain types of jumps will create more problems than others and this is where repetition is so important in the training process.

The horse needs time to gather information about the object he is looking at. He needs to assimilate the information and be allowed to go on at his own pace. Once he has learned that the object is safe, a shying episode is less likely to occur than without sufficient time to assess.

The quality of vision evolved by different animals is directly related to their need to survive. As a flight animal, the horse has vision that has evolved to assess danger in both good and poor light, protect body mass, and identify food and predators.

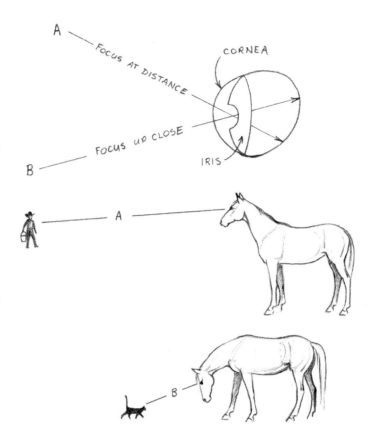

2.12 Equine vision, showing the focus functions of the horse.

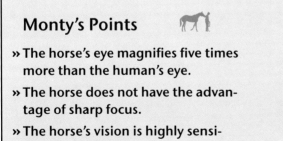

Monty's Points

» The horse's eye magnifies five times more than the human's eye.

» The horse does not have the advantage of sharp focus.

» The horse's vision is highly sensitive to movement.

» The horse uses his eyes first; smell is secondary.

» The horse is monocular in 285° of his vision.

» Memory connected to vision is not automatically transferred from one side of the brain to the other.

» To focus, the horse has to move his head.

The Intuitive Horse

In 1942, at the age of seven, I had a personal experience that brought a phenomenon to light that I believe was relatively unheard of before my time. I had a raw horse come to me and trust me to put on his first saddle. The adults around me were frightened by this event and seemed certain that I was flirting with disaster. I do not recommend that children experiment with raw horses, but it seems to me quite clear at this point in my career that horses can read the agenda of human beings far more clearly than most of us ever thought possible. It is likely, if you have been connected to the horse business for any length of time, you have had a story relayed to you where a child could successfully work with a horse where adults had failed.

It seems plausible to me that the horse can identify members of the human species who have no agenda to harm. In recent years I have been closely connected with therapeutic riding and I am constantly amazed at how horses respond to physically challenged children and adults. Recently, I was at a therapeutic riding facility where I met a man in his fifties who contracted Parkinson's disease and was seriously disabled at the time of our meeting. He was a full-sized adult who had been a school teacher whose mind was fully functional. The horses seemed to read that he was in trouble physically; they appeared to be attracted to and protective of him.

Equally interesting is that the predators of the world are inclined to act out violently toward the weak or disabled. I believe nature must be working to rid the environment of the weak and dysfunctional, acting exactly opposite to flight animals. The predator will often turn on individuals that he judges to be easy prey. There are examples of lions and bears turning on disabled trainers. One virtually never hears of flight animals attacking helpless humans.

We humans, being of the fight mode, have been known to take advantage of disabled members of our own species. It is not unheard of for counselors of abused children to ultimately take advantage and further abuse them. I have referred to rape victims as "stunned fish," recognizing that the male human predator will often re-victimize these vulnerable people. The stunned bait fish tossed into a school of millions of its own kind will give off the vibrations of vulnerability that are likely to attract the intended predator fish who selects them over the healthy ones. I believe that it is likely that horses have adopted or attempted to adopt vulnerable human beings. These facts might explain why horses seem quite comfortable around physically challenged people and able to respond to their needs, carrying them with a surprising awareness of this responsibility.

As we further examine the ability of the horse to detect the agendas of the human species, let us investigate another in the list of human ailments that seems to connect us somehow with the horse, a flight animal.

Autism

In the United States autism affects over 400,000 people. It occurs in approximately one in 500 births and five boys to every girl. It is the third most common developmental disability, following mental retardation and cerebral palsy. Shortly after my first book was published, I began to receive comments from the parents and caretakers of autistic children. One after another they seemed to echo the same message. They told me that my theories about communicating with horses had a very close relationship to the messages conveyed to the medical community by autistic people studying this problem. They made me aware that autistic people are often very much like flight animals. They are seldom sure that people with autism can fit into the society around them. Autistic people are often nonverbal and strong creatures of habit, prone to repetitive behavior that brings them solace.

Autistic people comforted by a world that revolves around routine and repetition often become distracted by minute details, yet are unable to focus on life's necessities. Like the flight animal, they dislike eye contact and find difficultly in approaching face-on, tending to come close only when outside a person's direct vision.

The horse is a visual thinker, responding only in the present to images the brain receives. Most nonverbal autistic people follow that pattern far more closely than humans with normal verbal capabilities. Therefore it is hardly surprising that horses are at ease with autistic people despite their sometimes bizarre behavior. I too think in pictures and this may be one of the reasons that I am so comfortable around horses.

The fact that autistic people are often nonverbal does not necessarily mean that they cannot communicate. I believe that they possess characteristics similar to horses that allow them to communicate through gestures and they are often quite fluent. I have had parents and special-needs teachers tell me that they could communicate with autistic children far more successfully when using gestures than through sound. Clearly there are many other similarities between the autistic person and the flight animal. The fear of sudden and loud noises will often evoke a ballistic flight response from the horse and the autistic person. It is a tendency of the autistic person and the horse to push into pressure and to fear confinement. The autistic person expresses these symptoms often more profoundly than the person who is not autistic.

Many disabled children want to be hugged but cannot handle the pain that the stimulation causes. Like the horse, a certain quality of touch is acceptable, but it must never be forced. Temple Grandin, a well-known animal behaviorist with a disability closely linked to autism, explains in her books, *Emergence* and *Thinking in Pictures*, her into-pressure feelings. She developed a "squeeze machine" which she learned to use. She was at once frightened by touch and stimulated by it. The soft touch, such as would be socially acceptable between people, was repugnant to her, but the squeeze machine made her feel comfortable if she could get over the intense stimulation it caused.

Curiously this links in with the same impulse to potential pain the horse feels around his body. The horse, once stimulated by pressure in any area, will push himself into the source of the pain, seemingly at a high emotional level. We see this phenomenon at the starting gates. In *Thinking in Pictures* (Vintage Books, 1995). Temple Grandin graphically describes this feeling, writing, "Many autistic children crave pressure stimulation although they cannot tolerate being touched.... When touched unexpectedly, we usually withdraw because our nervous system does not have time to process the sensation." Describing the squeeze machine in the same book, she says, "At first there were a few moments of sheer panic as I stiffened up and tried to pull away from the pressure, but I could not get away because my head was locked in. Five seconds later I felt a wave of relaxation."

Distractibility

For the horse to survive in the wild, he must be acutely aware of his entire environment always. The horse cannot allow a lion or a wolf to creep up on him and make a surprise attack. Everyone who rides or works with horses will know that they can startle at the slightest thing: a paper bag in a bush, a sudden noise, a shadow or the sudden appearance of a strange object. Once the horse has become aware of potential danger, he will focus on it, but never to the extent that he ignores the rest of his environment. In human terms this could be described as *distractible*.

2.13 The horse is a distractible animal.

Distractibility is the tendency therefore to be aware of everything happening in his vicinity. In the horse world, this is a great asset; in the human world, it is a disability. Modern man functions best if he can focus on one thing at a time. For example, it is important for the student to be able to block out the distractions of the classroom and concentrate on the task in hand.

Many children suffer from distractibility. It is not that they do not want to focus on one thing, they simply cannot. People who suffer from this disorder find it virtually impossible to screen out peripheral sounds. For some autistic people, external cacophony can become a nightmare. Their only defense is to retract into another world, closing off from the distractions around them.

Distractibility can, as we have implied, be an asset; it is to the horse. For those of you who have chosen to train horses or simply to ride and handle them for your own pleasure, it is useful to understand this phenomenon. If we become aware of its existence as a normal part of the horse's makeup, we will be far more tolerant of behavioral patterns that have angered many horsemen. It will serve us well to intelligently approach distractibility in the horse and learn to deal with it appropriately. Each of us who has spent significant time within the horse industry will recall horses

being hit or yelled at because they shied from an unfamiliar object. So often the human's first response to fear is to attack. If we are to be good horsemen, we need to modify this behavioral pattern within ourselves and learn to respond in a responsible fashion. I find myself stroking the horse on the neck and saying things like, "You silly boy, that's not going to hurt you." I would be distorting the truth if I told you that when a horse slams all four feet on the ground and jumps three feet to one side or the other that it does not startle me; it does.

What I must do, however, is pull my adrenaline down, relax and respond to the horse in a cool, unhurried fashion. Horses will synchronize with their rider or handler. If your adrenaline is up and you act out ballistically, your horse is apt to emulate your actions. Often this will escalate so that the horse and trainer simply alternate unacceptable behavior until there is an outright fight that never solves problems. Many horses have been permanently damaged by this phenomenon and good horsemen should seek to understand and control this response to fear.

It seems important at this juncture to investigate the positive uses of distractibility in the training of a horse. I often use the horse's characteristic of distractibility in the Join-Up. One of the first procedures where I use distractibility on a regular basis has to do with the horse wanting to buck with his first saddle. I will stand in the middle of the round pen allowing the young horse to express himself by bucking. I have learned to keep my pulse rate down, encouraging the horse to synchronize with my low pulse rate and calm demeanor. In fact, my demeanor distracts the horse from his feeling that the saddle could be a predator. The horse tends to forget the saddle and is distracted into becoming more comfortable and seeks me out as a safe place. I then distract him further by putting on the first bit and bridle of his life. The bridle is even less familiar than the saddle that has been on his back for two minutes or so. The bit is something brand new, thus distracting him from his desire to buck the saddle off.

Often, I find it quite difficult to put the first bit in the horse's mouth. It is a sensitive area of his anatomy and he tends to resist taking the snaffle bit between the teeth. To overcome this obstacle, I will place my right arm high on the crest of his neck and with my right hand on the upper portion of his forehead, I pass the crown of the bridle to the right hand allowing the bit to hang a couple of inches below the lips. I then hold the snaffle bit in the palm of my left hand and attempt to place it on his lower lip well outside his mouth. If he allows me to do that, I begin to distract him by scratching his upper forehead gently with my right fingertips. I watch as his eye rises to see what this is and I often observe that his ears will point toward my right hand. When I have his brain thinking about my right hand, I place my left thumb in the corner of his mouth. That normally causes him to open his teeth. When he does, I slide the bit into the mouth and with my right hand raise the crown of the bridle. A second later, the bridle is on and I have successfully used distractibility to accomplish my goal. Virtually every horse that I start will either fail to buck at all after the bit is on or at least buck less.

More on distractibility will be described in the chapter I call "Techniques I Find Questionable" and specifically in the section "Feeding by Hand."

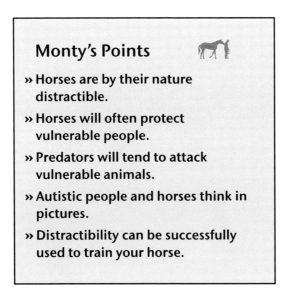

Monty's Points

» **Horses are by their nature distractible.**

» **Horses will often protect vulnerable people.**

» **Predators will tend to attack vulnerable animals.**

» **Autistic people and horses think in pictures.**

» **Distractibility can be successfully used to train your horse.**

Chapter 3

Building Trust

Trust

As a child I watched my father apply the principle, "You do what I tell you to, or I'll hurt you!" to the horses that went through his hands. He often applied the same concept to me. Did the horses feel the same resentment that I did toward the needless pain inflicted upon them? I do not recall learning anything through being physically punished except how to avoid such an incident. Even then, I questioned whether an environment dominated by pain, and therefore fear, was productive. I obeyed him because that was what my father wanted. I loved my horses and knew that I wanted good relationships with them, surmising that there might be a better way.

I was, therefore, from a very early age looking for a way to build a trusting relationship, a 50–50 partnership. Through my observation of the mustangs in the desert and being constantly around horses, it occurred to me, as I watched them moving about in a close-knit herd united for survival, that trust and communication were the keys to their success as a species. After much observation, I could put the rudiments of their language together. I believed that if the horse could trust me, then the whole learning process would speed up. I felt strongly that the answer was through communication. It was many years before I could share my methods with the public. I produced good horses and no one knew how. After my father died, I went public. The rest is history.

The desire to dominate is prevalent in man, the quintessential fight animal. It ruled my father, but if you want the best from your horse, you must trust. Join-Up creates trust and conversely trust must be established with the horse before Join-Up can occur. Trust is the basis of everything I accomplish with the horse, and Join-Up is proof of the existence of trust within that relationship. By establishing trust, I am creating a zone around me where the horse feels comfortable enough to willingly Join-Up with me. At the moment of Join-Up,

> *"Utnil he extends the circle of compassion to all living things, man will not find peace."*
>
> *—Dr. Albert Schweitzer*

the horse comes to me and says, "I'll stay with you; I trust you. I am a herd animal and I can only survive if I have friends."

Horses abused never forget what has happened to them. The best you can do is to reconstruct a friendship based as I do on the techniques outlined within this book. The horse will forever carry the baggage of his experience and will always be affected by that memory. With careful retraining and trust-building, the fear can be overlaid with a veneer of acceptable behavior. Horses quickly learn to manage their immediate environment, finding ways by which they can avoid what they think might be an unpleasant situation. They very quickly learn to distrust or trust their handlers. For example, when a horse feels pain every time a person mounts, he soon works out that in order to avoid the pain he can walk off when someone puts a foot in the stirrup.

Many people say that they would not have the patience to do Join-Up. My answer is that I would not have the patience to spend four to six weeks "breaking" a young horse to saddle, bridle and rider.

Trust is established by working around horses in an utterly predictable manner. The way in which I move, the quietness with which I work and the messages I give all imply that I am trustworthy. In building this trust I obtain the horse's cooperation.

When a horse refuses to load in a trailer or bucks his rider off, it means that he is resisting the goals of his rider or handler. At that point, one no longer shares trust and a common aim. It becomes a mutiny. The horse is saying, "I no longer trust you." Horses, as we have discussed, are far from stupid. They learn fast and are capable of conscious thought. Trust in any partnership is based on the premise, "I believe in you and I am prepared to trust you." When you have proven to the animal that your actions are inappropriate, you are opening the door to a breakdown of trust.

Many people express to me their innate fear of horses. "They are so big," they say, or, "I'm terrified of their hooves and teeth. How can you handle them without being afraid?" or, "They move so quickly; they are so nervous." Fear generally stems from a lack of understanding. The horse has no desire to hurt anyone or anything. Circumstances may cause the horse to react in a way that frightens a person. The answer is to understand their reactions to circumstances. I tell people who express great fear of horses to get to know them, study their true patterns before you brand them as dangerous. The more knowledgeable you become about the nature of horses, the more trust you will have. The less you know or want to know about horses, the more fearful and therefore distrustful you will be.

Those who fear often presuppose that the only way to overcome this fear is to cause a greater fear in the object found frightening. This method can never result in true trust. If we examine circumstances occurring in the world today, country to country, we will often find these precepts at work. If we seek to rule through fear, we do it at the expense of trust. It is the precise antithesis of a 50–50 partnership. It is a lose–lose situation as opposed to win–win.

I see and understand more, not less, through my exposure to the horse and I constantly refine my techniques. No one should ever be disappointed if a perfect Join-Up is not achieved or some obvious mistake was made. It takes a lifetime and then some. It takes practice and then more practice. Trust building is a never-ending process.

It can take time to learn how to rebuild trust. Once you have a working knowledge of the Language of Equus, you will accomplish tasks in far less time than you ever thought possible.

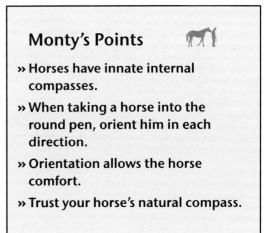
Equine Orientation

Horses have an innate internal compass. Animals in general will demonstrate a natural orientation. Horses can track themselves back from where they came and know in which direction they are going. I have ridden horses throughout long nights in the wilderness. I can recall often when I was certain that my horse was trying to take me in the wrong direction. I can remember arguments that I had with my horses, certain that I knew more about where we should be going than they did.

When I take a horse into the round pen, I move toward the center and face the horse in several different directions, rubbing his head each time I pause. This introduction allows the horse to orient himself, helping him to feel more comfortable in his surroundings. The horse has a directional mechanism so incredible that we human beings have difficulty in understanding it. The horse is far more likely to relax and accept his lessons if he is comfortably oriented.

Since the publication of my first book we have received many letters relating stories of horses that took their riders home. Some of these tales tell of quite frightening circum-

stances. Snowstorms and other harsh conditions will often leave the human less than completely competent to judge the appropriate direction to travel. Horses possess a vastly superior compass mechanism to that of a human being.

One lady recently sent us a story about getting lost on a mountain trail ride. She explained that when night fell she became very cold and her hands were so numb that she could not even hold the reins. She was paralyzed with fear as she buried her hands deeply in the pockets of her coat. Under the circumstances, she made the decision to completely trust her horse. Approximately seven hours later, she recognized the ranch headquarters; the horse had safely escorted her home. Once his head was free, her mount used his natural orientation. We should not view this as an exceptional feat. We should understand horses well enough to know that this is something they do quite naturally. Just as we use tracking dogs or homing pigeons, horses too can be used to enhance the human's limited sense of direction.

 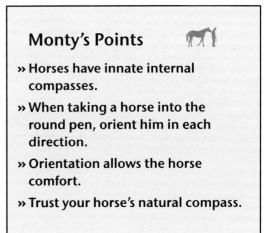

The Round Pen

I would advise that anyone using my methods become familiar with the round pen. It is true that you can accomplish Join-Up in almost any area, but a round pen is an extremely valuable tool. Round pens have been in existence for many centuries. There is evidence that they were used thousands of years ago on the Asian continent. Techniques in the round pen have varied, but a similar theme has survived through the millennia.

Wild horses were often gathered and driven into round pens. It was there they were lassoed, tethered and broken. It was from these techniques that training methods developed that became known as traditional. I watched these methods every day as a child. As the horse galloped round the pen in an attempt to escape his predator, the handler could easily get a loop over his head. The round pen was, in traditional horsemanship, a place of domination, a place where pain was inflicted to achieve submission.

Round pens have been constructed of many different materials: logs, planks, stones or even tires. They have varied in size. I have seen round pens 30 feet (approx.10 meters), and I have seen round pens 150 feet (approx. 50 meters) in diameter. On Flag Is Up Farms I built my round pens of solid plank walls approximately 8 feet high. I used a diameter measurement of 50 feet (approx. 16 meters). This is the optimum size for normal saddle horses of 14 to 16 hands. I work principally with Thoroughbreds, Quarter Horses and Arabians, and my 50-foot pens work beautifully. I have, in the past, dealt with significant numbers of Icelandic horses and Welsh ponies 11 to 12 hands in height. I find it easier to deal with these smaller animals in a pen approximately 46 feet (approx. 15 meters) in diameter. My work in Germany often requires me to deal with Warmbloods well over 16 hands, and I feel that

a diameter of 52 to 54 feet (approx. 17 to 18 meters) is more appropriate for these horses.

The factor that I observe most closely in determining pen size is the capability of the horse to canter, maintaining the same lead front and rear. I have noticed that most horses of, let's say, 16 hands, will tend to travel disunited (left lead in front and right lead behind, or vice versa) in a round pen of 46 feet in diameter. Those same horses will travel comfortably in a 50-foot round pen. It seems fair you could ask why I do not use a round pen of 60 feet (approx. 20 meters) for all sizes of horses, as this would provide an environment for proper leading across the full spectrum of breeds. While that conclusion is true, it requires the trainer himself to negotiate a circle

> "Horses take me for what I am, but they judge me by what I do."
>
> —Monty Roberts

much larger in the center of the round pen. So, it should be considered optimum when the round pen is as small as possible allowing for a comfortable canter. Having accomplished this, the trainer travels the shortest distance to complete his task. When I work in a 50-foot round pen, the circle that I personally use is about 8 feet in diameter. When I work in a 60-foot round pen that measurement increases to approximately 14 feet, resulting in a much greater demand on me. The increased energy output makes it far more difficult to operate in a comfortable and relaxed mode.

One of the most critical aspects of a round pen is the footing. Footing is important both for the safety and performance of the horse, and is critical not only in the round pen but in each area of training. It is with these facts in mind that I have devoted a section to it (see "Footing," on the next page).

As my career developed, I discovered that I needed to be able to move a pen around. In 1989, at Windsor Castle in England, a portable round pen was built for me. It was constructed of welded galvanized mesh. It was an effective design because it was light, safe and allowed viewers to see into the pen without having to be elevated. I demonstrated my work in this enclosure for Her Majesty, Queen Elizabeth II, and it was the first time that I had ever worked in such an environment. I was amazed at how the horses accepted this type of fencing and remained attentive to me, even though they could see through it.

In recent years, I have designed my own version of a portable round pen and it is what I now use for my demonstrations worldwide. To date, I have worked with more than 3,000 horses using this type of enclosure with virtually no injuries or significant mishaps.

My round pens are certainly not intended as places of trauma, quite the opposite. The round pen is my boardroom, my meeting place and my second home. This piece of equipment is important during Join-Up and is a place where the student of equine behavior can observe the horse's natural language. If given a horse, but no bridle, halter, line or round pen, I could still achieve Join-Up by communicating with the horse using my body language. I've proven that one can do Join-Up without the use of a round pen in open country; however, it takes longer and requires far more effort.

I am asked by many observers of my work why it is necessary to have the enclosure round instead of another configuration. While Join-Up can be achieved in a square or rectangular enclosure, the corners in them serve as spots that disrupt the flow of energy. Certainly a square pen with the corners paneled off to create an octagon can serve quite nicely as a substitute to a perfectly round enclosure. When the pen is circular, it encourages the smooth flow of uninterrupted motion which allows for communication without the distractions generated when the pace is significantly altered.

In the environment of the round pen I can set up response-based communication. The configuration of the round pen allows the horse to flee, yet remain at the same distance from me. If the pen is oval or rectangular, the horse could simply go to the point furthest from me. This would tend to break up the flow of motion and make smooth communication more difficult. The flight distance of the horse is the distance he is apt to use trying to maintain a safe distance from his pursuer. This usually amounts to about a quarter to three-eighths of a mile. Once flight is no longer his choice, the horse will instinctively begin to communicate with his pursuer, tending to circle. Nature has instilled the understanding that if the horse continues to flee he is likely to encounter another predator, eventually lacking the energy to successfully escape. Through survival of the fittest, the horse has come to realize that he is more likely to survive by conserving energy through communication and negotiation.

It should be noted that the predator must also be deeply concerned with energy conservation. The predator who burns more calories in pursuit than he consumes will eventually face starvation. It is with this knowledge that the horse comes to understand the value of negotiating with his adversary.

In a proper round pen a person can control the energy expended by the horse. Through communication one raises the horse's energy output and conversely effectively reduces it. When I am working with a horse, I fully understand that he is of a species who synchronizes with life around him. Synchronicity is key to communication. In its absence the conversation breaks down. I work to create an environment in which the horse can learn what I am about and come to trust me.

A round pen provides an appropriate place for learning to occur as it allows the trainer to offer leadership without confrontation. When we use the round pen properly, we can direct the horse in his own language. The animal always remains in a position to read communication, stay calm and come to trust.

Remember the horse has two goals in life—to reproduce and to survive. When the horse enters my pen he is not thinking about reproduction. As I send the horse away, I am demonstrating that he is on his own. The horse has to consider the possibility of joining up with me. Isolation is not a natural state for a horse. An understanding of the horse's language allows me to achieve Join-Up and thus an alternative to isolation.

As I communicate and respond to the horse in the round pen, I never lose sight of my objective, which is to offer the horse the opportunity to willingly allow himself to be saddled, bridled and ridden. The trainer must always remain objective. He should not personalize the horse's responses or become subjective. My round pen is a place where we are both wearing the same color jersey; we are on the same team.

We know that in many circumstances a horse comes into this environment with distrust, fear and/or anxiety. Through communication in a language the horse understands, we can create change to allay these phobias. It is important to increase the work load if the response you get is not the one you want. This effectively creates a contract, and one which the horse is apt to willingly consider. A response is the first step toward change and it is change that we are seeking. Any response should be viewed as a portal through which you can pass to create positive consequences and thus begin the process of negotiation.

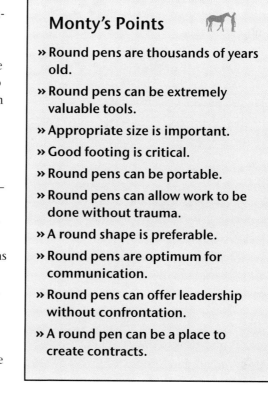

Monty's Points

» **Round pens are thousands of years old.**
» **Round pens can be extremely valuable tools.**
» **Appropriate size is important.**
» **Good footing is critical.**
» **Round pens can be portable.**
» **Round pens can allow work to be done without trauma.**
» **A round shape is preferable.**
» **Round pens are optimum for communication.**
» **Round pens can offer leadership without confrontation.**
» **A round pen can be a place to create contracts.**

Footing

Footing is an extremely important part of the process of training horses. I believe it is essential for a good horseman to study and be aware of footing before setting out to work with horses, no matter what discipline. Obviously, for those of you who may be trail and leisure riders, you are obliged to ride on the footing that is available to you. However, it is advisable for you to consider the shoes of your horse an important part of dealing with the given footing. If you have to ride on a stone-filled trail, it is important that you support your horse's foot with heavy steel shoes and perhaps include leather pads to prevent bruising from excessively rough ground. Wherever possible, each of us should try to avoid footing that could be harmful to our horses.

To educate the reader about my ideas on footing, I will confine my comments to the creation of footing for round pens, training tracks and other areas where regular riding is to take place. I will attempt to cover several disciplines with which I am familiar, and then generalize where I have had less experience.

It is my opinion that most activities involving the training of horses are best done on a surface that approximates the following: a well-drained area covered with a clay-like sub base of approximately 6 inches, with a 1½- to 2-inch coarse sand surface. If you are creating a training area from scratch, you may have to build in your drainage by laying down a foot or two of gravel as a sub base. This should be done sufficiently so that water below can escape the confines of the training surface. On top of the gravel it is advisable to lay down clay about 6 inches in depth. This will prevent your training surface from becoming too deep. The clay should be rolled while slightly moist to pack it firmly in place. With the two lower layers established, add 1½ to 2 inches of coarse sand to complete the training surface.

Crowning or sloping the grade of your training area can help you in creating drainage. It is essential to realize that when maintaining the surface you must not tear into the clay base, thus mixing the sand and clay. You should use a light harrow so as not to destroy the integrity of your footing. Maintenance should be confined to the sand area to maintain a level, firm clay base.

This surface is quite effective for disciplines such as jumping, hunter competitions, reining, working cow horse, pleasure, trail, equitation, dressage, hack classes, three-gaited, five-gaited and harness horses, also Tennessee Walkers, Peruvian Pasos, Arabians and general horse show competition.

The cutting competition may be done by increasing the depth of sand another ½ to ¾ of an inch in the area of anticipated herd work by

the cutting horse. Obviously, if you have a training ground for harness horses only, you should come back to about ½ inch of sand so that the vehicles can travel on a smoother surface.

Many equestrians feel that they want 6 inches of sand on their base. I have learned over my 60-plus years that this usually causes more damage to a horse than good. The strain of footing that is too deep can often affect the spine and pelvic attachments, and tendons and ligaments in the lower extremities.

If you are training the reining horse to achieve a sliding stop, you may want to keep your sliding areas a bit dryer than those portions of the training area where you would figure-eight, spin or work a cow.

A good trainer should remember that his surface can never remain the same. The sand is an ever-changing substance. Every step of a horse and every harrowing will fracture particles of sand, thus constantly causing your coarse sand to become finer. Once the sand has broken down, it will act more like the clay from which you have created your base. Care should be taken to remove and replace the sand when it begins to pack too quickly to remain friable footing throughout the day's training schedule.

It should be said that if you put the sand under a microscope, it should be made up of jagged particles and not round ones. There are many sources of round sand in North America and this type creates a surface that I have learned is quite dangerous for training horses. The round particles fit together too closely, becoming less than friable, and I have experienced far too many bowed tendons and fractures using round sand. Round sand is usually created by the actions of the sea. Beach sand is round, while river sand or crushed sand is jagged, thus creating the friable, gritty surface that I recommend.

If you get sand from a source created from

soft parent material, your sand particles will break down faster than if you find your material from a harder source. Granite is one of the hardest parent materials, providing the most desirable coarse sand for horse footing.

The type of machinery you use to maintain your surface is critical in prolonging the life of your sand cushion. A rototiller, for instance, beats the surface and breaks down the particles far more rapidly than a round-tooth harrow. It is essential to set your harrow so as not to disturb the clay base.

Having outlined for you the basic formula that I recommend for training surfaces, I suggest that there are many commercial substances on the market today that will improve the performance of your sand surface. "Equitrack" became very popular in the late eighties on some major racetracks of the world. It is a patented process in which a petroleum and rubber-like substance is mixed with sand so that each particle becomes coated. It increases the cushion and decreases the need for water. While my experience with it has been positive, I have interviewed many people who have said that they have chosen not to use it on their racetracks because of cost and the fact that it does tend to wear out. I have also talked with owners of jumpers and found that they are not pleased with it for their discipline.

Fiber sand is the name given when a wool-like synthetic fiber is added to the sand's surface to prolong "friability," give greater cushion and hold moisture. Allowed to dry out, the wind tends to separate it and pull it away from the surface, but I have found it to be useful in extending the life of the sand surface.

In many parts of the world bits of electrical insulation (*posada*) are chopped up and mixed with sand, which again increases cushion and prolongs the friability of the sand's surface. I have heard many jumping and dressage people sing the praise of insulation mixed into the sand. At home, on Flag Is Up Farm, I am ex-

perimenting with a new surface product that is ground-up sports shoes. It is a combination of canvas, rubber and plastic. I feel that it is working quite well and is one of the most effective surface additions available.

In conclusion, I would suggest keeping it simple. The basic formula I have outlined that does not include additional material is probably still quite effective.

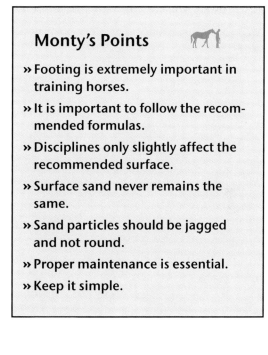

Monty's Points

» Footing is extremely important in training horses.

» It is important to follow the recommended formulas.

» Disciplines only slightly affect the recommended surface.

» Surface sand never remains the same.

» Sand particles should be jagged and not round.

» Proper maintenance is essential.

» Keep it simple.

Mouthing

The process of causing a horse to accept the bit and bridle is known, in most of the horse world, as "mouthing" the horse. I have heard the procedure called "bitting" the horse, "bitting up" the horse and "schooling to the bit and bridle." Whatever term you use for this procedure, it is causing the horse to accept communication from the hands of the rider through the reins, and ultimately the bit.

I call mouthing one of the most important procedures where training the young horse is concerned. It is critical to cause the horse to respond to cues from the reins and bit with the most subtle cues one can accomplish. The tissues over the bars of the horse's mouth in the area of the corners are precious to any horseman. They should be treated with utmost respect as there is no second chance to create sensitivity once this area has been damaged during training.

I am a proponent of mouthing the horse before saddling or riding. The definition of mouthing is to accustom the horse to bit and bridle (usually a snaffle). It is to cause the horse to be comfortable with wearing this device and responsive to being guided by it. It might seem strange to the reader who has seen my demonstrations to grasp this concept. I do not see the horses used in my demonstrations until the time of the event. With a few exceptions, I don't even know who owns them or where they come from. I want as much separation between myself and the horse as I can possibly have. This means that I would consider it inappropriate to even give instructions to the owner regarding mouthing.

To be given the chance to mouth a young horse before the start of saddling, bridling and riding is a high priority for me (outside of the parameters of a demonstration). For the past 40 years or so, I have taken every opportunity to acquaint the horse to the bit, bridle and reins before saddling and riding.

I am a strong advocate for using "black iron bits." These were the normal bits for thousands of years before the advent of stainless steel. I find that horses prefer black iron and perform better with it than stainless steel. I further recommend that the black iron bit has copper inlaid in the mouthpiece. The combination of black iron and copper seems to me to be preferred by virtually every horse I work with.

Since this segment of the book is devoted to mouthing, I will confine my comments to the use of the bit. It is true, however, that I

have used the hackamore, side pull and even the Dually halter, all of which are bitless. Here I have chosen to recommend the use of a snaffle bit for early training.

I recommend that you accustom the horse to the surcingle, which can be accomplished in the round pen or even in a box stall. Once the horse can cope with the surcingle comfortably, I begin the process of mouthing. You should always take care not to have protrusions from the walls or fences of the enclosure you use for mouthing.

I will place a black iron snaffle with a browband headstall appropriately on the horse's head. You don't need to have riding reins on the bit as a pair of side reins are used instead. The bit should sit in the horse's mouth so that it effects a slight smile on the horse. Once the bit is touching the corners of the horse's mouth, the handler should adjust it upward until it is about one-sixteenth of an inch higher than the corners would be in a natural state.

I suggest that the side reins be adjusted quite loosely at first. I recommend that the handler loose longe the young horse in the round pen in sessions approximating 15 to 20 minutes in length. You can execute this event using all three natural gaits of the horse. It should be noted that exhaustion is not a part of training and you should be careful to monitor the horse's comfort throughout the procedure.

After the horse has accepted the surcingle and the snaffle bit with loose side reins, the handler should then begin a process of shortening the side reins until the horse is nodding off the bit. Take care not to tighten before the horse is fully comfortable as he could object to the tension and potentially suffer injury by rearing or acting out in another negative fashion.

The side reins should be equipped with elastic to allow the horse a flexible tension and not a solid one. The handler might continue to loose longe, creating impulsion by simply tossing a light driving line behind the horse to move him forward. Be sure the environment is safe. One should study the footing and the walls closely so as not to create an environment that could be dangerous for your animal.

After two to three sessions, you can often introduce driving lines using the side rings on the surcingle at approximately the same position where a rider's knee might be. The handler should always be sensitive to how much work the young horse is doing and how he is accepting that work.

I recommend that mouthing should take place for 10 to 12 sessions before saddling and riding. The knowing handler will vary the length of time according to the needs of the horse. The nervous, fractious animal should be mouthed for a greater number of sessions than the quiet, cooperative one.

It is extremely important to use effective safety measures, only advancing when your equine student is fully prepared for it. I have provided an illustration here so that you can see each feature of the mouthing apparatus.

Many horsemen ask me how I suggest handling the horse that tosses his head while being ridden and I tell them that this mouthing procedure can be employed. It is most likely that a bad set of hands has caused this problem. I have found it effective to allow the horse to toss his head, simply meeting the side reins and stretching the elastics. Normally, horses will stop the head tossing after four or five sessions as recommended in this section.

I have used this method of mouthing a horse for well over 50 years now and have found it to be most effective. When I finally saddle and ride the animal schooled in this fashion, it is amazing how cooperative he is with his turns, stops and reining back.

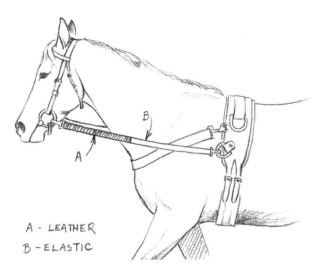

A - LEATHER
B - ELASTIC

3.1 Side reins with elastic to allow flexible tension on the breastcollar.

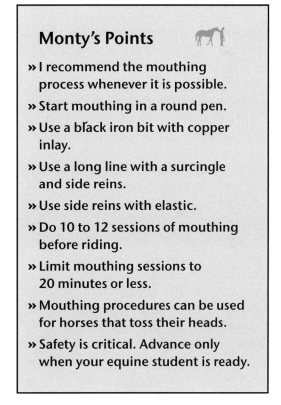

Monty's Points

» I recommend the mouthing process whenever it is possible.

» Start mouthing in a round pen.

» Use a black iron bit with copper inlay.

» Use a long line with a surcingle and side reins.

» Use side reins with elastic.

» Do 10 to 12 sessions of mouthing before riding.

» Limit mouthing sessions to 20 minutes or less.

» Mouthing procedures can be used for horses that toss their heads.

» Safety is critical. Advance only when your equine student is ready.

Chapter 4

Join-Up

The Process

Relatively speaking, there are few practical working horses left today. The vast majority of the equine world now revolves around sport and recreation. Plowing fields, pulling heavy loads and carrying messages at breakneck speed are no longer the primary duties of horses. Fortunately, the days of dead horses on the battlefields of the world are virtually a thing of the past.

The elimination of laborious tasks should not, however, lead us to conclude that man's journey with the horse is over. It is just beginning. We are now free to exist with horses without the pressures experienced in former times. At last, we can listen to our horses, enjoy the opportunity to learn from them and admire them for their many attributes. We have entered an era in which we choose to work and be with our horses; it is not a daily necessity. Entering the third millennium A.D., it seems appropriate to ask what kind of relationship we want with these animals and what we expect each species to get in return. These are important questions that I intend to address. They are central to my mission in life, to leave the world a better place for horses and people.

The practice of Join-Up is a commitment to a path that two species travel together in search of commonality, friendship and survival. This is my journey, what the horses taught me and what we have shared. It replaced my pain with joy and resentment with a willingness to serve. The process has no time constraints; it has no definable beginning or end. If you are involved with horses, then you should think horses, just as the astronomer has his head in the stars. The process does not begin when you arrive at the barn to meet your horse; it begins when you wake up in the morning and exists even as you sleep.

In demonstrations, when I first enter the round pen, I have simple goals. They are: Join-Up, follow-up and placing the first saddle, bridle and rider on the unstarted horse. Yet, as

> *"We always pass failure on the way to success."*
>
> —*Mickey Rooney*

I work, I am not consciously aware of these challenges. I place no importance on impressing my audience. If it is a good experience for my horse, the audience will be impressed. I hope my audience will learn something, but the primary goal is that my horse will learn that we can communicate. Should I cause a happy and successful horse, my audience will most probably enjoy it, too. I am committed to each stage of learning as if it was the only stage in existence. While I have my goal in mind, I work as the horse works, in the present.

Horses are not plagued with thoughts of failure, lofty aspirations or guilt. They have a flawless memory, but no ego or greed. They bring their memory into play whenever it is required to ensure their survival; the future is not contemplated by horses. Humans are vastly more complex and when I work with a horse, I must get simple. I believe that much of my success is due to my commitment to the process and not to the outcome.

Horses are reactionary and not actionary animals. It was believed for thousands of years that horses were not capable of conscious thought. Through Join-Up, I can prove that the horse can enter a mode of conscious thought. The early encyclopedias are now being rewritten to recognize this fact. The impact this news is having on the horse world is staggering. At last, the world knows for sure that inflicting pain on a horse to take it through the process of education is not necessary.

My level of respect increases with each horse I work. Their ability to come to terms with our shortcomings often astonishes me. I am truly humbled by the ability of the horse to continue reacting to our behavior, waiting for us to get it right. I watch repeatedly as horses take those first steps toward me. They are the steps to lead them to a better life, one of a better understanding of humans.

> ## Monty's Points
>
> » The vast majority of the equine world now revolves around sport and recreation.
>
> » We are entering a time where we can begin to truly enjoy horses.
>
> » The practice of Join-Up is a commitment.
>
> » Horses are simple; they have a flawless memory, but no ego or greed.
>
> » Horses are reactionary.
>
> » Horses have conscious thought.
>
> » Horses can react appropriately while waiting for the human to get it right.
>
> » Horses can lead us to a better understanding of our own species.

Join-Up

Join-Up is a title I have given to the body of work I employ in dealing with horses without violence. To define Join-Up, however, requires a narrower view of the term. Join-Up is that moment in which the horse decides that it is better to be with me than to go away. My wife, Pat, coined her own term when she named one of her sculptures "Moment of Join-Up." It is that magical instant when the horse voluntarily moves forward and reaches his nose out toward my shoulder. It was later decided by most of the people in my organization that the term Join-Up would be used in a broader sense to define my concepts in general. Join-Up can be achieved with all horses of any age or background. It is as effective on wild mustangs as it is on the gentle child's horse.

> *"Actions speak louder than words; Equus is, in fact, a language of actions, not words."*
>
> *—Monty Roberts*

If you intend to use Join-Up on an untrained mustang or a domestic horse that has not been saddled or ridden, you should practice until competent on safe horses. Working with untrained animals is not for amateurs. The raw horse should be dealt with by people who work with horses on a daily basis. These should be professionals who have had significant experience training horses. I recommend that anyone using Join-Up takes the time to comprehensively study the Language of Equus before attempting the procedure. Without a working knowledge of the language, it is unlikely that Join-Up will be successful. I think the first Join-Up attempt should be undertaken with the assistance of one of my properly qualified instructors.

Definition of Join-Up

Join-Up is a process based upon communication in a shared language to create a bond rooted in trust. It must be nonviolent, noncoercive and can only be accomplished if both partners have willingly entered the process. To gain Join-Up with your horse, it is necessary to step into his world, observe his needs, conditions and the rules that govern his social order. You should learn to communicate in the horse's language since we know he cannot learn ours. This process cannot be faked. Once understood, it is easy to use and can be mutually enjoyable for both you and your horse.

Join-Up is a tool, like a fine chisel, with which to carve a safe and comfortable environment for ongoing communication. The tool must be used with skill, which may take years to perfect, but in its basic form can be quickly learned. Join-Up works at any stage during this partnership between man and horse, whether it is a new one or one of long standing. Join-Up between you and your horse heralds an end to isolation and separation of both our species by bonding through communication. It is a procedure that should be precisely followed; there are no short cuts. Join-Up may bring out conflict and perceived resistance or even ambivalence. However, if the trainer is competent, believes in the concept and executes it reasonably well, the horse will respond positively. It is imperative that anyone employing Join-Up is totally responsible for their own actions.

VIOLENCE MUST HAVE NO PART IN THE PROCESS OF JOIN-UP.

Violence of any kind will destroy the effectiveness of the procedure. A trainer must move through the process keeping the conversation alive, always allowing the horse time to respond. Join-Up is *response*-based, not *demand*-based. The trainer should comply with two significant conceptual rules.

1. Time is not the important thing! Good horses are! An equine partner of the highest caliber should be our goal. We should enter the process of Join-Up with the idea that time is not limited. This attitude will maximize results in the minimum amount of time.

2. The second most important point to remember is that the trainer waits for the horse to do something right and rewards him. He does not wait for the horse to do something wrong and punish him.

Examine closely the list on the next page of recommended pieces of equipment and the ideal facility.

Join-Up
Equipment and Goals

Equipment
1. A round pen, 50 feet (16 meters) in diameter
2. Good footing (see "Footing," p. 31)
3. Saddle (type not important)
4. Bridle (type not important, could be bitless)
5. Long lines
6. One stirrup leather strap with buckle (to anchor stirrups together)
7. Halter (the Dually preferred; see Chapter 7)
8. Hard hat and appropriate footwear

List of Goals
1. Join-Up
2. Follow-Up
3. Vulnerable areas
4. Picking up feet
5. Saddle pad
6. Saddle
7. Bridle
8. Long lines:
   Full circles left
   Full circles right
   Stop, face away
   One step back
9. Rider:
   One full circle to the left
   One full circle to the right
   Stop
   Request one step back

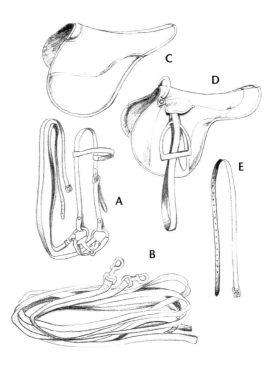

4.1 The necessary equipment for Join-Up: (A) bridle; (B) long lines; (C) saddle pad; (D) saddle; (E) stirrup leather.

Language of Equus, the greater the potential for success.

Before any of us begin to train horses for a particular purpose, we should reflect upon the fact that this species did perfectly well for 47 million years without us. Man was not around during this time to mold his behavioral patterns or alter his appearance through genetics. Each of us who chooses to influence the brain of a horse should contemplate with care that the horse has never stalked, killed or devoured flesh to sustain life. We should have it crystal clear in our minds that the horse means no harm to any other species and would rather flee than fight. When teaching the horse to accomplish a chosen task, we should know that to act out in violence will only drive adrenaline up and put the horse to flight (see "Adrenaline Up, Learning Down," p. 98).

I intend to describe Join-Up in this section

Absorb the content of these lists, then learn as much as possible about the Language of Equus before setting out to train your horse using this method. The greater your understanding of the as it applies to the young, domestically raised horse. By domestically raised, I mean a horse that now leads well, allows you to pick up his feet, and stands to be groomed or doctored without resistance. The highest percentage of my readers are working with young, domestically raised horses, causing them to accept their first saddle, bridle and rider. The procedure varies significantly when you are dealing with a mustang untouched by human hands or a remedial horse with a reputation for a particular phobia. It should be understood that the circumstances of Join-Up can vary. It is also surprising how predictable they are, no matter the breed or the geographic location.

BEFORE YOU BEGIN ANY WORK WITH YOUR HORSE, YOU MUST BE PERFECTLY SATISFIED THAT HE IS SOUND IN EVERY WAY. ANY PHYSICAL PROBLEM CAUSING PAIN COULD DESTROY THE JOIN-UP PROCESS. IT IS ALSO TRUE THAT IT IS INAPPROPRIATE TO TRAIN A HORSE EXPRESSING PHYSICAL IMPAIRMENT.

Join-Up Day One

I recommend leading your equine student with a 30-foot (approx. 10 meters) long line into the center of the round pen to initiate the procedure. I believe it is helpful to step in front of your animal and give him a rub on the forehead. This accomplished, turn the animal 90 degrees and repeat the process. Again, turn him 90 degrees, rub his head and then make a final turn that brings you back to the original position. What this means is that you have stopped the horse in the center of the pen and rubbed him between the eyes while facing north, south, east, and west. With this, you accomplish an orientation helpful to the horse. It is essential that you do not look the horse in the eye while doing this. It is best to look at a point near the shoulders or the forelegs.

At this time, I am prepared to release the

4.2 A rub between the eyes is a horse's reward.

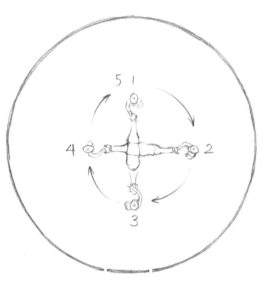

4.3 Orientation.

animal and begin the process of communication. I unsnap the long line and step away toward the rear of the horse. I do not allow even so much as a glance toward the horse's eyes. Taking care not to enter the kick zone, when I am at a point directly perpendicular to the rear flank of the horse, I then go into action.

I snap my eyes on the eye of the horse. I pierce his pupils with my gaze. Squaring my shoulders, I cause my body to assume a military stance of attention. I swing the line coils, slapping my shoulders, first one side, then the

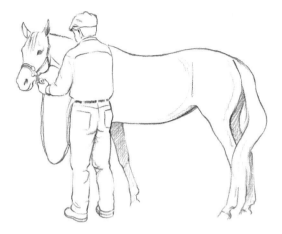

4.4 Unsnap the line.

4.6 Throw a line to send the horse away.

4.5 Step back to prepare to drive the horse away.

other, and the horse flees virtually every time. As my student runs away from me, I pitch the long line toward the rear quarters. My intention is to convey to the horse that I am perfectly happy with his decision to flee. My experience has taught me that the horse regards being sent away as an act of discipline. I learned in my early days that the alpha female assumed this role when disciplining the obstreperous adolescent.

My body language says, "Go away! Do not go away a little, go away a lot!" I keep my shoulders square with the body axis of my student, and I maintain piercing contact with my eyes on the eyes of the horse.

The flight distance of the horse is about ¼ to ⅜ of a mile (400 to 500 hundred meters). In a round pen 50 feet (16 meters) in diameter, the animal must negotiate between 4 to 6 laps in each direction. I try to negotiate 4 or 5 laps with my horse moving as swiftly as is comfortable and safe for him. I then step in front of his balance point, reverse him, and repeat the process in the opposite direction. Once I have my

4.7 Sending away,
from the horse's perspective.

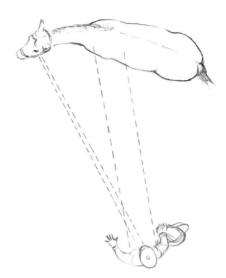

4.10 Correct angle between
horse and person to send the horse away.

4.8 Slap the line to
encourage faster movement.

4.11 Turn the horse to change direction.

4.9 Pitch the line to help send the horse away.

8 to ten 10 comfortably completed, I reverse my animal again. Remember, I am still working with my shoulders square, eyes on eyes.

The second reversal puts the horse back in the same direction that he traveled just moments before. I have found this to be of some comfort to the horse. He will now be more relaxed. I employ the gestures that reduce the pressure to leave, allowing the horse to slow (see p. 92). I will often put my line in my left hand and open the fingers of my right hand, with the horse circling to the right. I make sweeping movements through the air with my arm and extend the fingers in an aggressive manner. The horse appears to consider this a "predatorial" gesture and will usually maintain his position against the fence, as far from me as possible. It is at this point that the horse begins to communicate.

There are four gestures by the horse that I call desirable goals. It is not necessary to achieve each of these gestures, but Join-Up is enhanced if you do. The first gesture you will observe concerns the horse's ears. The horse will adjust the ear nearest you so that you can see into the open part of it. This ear will remain fairly constant while the ear furthest from you will move, picking up the sounds from the rest of the environment. I believe that this gesture means that the horse respects you. This suggests that you are important in his life though he is not sure why. Remember that you are still assuming your aggressive stance, eyes on eyes, shoulders square, all motions square.

The next gesture is nearly always second of the four desired. The horse will come off the round-pen fence, shrinking the size of his circle. At this point, you will often see the neck bend inward so that the horse views you more intently than he did at first. The neck will generally relax and soften compared to its condition early in the flight mode. This gesture means that the horse wants to stop going away

4.12 The first gesture of communication, ear "locked on."

4.13 The second gesture of communication, coming off the fence.

and to get closer to you. He would like to negotiate an agreement that would be mutually beneficial.

While the third and fourth gestures often switch order positions, I will list as the third gesture "licking and chewing." In doing so, the horse communicates that he is a herbivore and is eating. If he is eating, he cannot be afraid of the situation he is in. In fact, this can be considered a sort of smoke screen. The horse is testing the waters, so to speak, prepared to flee if necessary. I believe that this gesture is a later version of one expressed by foals when they snap their jaws open and shut at the sight of a strange horse, or have a frightening experience. I believe this gesture means that while the horse is eating he cannot be afraid. I think he is saying, "We have guard horses on our

4.14 The third gesture of communication, "licking and chewing."

4.15 The fourth gesture, head down as if to say, "I'll let you be the chairman of the meeting."

herds and when a predator is present we must stop eating. We must get our heads high and get ready for the run or we die." I often notice that the horse will defecate, lightening the bowel, in order to have a better chance of outrunning the predator.

The final desired gesture is the horse dropping his head and neck and moving so his nose is just about an inch from the soil. He will often flex at the poll so that the head synchronizes with his pace with a kind of nodding motion. If the trainer finds the horse does not drop his head, he can employ a gesture likely to evoke this response. To ask the horse to drop his head, you should make the following gestures: first, raise one hand with open fingers

and palm toward the horse. The arm, wrist and hand should be rigid at this point and rapidly moving left to right. Then, gradually close the fingers while simultaneously bending the wrist and relaxing the arm and bring the arm downward and toward the center of your body. With the arm relaxed, wrist and elbow bending, and fingers closed, bring your hand across your belt buckle to a point slightly beyond your body midline. This will often result in the horse stopping and dropping his head. Should you choose to send your horse onward again, you can employ your other arm to encourage the horse to continue circling the round pen (see p. 92). I believe that when the horse drops his head, he is saying, "If we could have a meeting

4.16 Gestures that send away, and invite back in.

to renegotiate our contract, I would let you be chairperson of the meeting." I do not believe that it is a message of submission, but one of wanting a partnership. It is one more request by the horse for a partnership without confrontation.

It should be your goal as the trainer to accomplish all four gestures, allowing him to begin the full complement of communication that will lead to Join-Up. First, turn slightly to move in the same direction in which the horse is traveling, but no longer have your shoulders square with the horse. One shoulder should point toward the horse's head.

Next, step a fraction ahead of the horse's balance point, casting your eyes slightly downward and away from the horse. This will usually cause him to halt and look inward. At this point, assume a passive stance, eyes downward, shoulders relaxed and on a 45-degree angle to the axis of the horse. Remain motionless at this 45-degree position, facing slightly away from the horse, not 45 degrees and toward the horse.

It is at this time that the trainer should remember to use communication to make the horse want to be with him. All movements at this time should be slow and smooth, never rapid or jerky. Fluidity of movement including those of your eyes is critical at this juncture. The mistake of a quick snap of your eye will almost certainly send the horse away.

At this time the horse will often advance, walking right up and reaching out with his nose to nuzzle your shoulder. This is the "moment of Join-Up" (Goal Number 1). It is critical that while

4.17 Bring the shoulder by, and go passive to invite the horse in.

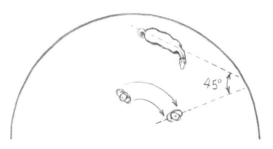

4.18 45° angle, bringing the shoulder by to invite the horse in.

4.19 The "moment of Join-Up."

in the passive mode you do not make eye contact with your student. You should, however, keep the horse within your peripheral vision to know where the animal is. If the horse feels the pierce of eyesight, he is likely to believe this is not a safe place to be and may even break away.

4.20 If the horse breaks, send him away and back to work.

If the horse fails to walk forward, you should move in arcs turning away from the horse and remaining passive. By making these movements you are saying in the horse's language, "I am a safe place to be." This will draw the horse toward your shoulder. It is critical at this point for the trainer to remember that if indeed all learning is zero to ten, the most important part of learning is zero to one. If we can just get our student to take one tiny step in the right direction and reward him, it is likely that he will soon want to remain with us.

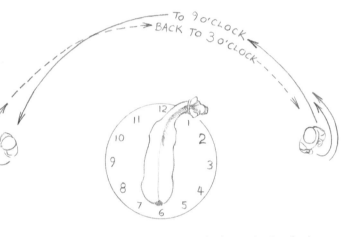

4.21 Arcing to invite the horse.

In either case, once Join-Up is accomplished, you should then turn slowly toward the horse and standing immediately in front of him, rub gently between the eye. Never during this maneuver should you make eye contact. I find that it is advisable to look down between the horse's knees. Once you have rewarded your animal for his positive actions, you can then walk away and expect follow-up (Goal Number 2) to occur. Equestrians would do well to remember that predators never walk away from their prey, so the horse has come to regard this as a nonthreatening gesture.

4.22 Reward.

4.23 Follow-up.

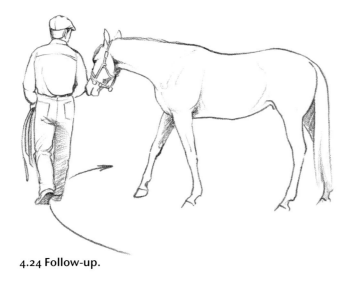

4.24 Follow-up.

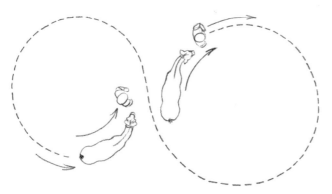

4.25 Follow-up on serpentine path.

I recommend walking in circles both right and left, stopping every few seconds to rub his forehead as a reward for following you (a positive action). You can walk in serpentine patterns so that the horse clearly expresses a desire to be with you by following your exact movements.

Having accomplished Join-Up and follow-up, the balance of the procedure to accept saddle, bridle and rider are virtually academic. (This is the point at which you would stop if you were dealing with a weanling or a horse you did not intend to ride for whatever reason). I snap the lead on, but I do not attempt to pull the horse to cause him to stay with me. I prefer to leave slack in the line so that the animal clearly stays with me because he wants to, not because he is forced. I believe that this is a critical issue and that if your horse wants to leave you, you have not successfully accomplished Join-Up. You might do well to reinforce it by repeating the process, reestablishing the Join-Up and follow-up phenomenon. Should you choose to follow this course, Join-Up is likely to occur in less than half the time it took originally.

If your horse remains comfortably with you, and most will, it is time to go into the vulnerable areas (Goal Number 3). I suggest rubbing the horse all over the back, withers and neck. This is the part of the body where horses are attacked by large cats. It is essential that your horse is still comfortable with you as your hands massage this part of his anatomy. I further suggest that you massage the under portions of the belly and the fore and rear flanks. These

4.26 This is where cats attack.

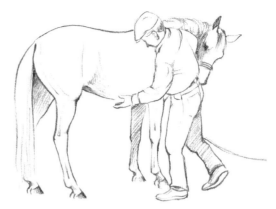

4.27 This is where dogs attack.

are the areas most often attacked by canine predators and are critically sensitive. Again, do not enter the kick zone during this work. Massage the vulnerable areas from the near-side, then passing in front of the horse and giving him a rub on the forehead, repeat on the offside.

I recommend that you return to the nearside of the horse again, rubbing the fore-head when passing the head and prepare to pick up the feet (Goal Number 4). First, you pick up the near fore, using safe and accepted procedures. Then progress to the near rear and lift it as though you were going to clean the foot. Pass again in front of the horse, giving a rub and then repeat the process on the offside.

With these four goals accomplished, I lead my horse to a point at the round pen fence furthest from the gate. I normally remove the line so that the horse is free to leave me if he chooses. The balance of the equipment can now be brought into the center of the round pen and placed on the ground. While not criti-cal, it is better to have an assistant bring it in for you so as not to lose the continuity of your Join-Up. Often, the horse will have an adrena-line rush at this point and may even break Join-Up with you. The sight of the equipment will sometimes frighten him and strain your relationship. This is normally short-lived. I rec-

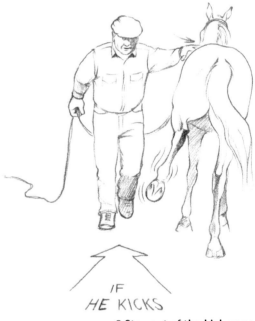

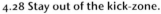

4.28 Stay out of the kick-zone.

ommend that you keep your adrenaline down and pay very little attention to this episode. I suggest that you walk between your equip-ment and the horse's head, encouraging him to stay with you rather than investigating the equipment.

Once your equine student will follow you comfortably, you should then again attach your long line to the halter, and stand with your horse beside the equipment. Pick up the

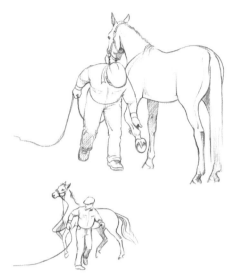

4.29 Carefully pick up the near-fore.

4.32 The reward as you pass to the other side.

4.30 Where your hands go to prepare to pick up the back feet.

4.33 Pick up the off-fore.

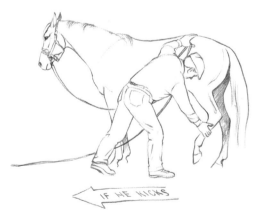

IF HE KICKS

4.31 Carefully pick up the back feet.

saddle pad and approach your horse, holding the pad close to your right hip. Stroke your horse's shoulder with your left hand and slowly place the pad so that it is slightly ahead of the withers (Goal Number 5). At this point, slide the pad back until it sits in the intended position. When the pad is correctly in place, pick up the saddle (stirrups up) with the girth (or cinch) placed over the seat. Move so that your left hip is near the left shoulder of your horse. Gently place the saddle on his back. Lift the girth and place it across his neck in front of the saddle (Goal Number 6). Now move carefully past his head to his offside, giving his forehead a rub as you pass. Stand near the right shoulder and take the girth down slowly and smoothly without hesitation.

Move quietly back to the nearside, rubbing the forehead again. Stand near the left shoulder and carefully reach under to pick up the girth. For an English-type saddle, place the front buckle on the front billet and draw it snug, reading your horse so as not to make it too tight, but tight enough to ride or stay with the horse if he should buck. Do not place the tongue of the buckle into a hole on the billet until you are comfortable that it is sufficiently tight to ride through bucking. If your horse should start to buck before you place the tongue in the hole in the billet, then the buckle will slide off the billet, allowing your saddle to be thrown clear. If you place the tongue in a

4.34 Introduction of the tack.

4.35 Snap on the long line.

4.36 Pick up the saddle pad.

4.37 Approach the horse with the saddle pad.

4.38 Place the saddle pad on the horse's back.

4.39 Place the saddle on with the girth lying over the seat.

4.40 A rub on the head for good behavior.

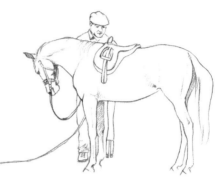

4.41 Check the offside of the saddle.

4.42 Use a hook to pick up the girth.

4.43 Now is the time to girth up.

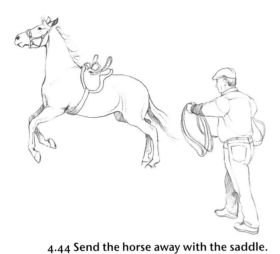

4.44 Send the horse away with the saddle.

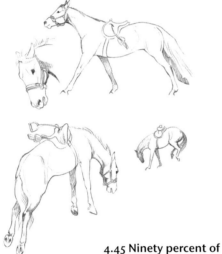

4.45 Ninety percent of horses buck with their first saddle.

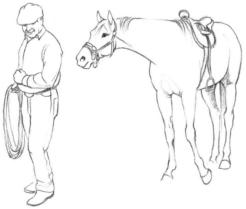

4.46 The horse joins-up once again.

4.47 Put on the first bridle.

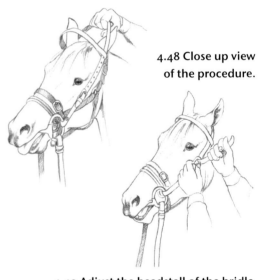

4.48 Close up view of the procedure.

4.49 Adjust the headstall of the bridle.

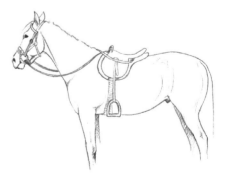

4.50 Where the reins go behind the saddle.

Chapter 4 / Join-Up

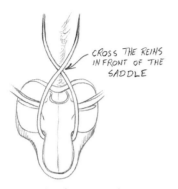

4.51 Rein placement from above.

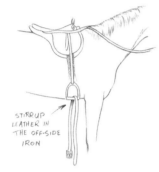

4.52 Place stirrup hobble in off-side stirrup.

4.53 Twist the stirrup leather.

4.54 Buckle stirrups in place.

billet hole before it is tight enough to ride the bucking, you could have your saddle turned under the horse which can be a dangerous and frightening experience.

With the front buckle in place, pull the back billet through the back buckle on the girth. I suggest that you draw it up one notch tighter than the first one and then go back to the front buckle and level it up with the back one. If you have chosen a Western saddle for this procedure, use established safe techniques for saddling your horse. I do not recommend a flank or rear cinch on the first saddling. Take care to draw the latigo snug with one flowing motion and attempt to get it tight enough to ride out any bucking. The use of a Western-style cinch is less safe than the English-type where first saddling is concerned. The Western saddle is generally heavier and far more top heavy, thus more prone to turn under your animal. In addition, the English-style girth provides a simpler method of attachment for the trainer saddling the first-time horse. This is why I have chosen to use the English-style girth exclusively in recent years.

Now, remove the line from the halter, stepping back cautiously and staying out of the kick zone. At this point, you can send your horse away and if he chooses to buck, simply put him to work, keeping your adrenaline down. When you can ask your horse to travel in both directions of the round pen without bucking, he is ready to Join-Up again. Go passive and invite your horse to be with you again. Reward him, and allow him to follow you for a short period. At this point, you can bridle the horse using safe procedures (Goal Number 7). I recommend that you place the reins under the rear of the saddle, or provide another safe attachment. The reins should have slack in them and not make contact with the horse's mouth while executing normal maneuvers.

Walk in circles again, and let your horse follow you while mouthing the bit. Bring the horse back into the center. Pick up the stirrup leather and drop it through the offside stirrup iron so that it hangs halfway through. Move to the nearside, carefully pick up both ends of the stirrup leather, putting at least one twist in it, and then buckle it through the near iron. This procedure causes the stirrups to be secure at the sides of your animal so that they will not flop up and down during long lining.

Long Lining

Next, take up both lines holding them at the snap ends. Snap one into the nearside training ring of the Dually halter and place the other over the seat of the saddle allowing the snap to just reach the ground on the opposite side. Cross in front of your horse to the offside, giving his head a rub as you go round. Pass the offside snap through the stirrup (back to front) and snap it into the offside training ring of the Dually halter. Take care to adjust the Dually ring smoothly under the bit and bridle. Return to the nearside and repeat the process with the nearside line. Pick up the two lines on the near side of the horse and move backward and laterally outside the kick zone toward the rear of the horse. At this point, you are prepared to drive your horse on the two lines (Goal Number 8). Swing the offside line over his hips, which places you well behind the horse and in the driving position. You should be experienced with long lining long before you execute this procedure with a raw young horse. I recommend that you long line many trained and quiet horses before you take on a young inexperienced one. If your horse accepts the lines well, you are now prepared to allow him to circle the round pen while you stand near the center guiding him. Your horse should successfully execute circles on each lead and turn comfortably away from you as you request.

When your horse is turning and accepting his work at the walk, trot and canter, you should stop your student and turn him outward facing the fence. You should allow the animal to stand for a moment and relax. Then, lifting the lines, you should encourage him to take one step backward as he draws the slack from the reins. I recommend that you always cause your horse to take a step back before going to the next goal in the training procedure. I feel that this is important, as it instills in the horse's mind a desire to relax at the conclusion of each maneuver. If you accomplish this with

4.55 Fix the long lines on offside.

4.56 Fix the long lines on the nearside.

4.57 Long lining from the Dually halter.

4.58 Prepare for long lining.

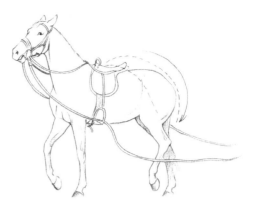

4.61 Swing the lines over the horse's hips.

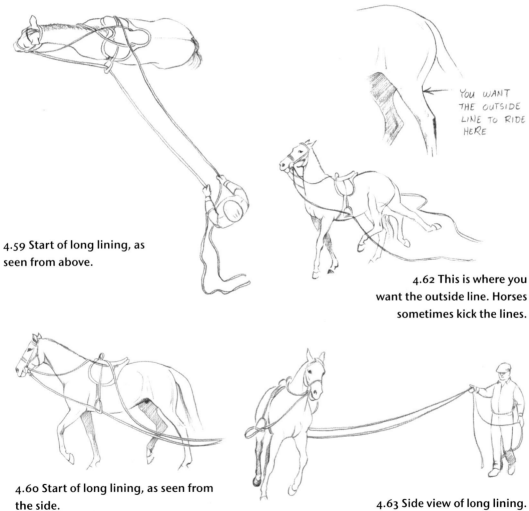

4.59 Start of long lining, as seen from above.

YOU WANT THE OUTSIDE LINE TO RIDE HERE

4.62 This is where you want the outside line. Horses sometimes kick the lines.

4.60 Start of long lining, as seen from the side.

4.63 Side view of long lining.

your horse, it is likely that you will never produce a horse that barges into the next procedure unilaterally; he is more apt to wait for you. I recommend driving, using the rings of the Dually halter once or twice (see Chapter 7), and then advance to the rings of the snaffle while long lining.

Next, remove the long lines and the stirrup leather. At this point in the procedure, horses that I start are generally ready to be ridden. It should be noted that I recommend that riders of horses that are being ridden for the first time are experienced in this activity. No matter who is starting the horse or how well he does his work, an untrained animal can be dangerous. Only a person accustomed to riding unschooled horses should attempt to mount at this point.

I do not want to leave you with the impression that I specifically recommend riding on the first day. Should you choose to repeat this process for several days before riding is accomplished, it is perfectly fine. You should be cautious not to repeat the Join-Up process so much that it becomes boring for your horse. I believe that just as with human students, horses need to move along in the educational process, keeping the work interesting.

I rode my own horses for about thirty-five years of my career. I began while in my forties to experiment with the use of an assigned rider. I discovered very quickly that it makes little difference whether I got on myself or I used another rider. In the Thoroughbred industry, most of the owners feel that riders should be very light. My early experience with using an assigned rider was with that in mind. There is no question that it is just as effective to have someone else ride for you.

In preparing your horse for riding, make sure all of your equipment is adjusted properly. It should be equipment that is sound, well-made and appropriate for dealing with young horses. Check the adjustment on the bit, and

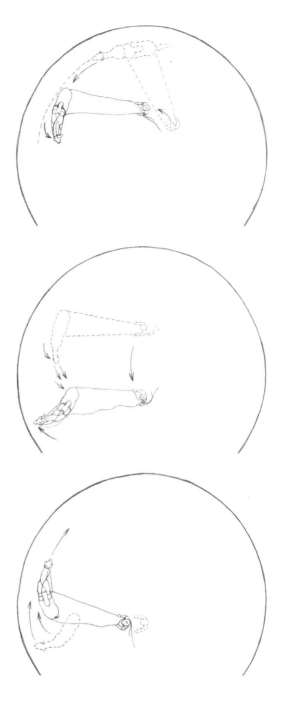

4.64 Overhead view of changing directions.

4.65 Overhead view as the direction changes.

4.66 Long lining resumes after changing direction.

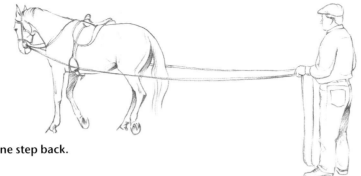

4.67 Take one step back.

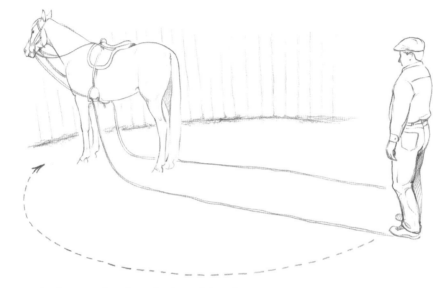

4.68 Drop the lines, and walk to the horse's head.

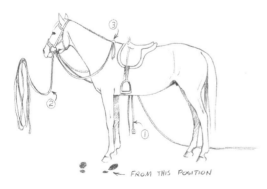

4.69 (1) Unbuckle the stirrup leather and let it hang; (2) pull the near line through the stirrup; (3) take the reins from under the saddle, and prepare them for the rider.

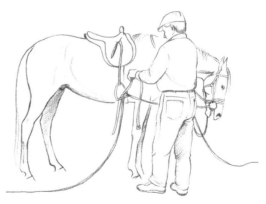

4.70 Remove the lines from the offside.

be sure that it is properly placed in the horse's mouth. Consult with the rider that the reins are acceptable. The girth, while not excessively tight, should certainly be snug enough to prevent the saddle turning. If you intend to ride the horse, it is at this point that I suggest you bring in an assistant to hold the horse and to leg you up (or hold for you to step on). For this book, however, I will complete the guide to Join-Up by describing how the trainer puts a rider on his horse.

4.71 Introduce the rider.

Mounting

Snap a line on the nearside bit ring. Give your rider a minute or two to get acquainted with the horse. He should rub both sides of the animal, and over the head and neck. At this time the rider should check the girth to make sure it has not loosened during the long lining. The rider should never raise his voice or act aggressively. It is advisable that your rider understands the concepts of Join-Up, and that his body language sends the correct messages to the horse. Jerky movements and aggressive body language could ruin the efforts you've made up to this point.

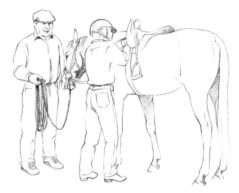

4.72 Be sure to check the girth for tightness.

I leg my riders up and I find it safer to belly them over at first. Next, I turn my horse left and then right, allowing him to feel the weight of his first rider. Should the horse want to buck, the rider can safely jump back away from the horse, which he could not do if he were sitting upright in the saddle. If the rider ejects from the belly position, he should stay forward of the horse and toward me. It is important that if this occurs, I bring the head of the horse toward me which moves his hips away from both the rider and myself. This will prevent the horse from kicking either one of us. It should be noted that an unintentional kick hurts just as much as an intentional one. The reason that I turn the horse first left and then right is because I want the horse to view my rider with each eye. I turn left first because that

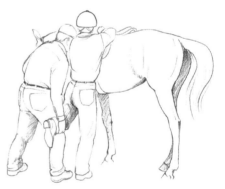

4.73 Leg-up the rider to belly over.

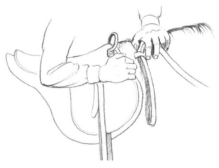

4.74 Where the rider should put his hands.

4.75 Belly over the saddle.

4.77 The rider's foot is guided into the stirrup.

4.76 Turn the horse's head left, and then right.

4.78 Send the horse and the rider away.

4.79 At the end, the rider requests the horse take one step back.

gives us the greatest control. Once I see that the horse has accepted this, I turn right so that the horse can see the rider out of the right eye. I am careful to control the horse and not allow him to take his head away from me should he start to buck as it could put my rider in jeopardy.

If the horse is comfortable with the rider lying over him, I will guide the rider's foot into the near stirrup and allow him to fully mount the horse (Goal Number 9). I then repeat the circles left and right. The reason being is that the horse will now see the head of the rider well above his back. This often frightens a young horse, and can evoke bucking. I repeat this procedure because I have found that if I can take my young horse through this now-familiar movement for the second time, I am less apt to get bucking with the upright rider. When my horse is relaxed and accepting the seated rider, I make larger circles so the horse gets a feel for walking forward with the rider up.

Once the horse is moving confidently, I quietly unsnap the line and help the rider by communicating with the horse that he should circle the pen once in each direction. I do not ask the horse to canter on the first day. I believe a walk and trot will suffice for the first experience. After each revolution, I like my rider to stop and rein back one step. I maintain that this reinforces what I accomplished on the long lines and sets a pattern for the life of the horse.

I ask the rider to request a step back and prepare for dismounting. The horse should be in a position well away from the fence. I attach the long line to the bit and throw the line behind me. I place one hand on the saddle at the withers as a precaution should the horse move

4.80 The proper procedure for the attendant to assist rider in dismounting.

LOOSEN THE CHEEK BEFORE PULLING THE BRIDLE OFF OVER THE EARS

PUT THE GIRTH UP OVER THE SADDLE BEFORE REMOVING THE SADDLE

4.81 How to remove the tack correctly.

toward me while the rider is dismounting. The rider should remove both feet from the stirrups and then bring the right leg clear over the back of the horse and dismount.

I untack my horse using safe procedures, and allow the rider to leave the pen, taking the tack with him. At home, I'm not a hero if my horse is not ready to be mounted; I save this last goal for another day. Remember, when I do my demonstrations, they must be completed in one session. If I took a long time or two sessions, the audience would have to return the next day. I also find that generally the horse is quite happy accepting the rider in about 30 minutes on average.

Join-Up will save you so much time that you will be well ahead even if you take several days before mounting. What is important is the quality of the work, and not how fast you accomplish it. By quality, I mean the level of acceptance and understanding the horse shows regarding the above goals. We all want well-behaved, happy and willing horses. It is on this that you will be judged, not the time it took.

It is well to remember that throughout Join-Up you want the horse to be a volunteer. You want your student to feel free to make choices, to choose to be with you and to be responsible for the consequences of those decisions. Never can a trainer excuse a deliberate act that causes the horse pain, and you always want to make it comfortable for him to be near you, rather than to be away. Discipline is an important part of Join-Up, but it should always take the form of work, never pain.

After your rider and equipment are clear of the pen and the gate is closed, you should create an environment that we at Flag Is Up Farms call "quality time." Crawford Hall, who has worked with me for almost three decades, believes that it is one of the most important things we do as part of the Join-Up process. You should simply stroke the head of the horse and walk away. It is likely that the horse will follow, but in the event that he does not, you should return and stroke the head and again walk away, crossing the line of sight of the horse, walking in circles. Most equestrians are surprised at how intently the horse wants to be with you. Some horses will choose to roll, and

there is certainly nothing wrong with this. You should simply wait for the horse to stand and then continue the quality time. We have come to believe that the quality-time session should last at least five minutes, but it does not hurt if it is ten or fifteen.

The full Join-Up procedure should be accomplished at least four times on successive days. This will start the horse's life of training in an exemplary fashion. With extremely difficult horses I have had to do the full Join-Up procedure as many as ten times. This is, however, extremely rare. I find that nearly all the domestic horses I start will be good students after four Join-Up sessions. There is no need to repeat the procedure an unreasonable number of times. Horses will eventually resent hearing the same story.

In the Stall

I often say to horsemen that once Join-Up is accomplished, we should live by the principles of Join-Up throughout the life of the horse. To explain that statement further, I think it is fair to give the reader two examples: one, the box stall; and the other, an outside enclosure such as a corral, paddock or small field. When you enter a box stall to catch a horse and remove him for riding or handling of any kind, you should use the principles of Join-Up throughout the procedure. If you enter the stall and the horse moves willingly toward you, you should drop your eyes to a point near the horse's forefeet and turn slightly to a 45-degree angle, thus inviting the horse to come near. At this time you can place the halter on the horse if you choose.

If you enter the stall and the horse is facing away from you and is reluctant to come to you, you should bounce the lead rope on your leg, square up on the horse, look him in the eye, and make moves as if you were trying to drive the horse away from you. Within a few seconds, the horse should turn slightly and look at you. With this, you should drop your eyes, turn to a 45-degree angle and invite the horse to turn off the back wall and approach you. If the horse is reluctant, you should repeat the process. If two or three of these episodes happen without the horse joining-up, you should consider returning to the round pen for another session. This procedure should be used in the box stall throughout the life of the horse.

In the Field

In an outside enclosure, you should utilize the same procedures as described for the box stall. In the larger enclosure however, you may have to walk some distance to effect the same result. Again, if the horse is not cooperative in two or three attempts, you should return to the round pen for more Join-Up training. Like the box stall, these procedures should be used in outdoor enclosures for the entire relationship that you have with the horse. My students often tell me that they believe these Join-Up sessions are even more important than the round pen session.

Monty's Points

» Join-Up is the most critical element of my concepts.

» Join-Up is the centerpiece of all communication when using my concepts.

» Violence must play *no* part in the process.

» The procedure should be precisely followed.

» Slow is fast; fast is slow.

» Goals should be set and met.

» Time is the least important thing.

» Always be safe.

» Equipment must be appropriate.

» Quality time is important after Join-Up.

» Principles of Join-Up should be used throughout the life of your relationship.

» Use principles of Join-Up in the box stall.

» Use principles of Join-Up in outdoor enclosures.

Questions and Answers _____

Q. Can you do Join-Up with a weanling?
A. I recommend Join-Up for a weanling when he is fully separated from his mother and has ceased calling out to her. Before you attempt a weanling, I recommend that you practice this art on some older, trained horses. A weanling should not be introduced to the Join-Up process more than two or three times. Once you have completed Join-Up, the horse should be turned out with other animals of the same age,

and allowed to grow up. You can live by the principles of Join-Up throughout the many months of rearing your foal. This simply means that you should always use the body Language of Equus when dealing with young stock.

Q. Does the size of the pen matter?
A. Sure, it matters. (See "The Round Pen," p. 29).

1 Monty introduces himself to the horse.

2 Eyes on eyes, shoulders square, Monty sends the horse away.

3 With eyes on eyes, Monty aggressively throws the long line for emphasis on going away. The horse moves away on his right lead.

4 Monty moves into a position to encourage the horse to reverse direction and take a left lead.

5 Monty again reverses the horse's direction back to a right lead for the second time around.

6 The horse continues to move off, but the right ear is now locked onto Monty, starting to show respect.

7 The horse is slowing down, with ear completely locked onto Monty now.

8 Monty folds his arm down with closed fingers and the horse starts to put his head down, as a gesture of readiness to negotiate.

9 Monty drops his eyes, brings his shoulder around to a 45° angle, to invite the horse to come in for Join-Up.

10 The horse starts to move off the fence, coming closer. Both ears are locked onto Monty.

11 The horse approaches Monty, while Monty remains passive with eyes down, inviting the horse to take that final step.

12 This is the "moment of Join-Up."

13 Monty invites the horse to follow-up, first turning clockwise.

14 The horse continues to follow-up with Monty in a clockwise motion.

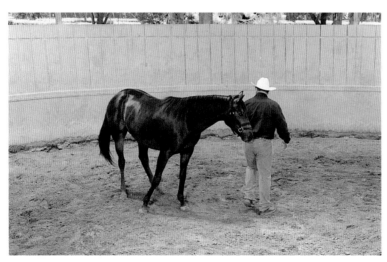

15 Monty reverses direction and invites the horse to follow-up in a counter-clockwise direction.

16 The horse is fully following Monty in a complete counter-clockwise direction.

17 Monty rubs the vulnerable areas where lions, tigers and leopards attack.

18 Monty rubs the vulnerable areas where wolves, coyotes and other canines attack.

19 Monty carefully picks up the near hind leg, while the horse stands quietly.

20 An attendant now brings in the tack. The horse looks it over closely to see if it is something that will harm him.

21 Monty tests the horse's trust by allowing the horse to choose to follow-up, despite being distracted by the tack.

22 The first saddle pad is put up on the horses's withers. He stands quietly.

23 Monty puts the first saddle of the horse's life over the saddle pad. The horse remains calm.

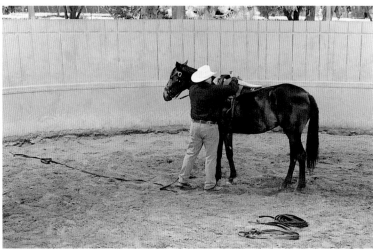

24 Monty now reaches under the horse to attach the girth. During this procedure the horse is standing with a loose long line.

25 With his adrenaline
low, Monty girths up
the saddle.

26 Acting instinctively,
the horse attempts to
buck the saddle off his
back. This is a very
normal reaction.

27 The horse reverses his
direction, but continues
to buck.

28 The horse volunteers
to Join-Up with Monty
once more, finding safety
in Monty's company.

29 Now it is time to put
the first bridle on the
horse. He accepts
it quietly.

30 Monty crosses the
reins behind the saddle
in preparation for the
long lining procedure.

Chapter 4 / Join-Up

31 Monty now attaches the stirrup leather to the stirrups. He puts a twist in the middle to take up some slack.

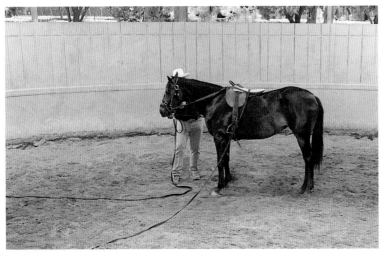

32 Monty moves to the offside where he attaches the long line through the stirrup and snaps it to the Dually halter or the bridle.

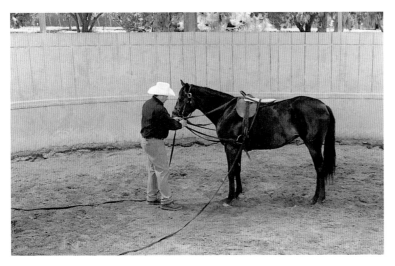

33 Monty now moves back to the nearside where he runs the left long line through the stirrup and again attaches it to the Dually halter or bridle.

34 Monty steps back and away from the horse in preparation to drive the horse on the long lines.

35 Monty flicks the offside long line down over the left hip and the long lining procedure begins.

36 This is what the long lining procedure looks like from the side as the horse moves away on his left lead.

37 Monty reverses direction to put the horse on his right lead.

38 Monty asks the horse to stop and take one step back.

39 After the horse volunteers to take the step back, Monty loosens the long lines and drops them.

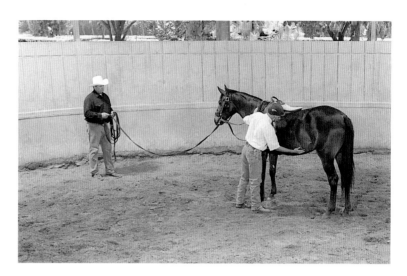

40 Jason Davis, the rider, now introduces himself to the horse, while Monty stands back quietly watching.

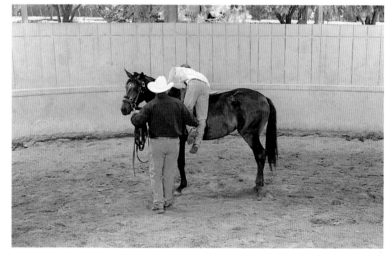

41 Before mounting, Monty assists Jason in bellying over the horse to accustom him to the weight and to see the rider on his back.

42 Jason rides the horse off in a quiet fashion, giving the horse the chance to feel comfortable with his first rider.

43 Jason gives the horse a reward for a job well done.

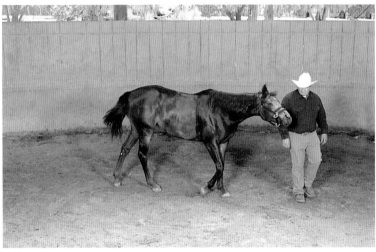

44 A very contented horse, he continues to want to be with Monty, following him around the pen.

45 Monty is giving the horse some "quality time." This is what Crawford Hall calls the moment of relaxation upon completion of the starting.

Join-Up
Days Two Through Four

I advise that once started with Join-Up, the process of a horse's education should continue uninterrupted. It is not a good idea to start the horse, give him a day or two off, and then expect him to pick up where you left off. Through these concepts, it is fair to expect improvement each day if the work is done on consecutive days. Using between four and ten full complement Join-Ups is appropriate. One should execute at least six consecutive sessions before giving the horse a day off. If four full Join-Ups are employed, then the last two sessions would be simple communication, living by the concepts of Join-Up.

If you have followed to the letter the procedures that I described in "Join-Up Day One," you are prepared to go on to "Day Two." For our purposes herein, we will define Day One as the first day when the horse is ridden.

Day Two
Bring your horse to the round pen having in mind all of the admonishments connected to Day One. Follow the Day One procedures virtually identically. You are likely to find that each goal is accomplished quicker and is easier to meet. When you reach the point at which you have your horse on long lines, I suggest that you extend the length of time you work with your horse in this format. Trot and canter more. It is likely that you will find your horse more willing to rein back while on the long lines. Be soft with your hands, but ask a bit more of him in this area. After mounting, it is likely, but not necessarily always true, that your horse is ready to canter on the second day. If you think that your horse is inclined to buck, save the canter for the third or fourth day. I have had some real challenges in my career who were not safe to canter until the eighth or tenth day, but those are very rare.

On Day Two, most horses are ready to cross through the center of the pen being directed by their rider at a trot. I feel that it is appropriate to extend the length of time in the round pen on the second day so that you spend about 45 minutes on average, rather than the 30 minutes on average that you spend on the first day. Remember, it is important to end each of your procedures, and the day, on as positive a note as possible. Take your rider off and close out Day Two in a similar fashion to Day One.

Day Three
With the average horse that I start and train, Day Three is one of the most interesting. It is often a day when the horse will experiment more than in Day One or Day Two. He has now learned to carry the rider's weight and be a bit more comfortable with the challenge of carrying saddle and rider. Often the horse that chose not to buck in the first two sessions will try it in the third session. Thus, it is important to follow the rules regarding the rider throughout the first five or even ten rides, depending on the horse. As I have studied the horse industry throughout my life I have found that this is the case no matter which procedures of starting or breaking are used. I say this not to frighten the reader, but to advise against being lulled into a sense of security and then surprised by your equine student.

Day Three should proceed much as Day Two, however the early procedures of Join-Up, follow-up, and vulnerable areas are apt to take less than five minutes. It then becomes a matter of saddling, long lining for even a greater length of time than in Day Two, and riding and building on the procedures of Day Two. If your horse canters well on Day Three, you are probably ready to introduce him to a saddle horse in the round pen at the same time. Preferably a gelding, this horse should be well-trained and easily manageable. Your young horse should become acquainted with the saddle horse and given the chance to follow him round the pen at a walk, trot and canter in each direction. At this point, the rider can begin to use fairly obvious leg aids and guide the horse more overtly with the bit and bridle. If you are worried about your saddle horse kicking either the young horse or the rider, one should pull the rear shoes on the saddle horse and have him go bare-footed behind through these procedures. Finish off Day Three as positively as possible, and by this time you might be in a position to allow the rider to dismount without assistance.

Day Four

Day Four is usually a type of graduation day in my operation. The average horse that I start is ready on Day Four to leave the confines of the round pen and go on to a larger training area, in my case, an arena. Day Four should go much as Day Three, but spending a longer time with your saddle horse in the pen with your student. If the young horse is following the saddle horse comfortably and your rider can stop, turn left and right, and rein back, then you can go on to the outdoor or larger training area. If there is any doubt in your mind that this procedure can be done safely, take an extra day or so.

Remember, your outdoor training area must have safe footing and safe fencing. It is advisable to have a third person to handle the gates of the two areas so that there is no interruption in your transition to the outside area. The outside enclosure should be free of things that would spook a young horse. These might include loose animals nearby, an uncontrolled dog, or a plastic bag hanging from a tree or fence. The first day outside should consist entirely of following the saddle horse and include the walk and trot in both directions and a reverse by creating a large figure-eight. It is not necessary to canter outside on the first day, which might be best reserved for another three

to five days. I recommend that both horses and riders return to the round pen before dismounting, and in my operation it is not until about the tenth day on average that I have the rider dismount outside.

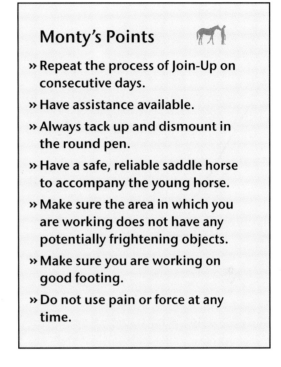

Monty's Points

» Repeat the process of Join-Up on consecutive days.

» Have assistance available.

» Always tack up and dismount in the round pen.

» Have a safe, reliable saddle horse to accompany the young horse.

» Make sure the area in which you are working does not have any potentially frightening objects.

» Make sure you are working on good footing.

» Do not use pain or force at any time.

Join-Up Problem Solving _____

Q. My horse won't Join-Up. What should I do?
A. If I have a human student in front of me, I can react to what I see as a shortcoming in his procedure or a need to modify. When writing a book, however, I do not have the privilege of seeing my reader at work, thus I must generalize my comments. It comes down to the fact that I must answer practically every question with the admonition to study harder and practice more because these are the only two ways we can become better at learning Join-Up.

I have been dealing with the principles of Join-Up since 1942. In 1947, I began my work with mustangs. I feel that dealing with these horses who have a communication system that is pure was the real beginning of my understanding of the Join-Up phenomenon. The mustangs use a language with one another that is unaffected by human contact. I observed first their exchanges horse to horse, and then I watched as they dealt with predators. Subsequently, I used forms of the gestures that I had seen in an attempt to create communication between myself and horses. I was amazed to find that it was possible. By 1952 or 1953, I was what I would call "street conversant." I have continued to hone my skills and understand more about the Language of Equus so that communicating Join-Up has become increasingly more fluent. Now, with more than 12,000 horses on my list, I attempt to teach this skill to entry-level horsemen. While I feel that I can give students a great leg-up in the learning process, there is still much education to do. I had to learn through trial and error.

I do not know of any language that can be learned overnight. I am not aware of a worthwhile skill that just falls into your brain like a flake of snow from the sky. You need to educate yourself to the Language of Equus which allows you to accomplish Join-Up. Often, I have people come to me and say, "I tried to Join-Up with my horse, but it does not work with him. I guess he is stupid or something."

I am quick to answer, "Please do not blame your horse or call him stupid." Wherever there are shortcomings in the training process, one should look inward to find the reason. I normally ask how many horses they have attempted Join-Up with, and I generally get numbers like one, two, or three.

I relayed a story to my students about my being in Paris in the early 1970s. Once, I found myself hopelessly lost in a rented car. When I saw a police officer standing on a corner, I decided to pull to the curb and ask how to get back to the George V Hotel. I used several sentences of my best French to glean an answer from him. It did not take long to figure out that this police officer was very angry about my parking the car in a restricted area. His tone of voice, waving of arms and shouting at the top of his lungs made it clear to me that he did not understand my French at all and wanted me out of there immediately. I drove to the first hotel I saw and secured the services of a bilingual taxi driver to negotiate the way to the George V Hotel with me following in my rented car.

Prior to my trip to France, I had taken a one-week course in the French language. I use this story as an anecdote to prove to people who come to me that it is essential to spend time learning the nuances of Join-Up. I suggest to them that they use an older, trained and gentle horse while learning the process, as I often find that students will expect to be successful with the raw horse at first asking. Like anything else in life, we should crawl before we walk and walk before we run.

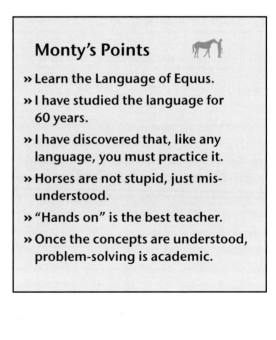

Monty's Points

» Learn the Language of Equus.
» I have studied the language for 60 years.
» I have discovered that, like any language, you must practice it.
» Horses are not stupid, just misunderstood.
» "Hands on" is the best teacher.
» Once the concepts are understood, problem-solving is academic.

More Questions and Answers _____

Q. My horse gives me his gestures, but he does not seem to understand mine and refuses to Join-Up with me.

A. This is a situation almost identical to myself and the police officer. He understood French perfectly well, but he did not understand my French and obviously I needed to learn it better before expecting him to understand. I suggest that you do Join-Up with ten to twenty head of trained horses and then try your horse again. You will probably laugh at how easy it can suddenly become. Meanwhile, it would be good to study the principles through my videos and books.

Q. I can get my horse to Join-Up fine, but he will not follow. What should I do?

A. When I hear this query, I find that the student is telling the horse not to follow with the gestures he or she uses. Most often, it will be bad eye movements. The student will take a step or two and then snap his or her eyes back toward the horse to see if he is following. This tells the horse not to follow. I often explain that within a few minutes I have no doubt this horse would follow me. This means that my movements better execute the Language of Equus.

Q. I find that after a few minutes of dealing with my horse he tunes me out. He becomes what I would call resistant. He ignores me and I cannot seem to get his attention. What have I done wrong?

A. A horse will only give you a few tries to get it right and then it seems that he says "He does not understand my language; I'm going to stop bothering myself about it. I am just going to tune him out." Again, more study and more practice is the answer to getting it right.

Q. I have studied Join-Up extensively. I have watched the tapes and I believe I know what I am supposed to do. I go in the round pen and while working with my horse I see the signals that I have trained myself to observe. But, when I attempt to transition to the next step, my horse is nonresponsive. Why is that?

A. I am pleased that you have taken the time to study the process thoroughly. I believe the problem here is that you have not practiced sufficiently with live horses to get your timing right. Often students will become quite knowledgeable as to the procedures they need to follow. However, watching them in the round pen, I realize that the flow of their movements and the timing of their gestures are out of synchronization with their horses. Often, a student will observe the gesture made by a horse and then walk a few more steps thinking about exactly what to do to execute the transition. By the time he does, the horse is off on another subject. We have had several students in our school that pass the written tests successfully. Later in the round pen, I observe a person who is unable to execute the simplest elements of the Language of Equus. In a case like this, we will try to assign him a young horse to hone his practical skills. I have adopted several mustangs who serve as the greatest teachers available for students who fit this category. If you have the academics down, the likelihood is that you need more "hands-on" time with live horses to perfect your skills.

Q. Can you tell me why my horse just canters around and around without apparently seeing or responding to me?

A. Without personal observation, I can only speculate about why this is occurring. I answer this question quite often, however, and I will attempt to base my answer on what I find to be the seat of the problem. A primary condition that leads a student to ask this question is that the horse has been extensively longed. He has learned that he has to stay out there and run around the pen until the trainer cues him to stop. One reason I dislike single-line longeing is that it goes against the nature of the horse. I can always tell when a horse has been longed that way because he exhibits many idiosyncrasies that single-line longeing tends to create (see "Single-Line Longeing," p, 104).

Other Common Problems

Orphan foals that have been raised on a bottle seldom learn the Language of Equus fluently, therefore using the Language of Equus in Join-Up is relatively ineffective. I do not know of any other procedure that works well on bottle-raised foals either, because it is difficult to communicate with them. I advise people to use alternative techniques when raising orphans. First, it is important for humans to have as little contact with the foal as possible. I also recommend raising them with other foals. A well-grafted nurse mare can be very effective and will often raise you a foal that you would not know was an orphan. Goats can help you in this process too, and I have found their milk to be significantly superior to cows' milk to nourish a young horse. A goat, along with several foals to run with, and close attention to the use of alternative concentrate feeds, can help you raise a well-adjusted animal.

Without a doubt, the greatest contributor to raising an abnormal foal happens when the humans allow emotion to enter the scenario. They will often fall in love with the baby and find it gratifying that the young horse comes to rely upon them to sustain life. The inevitable outcome of this activity is the production of a young horse that believes that he is part human. It is curious that with this mind-set the foal will virtually always become mean eventually. Associating food with the human body, and believing that he is somehow close to being the same species, will create the expression of anger within the foal.

Aggressive males can be a serious problem for the practitioner of Join-Up. This is not to say that they are not a serious problem for any

other method, but you could be laying yourself open to injury if you place your trust in an aggressive young male horse. It is not by accident that aggression in young colts becomes a part of their makeup. There is a high probability that mistakes have been made by people that cause this problem. That, however, does not mean you should consciously expose yourself to potential injury in an attempt to do Join-Up with this sort of animal. Young stallions should be handled by professionals, not by amateurs. An aggressive young male should be treated as a remedial horse before any attempt to do Join-Up.

The alpha female can, in rare cases, be as dangerous as the aggressive young male. If you identify alpha female characteristics in a filly, then she should be treated in much the same way as an aggressive male.

Monty's Points

» Orphan foals raised on a bottle seldom learn the Language of Equus.

» If possible, raise orphans with other foals.

» Nurse mares and goats greatly help in raising orphan foals.

» Keep human emotion out of the scenario.

» Associating food with the human body should never be allowed.

» Aggressiveness in young males is a serious problem and should be handled only by professionals.

» Aggressive young males should be treated as remedial horses.

» Alpha females sometimes exhibit aggressive tendencies.

The Dictionary of Join-Up_____

1. Human Gestures as Seen by the Horse

Eyes on eyes. — I am sighting my prey. I am hungry.

Eyes on eyes, shoulders square. — I am getting ready to be "predatorial."

Eyes on eyes and arms out, fingers open. — I am getting ready to pounce.

Fist closed, arms lowered toward body. — I am not "predatorial."

Eyes down, arms folded around front of midline. — I am resting.

Shoulders at 45°, arms down and folded across midline, eyes off eyes. — I am inviting you to feel safe around me.

2. Sending the Horse Away

1. The initial gesture to send the horse away
6. The optimal collection of gestures to send the horse away

1. Eyes on eyes is the initial gesture to send the horse away.

2. Eyes on eyes and shoulders square is more effective than #1.

3. Eyes on eyes, shoulders square, arms out, is more effective than #1 or 2.

4. Eyes on eyes, shoulders square, arms out and fingers open is more effective than #1, 2 or 3.

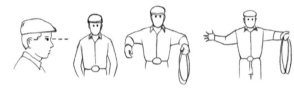

5. Eyes on eyes, shoulders square, arms out, fingers open and throwing the line is more effective than #1, 2, 3 or 4.

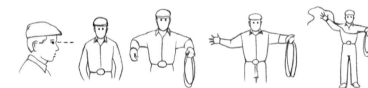

6. Eyes on eyes, shoulders square, arms out, fingers open, throwing the line and advancing is more effective than #1, 2, 3, 4 or 5.

3. Inviting the Horse to Join-Up

1. The initial gesture to invite the horse to Join-Up
6. The optimal collection of gestures to invite the horse to Join-Up

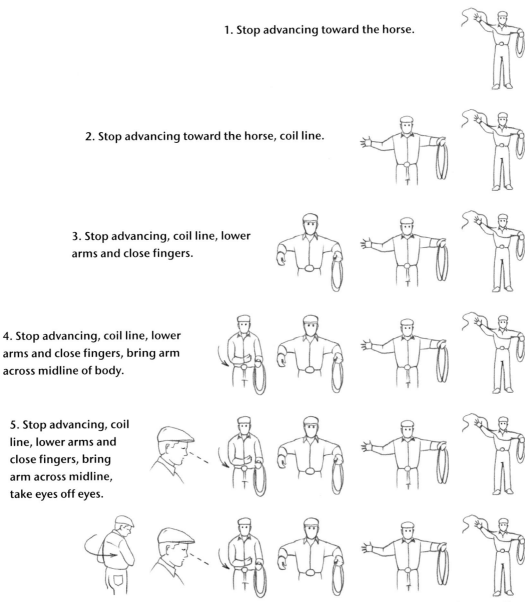

1. Stop advancing toward the horse.

2. Stop advancing toward the horse, coil line.

3. Stop advancing, coil line, lower arms and close fingers.

4. Stop advancing, coil line, lower arms and close fingers, bring arm across midline of body.

5. Stop advancing, coil line, lower arms and close fingers, bring arm across midline, take eyes off eyes.

6. Stop advancing, coil line, lower arms and close fingers, bring arm across midline, take eyes off eyes and stand with your shoulders at a 45° angle.

4. Sending the Horse Away

Arrows indicate the direction from which the gesture is made

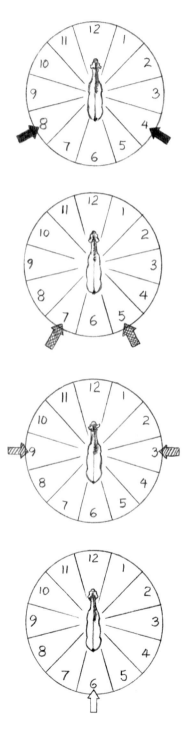

1. Sending the horse from near 8 o'clock or 4 o'clock is optimal.

2. Sending the horse from near 7 o'clock or 5 o'clock is less effective than #1.

3. Sending the horse from near 9 o'clock or 3 o'clock is less effective than #1 or 2

4. Sending the horse from near 6 o'clock is less effective than #1, 2 or 3, and not recommended.

5. Drawing the Horse Toward You

Arrows indicate the direction from which the gesture is made

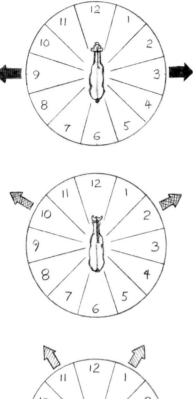

1. Drawing the horse toward you from near 3 o'clock or 9 o'clock is optimal.

2. Drawing the horse toward you from near 2 o'clock or 10 o'clock is less effective than #1.

3. Drawing the horse toward you from near 11 o'clock or 1 o'clock is less effective than #1 or 2.

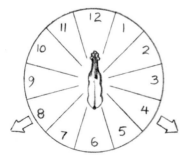

4. Drawing the horse toward you from near 4 o'clock or 8 o'clock is less effective than #1, 2 or 3 (6 o'clock is not recommended).

6. Sending the Horse Away by Snapping Your Eyes

Snapping your eyes is the most effective eye movement to send the horse away

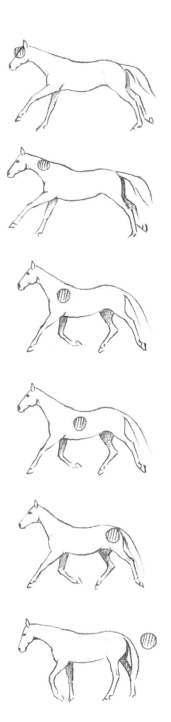

1. Snapping your eyes, from a location away from the horse, to the eyes of the horse, is the optimal initial gesture to send the horse away from you.

2. Snapping your eyes, from a location away from the horse, to the neck of the horse is less effective than #1 in sending the horse away from you.

3. Snapping your eyes, from a location away from the horse, to the shoulders of the horse is less effective than # 1 or 2 in sending the horse away from you.

4. Snapping your eyes, from a location away from the horse, to the ribs of the horse is less effective than #1, 2 or 3 in sending the horse away from you.

5. Snapping your eyes, from a location away from the horse, to the hips of the horse is less effective than #1, 2, 3 or 4 in sending the horse away from you.

5. Snapping your eyes, from a location away from the horse, to behind the tail of the horse is less effective than #1, 2, 3 4 or 5 in sending the horse away from you.

7. Dragging Your Eyes To Speed Up the Horse

This gesture is less effective than snapping the eyes

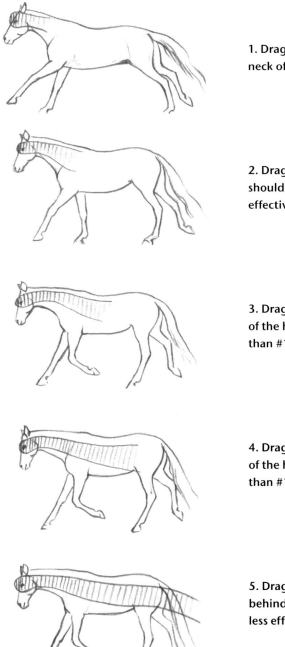

1. Dragging the focus of your eyes from the neck of the horse to the horse's eyes is optimal.

2. Dragging the focus of your eyes from the shoulder of the horse to the horse's eyes is less effective than #1.

3. Dragging the focus of your eyes from the ribs of the horse to the horse's eyes is less effective than #1 or 2.

4. Dragging the focus of your eyes from the hips of the horse to the horse's eyes is less effective than #1, 2 or 3.

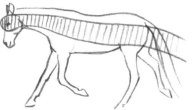

5. Dragging the focus of your eyes from the behind the tail of the horse to the horse's eyes is less effective than #1, 2, 3 or 4.

8. Dragging Your Eyes To Slow the Horse Down

Dragging your eyes from the eyes of the horse to a point on the horse's body is effective in slowing down the horse

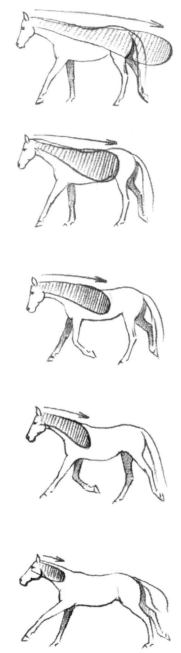

1. Dragging the focus of your eyes from the eyes of the horse to behind the tail of the horse is optimal.

2. Dragging the focus of your eyes from the eyes of the horse to the hips of the horse is less effective than #1.

3. Dragging the focus of your eyes from the eyes of the horse to the ribs of the horse is less effective than #1 or 2.

4. Dragging the focus of your eyes from the eyes of the horse to the shoulder of the horse is less effective than #1, 2 or 3.

2. Dragging the focus of your eyes from the eyes of the horse to the neck of the horse is less effective than #1, 2, 3 or 4.

9. Hand and Arm Signals Sending the Horse Away

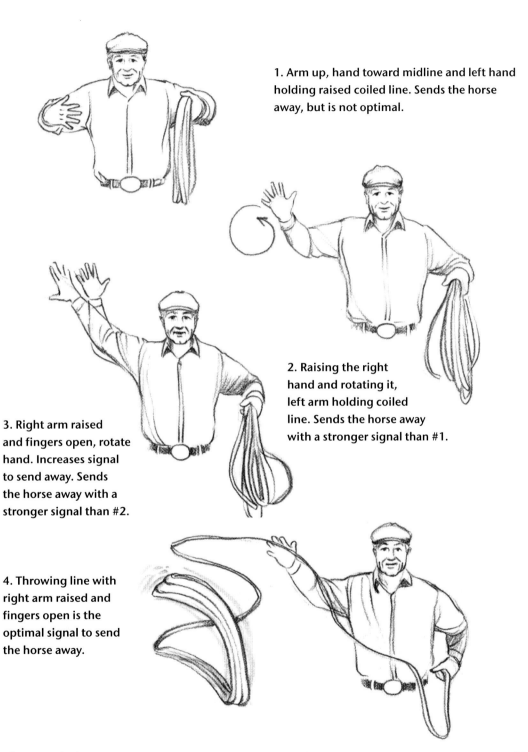

1. Arm up, hand toward midline and left hand holding raised coiled line. Sends the horse away, but is not optimal.

2. Raising the right hand and rotating it, left arm holding coiled line. Sends the horse away with a stronger signal than #1.

3. Right arm raised and fingers open, rotate hand. Increases signal to send away. Sends the horse away with a stronger signal than #2.

4. Throwing line with right arm raised and fingers open is the optimal signal to send the horse away.

10. Hand and Arm Signals Slowing the Horse Down

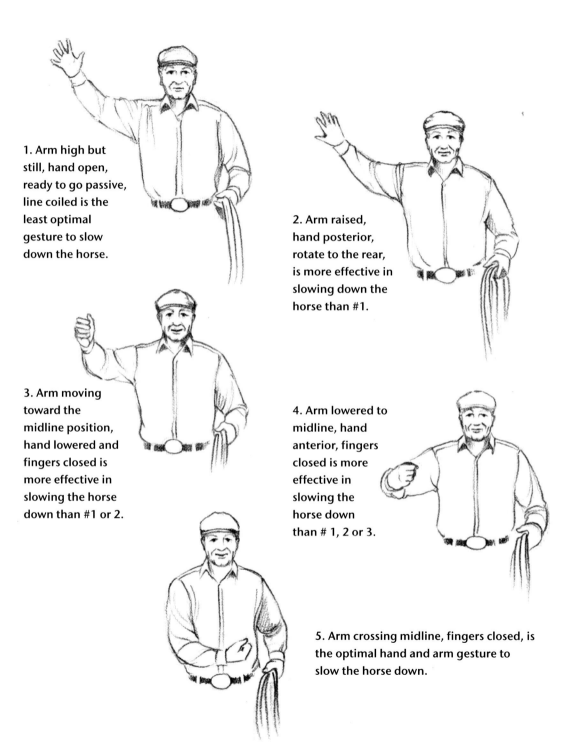

1. Arm high but still, hand open, ready to go passive, line coiled is the least optimal gesture to slow down the horse.

2. Arm raised, hand posterior, rotate to the rear, is more effective in slowing down the horse than #1.

3. Arm moving toward the midline position, hand lowered and fingers closed is more effective in slowing the horse down than #1 or 2.

4. Arm lowered to midline, hand anterior, fingers closed is more effective in slowing the horse down than # 1, 2 or 3.

5. Arm crossing midline, fingers closed, is the optimal hand and arm gesture to slow the horse down.

Chapter 5

Forming Partnerships

Creating a Willing Horse

I always say that there are no problem horses, only horses that have problems with the actions of people. Horses are not stupid. They do not possess an ego, so have a simple view of life—to procreate and to survive.

Use of my concepts (see the introduction) doesn't only solve the problems caused by inappropriate handling, but by learning the principles behind them, teaches people to retrain themselves in the way in which they work around horses. This way, a recurrence of the problems is often prevented.

When I was in the eighth grade, I had a great teacher. Sister Agnes Patricia used to say to the class, "Knowledge cannot be pushed into the brain by the teacher; it must be pulled in by the brain of the student." Her advice— a key to something so valuable to me—has helped to form the core of my concepts. That key is for the teacher to create willingness. I wait until the horse has decided he is ready to take in the information I am offering. When a horse is willing, he will learn for himself. He will make a decision to cooperate. Once you have harnessed his willingness, you have the solution to virtually every training problem.

The creation of willingness within your horse is possible only in an environment free of fear and resentment. To create a place free of these two elements, you must eliminate violence and force as an option and establish parameters of cooperation using discipline that is acceptable and bilaterally agreeable. I have concluded that the best way to do this is to establish a system of contracts. With people, you can have verbal contracts or written contracts. With horses, your contracts must take place with actions speaking as loudly as the spoken or written word. The effective equestrian will create these contracts so that when lived by, a path of least resistance is set up. This path is then designed so that the horse willingly takes you to the goals you want for him.

The idea of the contract system was first introduced to me by a horse I had from 1942 to 1953, called Brownie. In 1948, I was 13 years old, and had already won some championships. With youthful exuberance, I considered myself a competent rider. This horse proved to me that I still had a great deal to learn. I showed Brownie in the Western division and he was an incredible all-round performer. Like any horse he had his strong and weak points. Brownie's sliding stops were his trademark. His spins, Western pirouettes, were exemplary, but changing leads in his figure-eights would usually cost a point or two. I recall that I worked very hard to improve Brownie in this regard. It seemed that the harder we worked, the more problems we had.

I sought advice from top trainers and was told that I should back off and give him a rest. He was going sour. An idea came to me one morning as I was cleaning stalls. I chose a strategy and concluded that I would discuss it with Brownie when I got to his stall, which was the last on my list. I recall, as if it was yesterday, that I entered his stall and began to talk with him. "I know you do not understand my language," I said, "but someday, I will understand yours. Meanwhile, I will communicate with you the best way I can. I will attempt to let you know what I am thinking and do that through my actions. They tell me you are overtrained, so I have a new deal for you. I will agree to train far more lightly Monday through Friday, if you promise to give me one hundred percent on the weekends. I guess I have been asking you for championship performances Wednesday and Thursday, and then demanding them Saturday and Sunday. I promise I will ease up if you will go after it when the competition is on."

Of course, Brownie did not understand one word I said, but he did understand the concepts when they were in place. It is a contract system and it is all about rewarding the positive and causing the negative to be less comfortable. The secret behind the success of my work is to make it extremely comfortable for the horse to do what I want and uncomfortable when he does not.

5.1 Monty riding Johnny Tivio in a cutting horse competition. Johnny Tivio was the Pacific Coast Cutting Horse Association Champion in 1966.

This is a simple idea based on the behavioral principles of positive and negative reinforcement. I should clarify here that pain must never be synonymous with uncomfortable. To create discomfort, I like to use a system of putting the horse to work. The flight animal is generous and will, under normal circumstances, enter a work mode willingly and energetically. If you are sensible and you learn to require an amount of effort appropriate to the misdeed, you will seldom create resentment in your horse. Be quick to heap praise on him, and stop work when your horse enters a positive mode.

Negative Reinforcement

To give my reader an understanding of the origin of these principles and what caused them to be instinctual in the horse's makeup (see Chapter One), I will go over the salient points. If the predator's defense is to attack, the horse's defense is to flee. Flight is the first line of defense and therefore the key to his survival. For the horse, that period of intense exercise is, unlike the lion, not rewarded with a trophy, but with rest from flight and a return to his natural lifestyle—grazing peacefully.

When the matriarch mare sends the mischievous colt out of the herd, she makes his life uncomfortable. He is afraid he will be eaten by predators and is anxious to rejoin the safety of the herd. The herd affords protection and comfort to each horse. The matriarch will allow the youngster back in when he shows signs of respect. All my concepts make it difficult for the horse to do what I think is wrong, and easy for him to do what I think is right.

I do use some extrinsic training equipment. The Giddy-Up rope, a length of thick cotton braided rope that is swung back and forth behind the rider's leg, introduces movement to the peripheral vision of the horse. This movement will be perceived by the horse to be dangerous and yet no pain comes of it. The horse is likely to advance quickly, moving away from the perceived intruder. The rider should be quick to praise the horse for moving forward and take great care to not require significant effort in the early stages. Too much work will reintroduce an unwilling attitude on the part of your horse. Very gradually increase the workload until your horse has regained confidence and enjoys the chosen discipline.

The Dually halter (the practical application of which is described in Chapter 7) creates an uncomfortable environment when the horse is negative. When the horse does respond to this piece of equipment, he is doing so willingly because he has learned to cooperate with, instead of resist, the action of the Dually halter. When I first work with the Dually, a horse will often pull back, resisting my request to come forward. Sometimes he will even rear and strike out with his front feet. Many observers classify this action as failure on the part of the horse. In fact, if the horse wants to resist, this can be overcome by allowing him to express his resistance and then learn that it is uncomfortable and therefore unacceptable. This creates a

perfect opportunity for the horse to learn that coming forward to cooperate with the Dually is far better than acting out against it.

I find it hard to believe that there is anything on earth that fits the definition of *failure*. For me, those things that most people consider to be failures are simply opportunities to learn. There is another category of so-called failure that I would like to address here. It is what I call "unavoidable conditions in nature." Death, for instance, is the ultimate failure of an animate body to continue to function as a live being. Is it really failure, or is it the success of nature to clean up and prepare for a fresh start—to create an environment of improvement through a phenomenon of one generation learning from another? Through survival of the fittest, I believe that nature has created a wonderful method of revitalizing this earth through the principles of birth and death.

Throughout our lives, living and dealing with the minds of horses, we are constantly bombarded with actions from them that are less than desirable. We can respond to these actions with an attitude of anger and frustration if we choose. We can grab a whip and "work them over," demanding what we perceive to be acceptable behavior. This, after all, is essentially how we have dealt with horses throughout the 8,000 years since domestication. I have learned, however, that it is far more effective to observe these sessions of unacceptable actions by our horses in a calm and cool fashion.

A horse cannot contrive. Once you can accept that the horse is also a proactive thinker and will respond to an action by the trainer with his own thought process, then acting out violently is exactly the opposite of what in the long term will modify his behavior. Allowing a horse to fail is an important part of the learning process. When a horse bucks with his first saddle, is he failing? Certainly not! The horse believes that he has a predator on his back, and in order to survive he must buck the predator off. If you stand back and allow the horse to think through what is happening, then as the adrenaline goes down, the horse will be able to reconsider the situation. Whipping the horse will only confirm his first impression that he has indeed got a predator on his back. In the end, the horse will realize that by repeating a certain unacceptable behavior he is not finding much comfort. He learns very quickly.

The horse trained to safely carry a rider is accepting an enormous responsibility. Horse and rider are partners in whatever discipline they enjoy. Partners means 50–50, not 49–51.

I have, over the years, designed and adapted tack and equipment that has helped me with my concepts. I will be sharing with you how I use these designs: the Dually halter, my blanket for protecting horses going through the starting gates, long lines, and others to make life more comfortable for you and your horse. I should add that the most important part of any equipment is the hands that hold it.

Monty's Points

» **Make it uncomfortable when the horse is negative.**

» **Make it comfortable for the horse to do what you want.**

» **Make fair contracts with your horse.**

» **Respond immediately to the signals the horse gives you.**

» **Use the Language of Equus.**

» **Never lose your temper.**

» **Be consistent.**

» **Work to achieve a 50–50 partnership.**

» **Use well-designed equipment, in good condition.**

Training with Choice

The late Greg Ward from Tulare, California, was in my opinion one of the greatest horse trainers in our Western disciplines. He died of cancer in November 1998, at 63. He produced 14 world champions, and many millions of dollars worth of high-quality winning horses in the show ring.

Greg and I were university classmates in the late fifties. He came to college a very inexperienced horseman, and I worked with him during his early days as I had a good deal more experience in competition then. Greg was a thoughtful and observant man, possessing an open and inquiring mind. He and I shared much the same philosophy concerning horse training.

In 1995, I visited his operation, and I was interested to find that he and his son, John, had developed the ideas of non-confrontational training. Greg told me that when he arrived at the decision to invite his young equine students to learn through an environment of complete freedom, his success level escalated appreciably. I felt that I had been doing a great service to young horses by releasing them in a round pen, allowing them to follow a path by which they were responsible for their own actions, but controlling their directions within a matter of thirty minutes or so. What I discovered with Greg was that he was taking this concept a great deal further by allowing them twenty days of freedom to make their own choices.

The handlers of these young horses would not pull on the lead rope to get them to go in a particular direction. Instead, they would walk with them, encouraging them to go where they wanted, but never forcing. Once the horses were saddled, the riders spent an hour or so in a controlled safe area, but never directed the horses in any way. They would stop and eat, they might paw at the ground or even

5.2 Greg Ward with daughter up behind, and Monty on Night Mist—
co-winners of a major cow-horse championship in the mid-sixties.

ment in the process of learning is communication.

Greg was drawn to a particular two-year-old colt he nicknamed Magic. He felt he could win the Snaffle Bit Futurity on him. Greg's doctors informed him that he only had weeks to live. Greg made a choice. He could go home, go to bed and die, or he could work hard, compete on Magic and die. Greg chose the latter. He made the choice to compete on Magic. Greg and Magic won by the greatest margin ever before awarded. Greg and Magic's victory was achieved in late September 1998. He died sixty days later.

lie down, but were never directed to fulfill the wishes of the rider.

Still, within the first twenty days, if they were negative, the only discipline applied was to put them to work. They were given positive reward through rubbing, stroking and easing-up on the workload. By workload, I am referring to the schooling required for a horse to compete in Western show disciplines.

Training is a fine line between creating new challenges and establishing a safe environment. The challenges pose questions and the safe environment is one in which learning can take place. Training is accomplished through that balance of introducing new tasks and repeating already established ones. Success is tempered by the ability of the trainer to teach and the horse to learn. The primary ele-

Throughout his working life, Greg lived by the theory that his horses would be trained with a freedom of choice. This resulted in a career studded with extraordinary success. The last few months of Greg's life verified all that he stood for. He was only able to work the one horse a day, but Greg made every moment with Magic truly quality time. Clearly he had the knowledge, the ability and the horse.

My discovery of the horse's language has extended the idea of choice into the starting and training process. We know it is effective as Greg could show us. We know that if you trust a horse to make the right decision, you can build a valuable and productive partnership.

By taking away a horse's choice, we threaten his survival. There is no more dangerous "button to press" than that one. My concepts provide a path through the natural survival instincts to communication, trust, a methodology allowing the understanding of the nature of the horse, and thus a route to success.

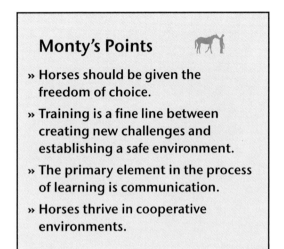

Monty's Points

» **Horses should be given the freedom of choice.**

» **Training is a fine line between creating new challenges and establishing a safe environment.**

» **The primary element in the process of learning is communication.**

» **Horses thrive in cooperative environments.**

Adrenaline Up, Learning Down; Adrenaline Down, Learning Up

I use the phrase "adrenaline up, learning down; adrenaline down, learning up" to describe, as graphically as possible, the enormous importance of staying calm to promote learning. It is a huge mistake for a horse trainer to panic or become angry. These conditions will not promote communication or learning. Probably the greatest learning tool is a calm state when it comes to educating the flight animal. If a horse senses fear, panic or anger, any task will take much longer and will likely end in failure.

Adrenaline is a secretion from the adrenal gland that increases the heart rate. Its primary use is to stimulate a response that will prepare the animal or human to fight or flee. It is in the very nature of humans and horses for fear to increase adrenaline levels. As the predator stalks its victim and gets ready to pounce, its adrenaline will begin to rise to meet the demands of the imminent attack. Adrenaline will raise the heart rate, providing the muscles with an increased supply of oxygen.

Horses, and most flight animals, have an interesting response to adrenaline. As it enters the system, alerted by signs and signals, the spleen responds by releasing extra hemoglobin (red blood cells) into the blood. This provides the horse with a greater capacity to carry oxygen, giving the horse the best chance possible to escape a predator. This increases the viscosity of the blood, and has the potential to cause the unfit horse to rupture the capillaries surrounding the alveoli of the lung sacks. Man does not have this response, and dogs only very slightly increase their red blood cell count at the onset of adrenaline.

When a racehorse, for example, is led onto a track or training ground, he is likely to get extremely agitated, often bucking, twisting, whirling around and becoming difficult to handle. This is a direct result of the increased supply of adrenaline in the blood. He is, quite literally, ready to go.

When a horse senses the rising adrenaline in his handler, or in another horse, he knows that there is danger nearby. Fear is instantly transmitted through a herd so that they are all ready to flee together. Any horse left behind is apt to fall to predators, therefore they have evolved by natural selection to flee at the first sign of danger.

The term I use to describe the levels of adrenaline is not clinical. Technically, low adrenaline could mean a coma or sleep. High adrenaline could refer to extremes of panic. What I am implying by this statement "adrenaline up, learning down; adrenaline down, learning up" is that when a horse is traumatized to the extent that he enters the flight mode, his capacity for learning is reduced. At this point, the horse may register images of traumatic incidents and store them in the brain for use later to avoid similar dangerous circumstances. If you were to consider this as learning, then, in fact, the horse is learning with his adrenaline up. This phenomenon is not effective in the area of learning those things that horsemen consider essential in the training process. For the Western horse to learn how to place his feet for the best sliding stop to turn a cow, it is essential that he can think it through in a calm, intrinsic fashion. The show jumper must learn how to measure his stride for optimal take-off and landing—he too must be calm and measured as opposed to harried and anxious. Suffice it to say, for my methods, I mean that when adrenaline is up, the training environment, hence the potential for learning, is down. I do not mean that the sleeping horse with a low adrenaline level is, at that moment in time, learning. Conversely, I do not mean that in the natural world a horse can learn nothing while he is frightened by a predator.

If we are to be successful in training the horse, in the world as we know it, we are obliged to execute the educational process with as low an adrenaline level as possible in ourselves and in our horses.

When a horse does something wrong, just smile. Smile, because if you smile, you will be less likely to get angry. No matter what the horse does, all you have to do is stay calm, and then you can turn the mistake or incident into a learning situation. The horse will learn from his mistakes if you use my concepts. Do not allow your adrenaline to rise. Seldom does the horse mean harm. If the horse reacts in a negative way, it is probably because he perceives the situation to be threatening.

Early in my career, I had the good fortune to work with a man whom I considered one of the masters of our time where horsemanship is concerned. Don Dodge, while I was growing up, lived near Sacramento, California. He was the consummate showman and achieved extreme success from the 1940s through the 1970s working in many disciplines. I recall that Mr. Dodge used to tell his students something that no one would recommend today. In fact, however, the premise was sound. Don would advise his students when they were having difficulties and felt anger creeping in, to get off their horse, sit cross-legged on the ground in front of their equine student and smoke a cigarette. He would say that it takes at least five or six minutes to smoke a cigarette, and by that time you would have regained your composure and could continue to work with the horse without being agitated. Cigarettes have been proven, since then, to be injurious to one's health. I am sure Mr. Dodge would not make that recommendation today, but his principle of stopping the process until your adrenaline level is normal is very appropriate.

As I circle the globe to work with horses that are difficult in the starting gates on the racetracks of the world, I constantly observe the value of remaining calm. The natural instinct of the flight animal is to synchronize with the animals nearby. I need to be ever mindful of this phenomenon to cause my equine students to relax and remain in a learning mode.

I can always control my pulse rate. Even if I am in a situation where I have to move quickly, I can still bring my heart rate down. The horse will perceive that there is no reason to be afraid. The message I convey is that this is not a survival situation, but a learning one.

I first became acquainted with the principles of pulse rate and adrenaline control when I was 13 years of age. I was in the eighth grade and my teacher, Sister Agnes Patricia, was not only interested in my work, but was an accomplished student of biology. She told me that there was great value in learning to breathe properly when attempting to relax, lower your pulse rate and reduce adrenaline levels. Sister Agnes Patricia encouraged me to study these techniques with a singing instructor by the name of Sister Julie. I was at once fascinated by what I could accomplish through appropriate breathing. It is necessary to lower the diaphragm on inspiration, allowing it to lift on expiration. I will not go further with this here, but suggest to you that one can find help with singing, acting and public-speaking teachers in this area. The knowledge of this phenomenon and the ability to execute it appropriately has played a major role in my career with horses.

> ## Monty's Points
>
> » Adrenaline down, learning up.
> » Adrenaline up, learning down.
> » Adrenaline increases hemoglobin.
> » Flight animals sychronize so that the herd is ready to flee together.
> » When you think your horse does something wrong, just smile.
> » Take a break if you feel anger or fear coming on.
> » Learn to control your pulse rate.

Chapter 6

A Look at Tradition

Techniques I Find Questionable

I explore many concepts in this book that I consider to be acceptable. These are heartfelt, well-thought-out practices that every student of my work will want to understand. But I think it is also appropriate for me to identify training techniques that I find questionable, not to point a finger of blame, but to give you an idea of just how much my concepts vary from what is considered traditional. I believe it will be helpful to identify the training procedures that I consider unacceptable, and against the horse's very nature.

It is with that in mind that I have created a chapter for those things that I suggest that you eliminate from your training routines. This chapter of this book will deal with three of the most often committed errors against my concepts—use of the whip, single-line longeing, and feeding by hand.

There are, in my opinion, no bad horses. Equus, the flight animal, simply cannot be born bad. If a horse is bad, he has been made that way by people. The knowing trainer will endeavor to study those actions likely to cause a horse to go wrong.

The Whip

Since the publication of my first book circumstances have caused me to be present at many of the world's largest equine gatherings. Most of these events include a very large section best described as a trade show. Hundreds of booths display both new and old innovations from the world of dealing with horses. I find them quite educational. New discoveries in tack design and inventions in the area of equipment of husbandry fascinate me.

It was during those visits that I saw literally thousands of people carrying whips purchased at the trade show. According to tack shops, the whip is always the number-one selling piece of equipment around the world. It amazes me that we have dealt with horses for approximately 8,000 years, yet failed to learn that the whip is probably the most ineffective tool. If our goal is to create resentment in a horse, then I suppose I would have to change my view, but if cooperation is sought after, the whip is certainly the wrong choice of equipment.

Recently, I was asked to write an essay on the use of the whip in the racing industry. I did and have decided to include it in this book. Please read it bearing in mind that the whip is still a whip, no matter what discipline, and that a horse is still a horse, no matter what his breed or lifestyle. You should realize that when I speak to the issue of the whip, I am dealing with the use of it where the intention is to strike the horse causing him pain. I understand that there are disciplines where the whip can be used strictly as an instrument of communication. Dressage is a discipline where the whip is often used only with a touch to convey a message. Certain competition driving is conducted in a fashion where the whip is an effective method of communication. Please assimilate the information I am offering with the understanding that my objections refer solely to the whip's use to inflict pain.

The Whip in Racing

To do a dissertation on the whip in racing, I feel the first thing a horseman should say is, "It does not matter whether it's racing or any other discipline, the whip is the whip."

Equus, the flight animal, is about 50 million years old. If you accept the discovery by Dr. Louis Leakey of Lucy in the Olduvai Gorge, then humans are approximately 3.2 million years old. We must conclude then that horses got along just fine without human beings for 47 million years. We are quick, however, to use the term "problem horse," a quite pompous statement from a species so junior.

A scientific fact is that horses are flight animals and, as the reader knows, they only have two goals in life (survival and reproduction). Horses do not often think strongly about reproduction during a race, which leaves us with only one facet of a horse's existence, his goal to survive. Consider for a moment that we are human beings dealing with horses under circumstances extremely demanding and frightening to them. Knowing that they are vitally concerned with their own survival, we often conclude that the best course of action is to whip them and cause them pain in the hopes that it will get them to run faster.

> *"My greatest accomplishment was learning to be gentle; without that I feel I would have achieved nothing."*
>
> —*Monty Roberts*

I submit that this is not only a bad decision from a humane standpoint, but a worse decision where its effect is concerned. Horses are "into-pain" animals. Their natural tendency is to push into pressure, like a child does biting on hard bread when cutting teeth. We may frighten a horse the first few times we whip him in a race, but very soon he may resent the whip and back-up to it, actually causing him to run more slowly.

You so often hear the statement, "We need the whips for safety's sake," but, in fact, nothing could be further from the truth, because far more accidents are caused by whips than are ever averted by whips. In fact, if a jockey felt the need for a whip to guide the horse, why not use a spongy, nerf whip so that no pain could be produced?

In a recent conversation with Trevor Denman (a race announcer at the Santa Anita race track), he said to me that he felt it would be a good idea if every time there was a disqualification, the newspaper should read that, "the horse ducked from the whip and interfered with the progress of another horse and was thus disqualified." Trevor suggested that an extremely high percentage of disqualifications were caused by using the whip. Further, he said that if the bettors could understand that, they would be less apt to insist that jockeys use the whips to verify that they are trying.

Aside from whether it is effective or not, let us examine for a moment how we stand with the rest of the world on this issue. Nearly all the racing countries of the world are dealing with the issue of the whip in ways that suggest it will soon be obsolete. I believe Great Britain is down to five strikes now, while Sweden has restricted the use of the whip severely, and, I think, only in front of the girth. In Germany, it is interesting to note that all two-year-olds are ridden only with a soft nerf whip, which is handed to the jockey as he leaves the weighing room. The United States is virtually the only country to fail to act on what has become an important issue to race fans the world over.

The third facet, and possibly the most important, is in the area of public perception. We, in racing, need to be pro-active. We need to realize that many potential race fans abhor the use of the whip and are turned off by our sport. What if we had whipless racing? Someone would be first, someone would be last and someone would be in the middle, exactly as it is with the whips. As for finding the genetic aptitude for racing, would you not prefer the winning horse to run out of a natural desire, rather than running from pain? And, wouldn't we be more acceptable to our audience?

I believe the number of race fans would increase with a strong promotional program featuring whipless racing. As racehorse people, we often say we are giving the horse a chance to do what he loves best, run. I believe that is a true statement, but if it is what he loves best, why do we have to whip him to do it? We do not.

It is my opinion that the best jockeys would still be the best jockeys, and in fact, true horsemanship skills would come to the front if we were to eliminate whipping.

I sincerely believe that the buggy whips used at the starting gate cause far more trouble than good. I have spent a good deal of my life studying equine behavior at the starting gate and I am absolutely convinced that the elimination of the whip would actually make life easier for the starting-gate crews.

People love animals, and we are supposed to be a civilized species. Is it not time for us to consider changing some of our retained barbaric ways? We have stopped lashing prisoners and whipping small children. Is it not time that we stopped whipping our horses, flight animals, who have no intention to hurt anyone? My goal is to leave the world a better place than I found it—for horses and people too. Racing could lead the horse industry in this truly important area of humane treatment.

Monty's Points

» **The whip is the number-one piece of equipment sold throughout the world.**

» **A horse is an "into-pain" animal and while the horse may run from the whip a few times, he will come to resent it and actually may run slower.**

» **Most disqualifications at the racetrack are caused by overusing the whip.**

» **The United States is virtually the only country to fail to act on the important issue of the whip in racing.**

» **The racing industry needs to recognize that the whip has a negative connotation among racing fans.**

» **Racing needs to be pro-active in this issue.**

» **Many disciplines use the whip for communication, and not pain. This is acceptable.**

» **Whatever the discipline, the use of the whip to produce pain is unacceptable.**

Single-Line Longeing

Single-line longeing is a practice inherently bad for your horse. By single-line longeing, I mean the method of longeing using a single line attached to the head of your horse. Sometimes, horsemen attach it to a longeing cavesson, which is a contraption reinforced with metal around the nose area, and three rings on which to attach the longeing line. The line is often attached to the top ring on the cavesson, and the horse is sent away from the handler to travel in circles at the walk, trot or canter. The horse cannot possibly balance himself with the unilateral (one-sided) action of the weight of the line, let alone with the weight of the person pulling on it. If a horse is subjected to this treatment for an extended period, he will probably modify his gait to compensate for the unilateral pressure.

Head carriage will almost certainly be negatively affected. A horse who has been subjected to longeing like this will usually negotiate the circle with his head held outward to his body axis. Most horsemen agree that it is desirable for the ridden horse to negotiate a circle with his head slightly inward of his body axis, and for his neck and poll to be relaxed, allowing for the inside hand of the rider to direct the horse's head slightly inward of the circumference of the circle. This gives the appearance of being more cooperative, and will enhance the rider's ability to control the horse's direction. When the horse's head is carried outward of the circumference of the circle, it not only gives the impression of rigidity but makes it more difficult to direct the horse with a soft feeling. The single-line longed horse will change his natural head carriage by curving his spine slightly in a counter arc to the circle's circumference. Good horsemen agree that the spine of your horse should approximate the circumference of the circle you are creating. Experts will verify that this aids the horse to

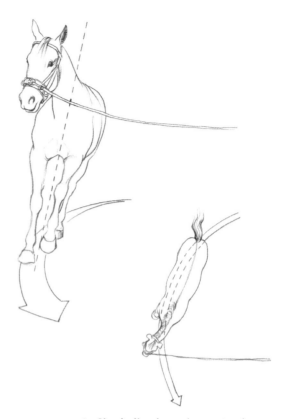

6.1 Single-line longeing puts a horse off-balance, with his spine in a counter arc.

use his muscle structure in a harmonious fashion with his skeleton. The horse that is traveling with a counter curve to his spinal column is working "muscles against skeleton" in an unnatural way.

In recent years, I have been asked to work with equine chiropractors concerned with Thoroughbred racing and cutting horse competitions. They expressed strong agreement with my concepts, and told me that they often work with horses expressing maladies resulting from these and similar actions.

Single-line longeing also affects the pelvic girdle and hindquarters. When a single line is attached to the horse's head, and he is asked to canter on the end of that line, centrifugal force will dictate that he moves with an outward pressure on the line. The handler holds the

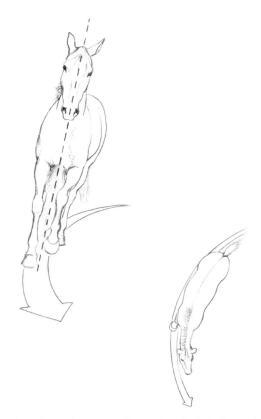

6.2 A loose horse moving naturally is balanced, and moves in a natural arc.

invariably travel with his head and neck substantially to the outside of circles or turns that he makes. His spine does not travel on the turns, and you will often see his head slightly tipped at the atlas, so his nose is further from the center of the circle than his ears are. The horse is at risk of developing back problems, and moves with reduced efficiency.

Conversely, if you watch a horse that hasn't been single-line longed running around a pen, free to balance himself, you will see that as he canters or trots, his head is comfortably in front of his body expressing actions anatomically normal. His neck and head point, most of the time, in the direction he is traveling.

Throughout my career, I have dealt with horses that have had the misfortune of being single-line longed. Some have been racehorses, some being prepared for jumping or hunter careers, and others destined for the Western show ring. I have also dealt with many horses longed on a single line as yearlings. Even if this single-line longeing has been done for as little as thirty days, it can, and generally will, be apparent throughout the life of the horse.

Let's explore, in order, the ways that you might exercise the horse instead of single-line longeing. I have literally watched horsemen single-line longe in a round pen with solid walls more than six feet high. I suggest that it would be far better to longe *without* the line under such conditions, and to communicate with the animal to encourage his pace and direction. I am told quite often by horse owners that they do not have an appropriate enclosure and that they single-line longe to accomplish what they want. If those people did nothing more than relocate the line attachment on the longeing cavesson from the top of the nose to a ring under the chin, there would be a slight improvement in the negative aspects of single-line longeing. I still do not recommend it, but at least from beneath the chin, the horse's head is not tipped as much. If the person

head a specific distance from the center of the circle, which results in the hindquarters moving slightly outside the circumference of the circle. Moving in this fashion encourages the horse to lead with the outside hind leg. The line will invariably cause the horse to canter on the inside lead in front. The result is that the horse travels disunited, one lead in front and the opposite behind. Cantering this way is detrimental to the horse's anatomy. It puts the pelvis in such an abnormal position that it strains some important ligaments, tendons and muscles. The damage, psychological (due to the stress of pain) and physiological, is critical in the immature animal of less than three years of age.

The extensively longed horse, when released in an area to exercise on his own, will longeing with a single line would use a bit and bridle, place a surcingle on a horse, use side reins with elastic, he would have the opportunity to encourage the horse to move in a much more symmetrical fashion than without the side reins. Ideally, I feel that the use of two lines, one on each side, would be far more appropriate. With your hands directing both sides of the horse's head, you can encourage symmetrical travel. I recommend a driving surcingle with guide-rings about where the rider's knees would be, or use the stirrups fixed with a leather to hold them next to the animal's sides (see "Long Lining," p. 54).

During my sixty-year career in the show ring, I watched and studied many outstanding trainers. One of the greatest horsemen I knew was Jimmy Williams. Throughout the latter part of Mr. Williams' career, he was the trainer at Flintridge Riding Academy in Southern California. One of the many things that I learned from him was the use of an innovative longeing surcingle. Jimmy felt that it was important to create a surcingle that had a metal semi-circle attached to it which was elevated about a foot over the horse's withers. It had a series of rings attached to the upper side of it through which you could pass two long lines. Mr. Williams believed that this placement most closely approximated the position of the reins as if they were in the hands of a rider. Jimmy Williams could absolutely "play a tune" with a horse with this equipment in place. He was a genius with long lines attached in this fashion and could stand in the middle of an open area and put a horse through paces as brilliantly as I've ever seen. I observed him schooling horses to execute flying changes using this equipment. Stopping, backing-

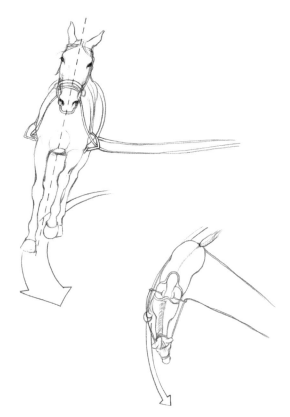

6.3 The long lines are balanced, and the horse is moving as he would naturally.

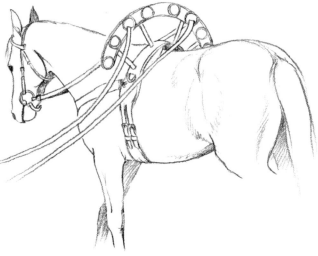

6.4 The Jimmy Williams longeing surcingle.

up, a pirouette, and even jumping were accomplished with the surcingle in place.

We had many conversations about the use of single-line longeing attached to the top of the nose, and Jimmy would admonish me not to tell other horsemen how bad it was. "I am in the hunter/jumper business," he would say. "This industry is full of people who make the mistake of single-line longeing. I have an edge over those horses and I would just as soon they all kept doing it."

Jimmy Williams was one of the most accomplished hunter/jumper trainers the American Horse Show Association has known. He was also a top-notch trainer in the Western division, showing some of the best reined stock horses of that era.

I see horses all over the world being negatively affected by single-line longeing. I would simply enjoy seeing them have a better life by eliminating this counterproductive activity.

Monty's Points

» Do not single-line longe your horse.

» Single-line longeing:

Throws the horse off balance.

Causes the horse to cross canter.

Damages ligaments, tendons and muscle.

Feeding by Hand

The predator and herbivore are two different animals. The predator lives on the flesh of the herbivore; the herbivore lives on available flora. Predators finding themselves hungry must search out their prey, stalk, attack and bag it, usually after some effort. The prey is therefore its trophy. Food comes as a reward after much effort. The herbivore, our friend the horse, lives in quite a different way by grazing. It is a constant search for ample forage. For horses, food is not a trophy; no blade of grass has ever run from them.

Of the three most common mistakes people make around horses, one is to feed them from the hand. In front of an audience of two thousand people, I was recently asked to deal with a horse that had some very common problems. The owner said that the horse would bite, buck with the saddle, buck with the rider, and rear up dangerously. Each of these serious behavioral patterns requires significant modification if you are to live with this horse in any reasonable fashion. I decided to show the audience how to deal with a horse that bites, recognizing that the owner was in big trouble. It was not hard to tell that all these remedial problems were likely caused by human error. The owner admitted to feeding the horse from her hand, and when asked why, she said she did it because she loved him so much. I could not resist the temptation to ask how she could love a horse that much who bites you, bucks with the saddle, bucks when you mount, and then rears dangerously. It was beyond me to detect what was left to love.

I often hear similar stories. Owners do, in fact, love their horses, but it does not mean that they understand them. This horse was finished with his biting in all of three or four minutes under my tutelage. In the end, I was offering him my arm and my hand; he was no longer in the mood for biting. If I were to check back on him today, it is likely the owner has this poor horse biting again.

While in Vancouver, B.C., in 1999, I met a lady who owned a horse she had lent to a local television station to be a companion for me at an interview. He was an "alligator!" He came up to me with every intention of biting me at a rate of about twenty bites a minute. "Wow!" I said. "What has been going on with this horse?" Nobody uttered a word. I began to school the horse in the fashion that I recommend. After a couple of minutes a young lady who was a groom at the boarding stable spoke up, "Tell Mr. Roberts what you do with Freddie. Tell him about your bag of mints." With that a lady in her sixties stepped from the back of the group with a beet-red face. "Oh, I know," she said. "He is such a brat, but I love him and I want him to recognize me when I arrive at the stable." The young lady spoke up again, "He recognizes you all right and you have seen the doctor three times already for the bites he has given you."

I continued to school Freddie, and as I did I admonished all the onlookers that when people feed horses from their hands they open the door for the behavior that I was experiencing. Within about ten minutes, Freddie was no longer a threat to me and we did the interview without serious incident.

There are professionals who use food to train their horses. This activity has been going on for hundreds of years and it is quite amazing to me that a knowledgeable professional will do this. I do not use food as a reward and it is a practice I would not teach my students. I feel certain that professionals trained in this art can accomplish their work without the side effects that the untrained person experiences.

Unless you are a professional who is trained to do this, do not train horses by feeding them from the hand. If you have treats, put them in his feed tub and let him find them. If, for whatever reason, your horse bites you or attempts to bite, do not hit him on the nose. When you hit the biting horse on the nose, several undesirable things occur. The horse will often bite and then, with your skin in his mouth, remember that he is probably going to get hit for it, jerk back quickly, and cause you more pain. An additional negative result is that the horse becomes head-shy. He resents the treatment, and it is rarely successful in stopping the habit, anyway.

> "No blade of grass has ever run from a horse."
>
> —Monty Roberts

The action I recommend you take is to watch closely, and when your horse reaches to bite you, swing your leg and bump him on the shin with your boot. If you are standing next to his shoulder, you can step on his coronary band with the heel of your boot and let it slide down his hoof. I am not recommending that you look down at his leg and violently kick him in the shin. What I am suggesting is that you continue to look wherever you were originally looking and swing your leg, as if by accident, bumping him on the shin. This is not meant to produce great pain and you will never injure a horse correcting in this fashion, but the result will be that after about six to eight repetitions, your horse will reach to bite you and then look down at his shin. What you have effectively done is to habituate to the extent that the horse connects the act of biting with another part of his anatomy. It is very effective.

The use of this procedure plays directly on the psychological phenomenon of *distractibility*. As I told you earlier, the flight animal is, by nature, very distractible. The experienced trainer can use distractibility to his or her benefit if he takes the time to learn the thinking process of the horse.

Monty's Points

» **Do not feed from the hand.**

» **A horse should not associate food with the human body.**

» **Some professionals can train by this method.**

» **Take action by bumping the shin as the horse reaches to bite.**

» **Horses are distractible, and this can be used advantageously.**

Chapter 7
The Wonders of the Dually Halter

How To Use the Dually Halter

For best results, I recommend that your horse be well joined-up before you start any work with the Dually halter. It may require two or three sessions of Join-Up to achieve full co-operation.

Work with the Dually halter should proceed on good footing in a safely fenced enclosure. The footing should be a loose, friable cushion of at least an inch and a half and the surface should be gritty with good traction. There are some rules that must be observed:

» Never tie your horse using either of the schooling rings.
» Never leave your horse unattended while he is wearing the Dually.
» Never leave your horse in a box stall or in a pasture with the Dually halter on because the schooling rings could become entangled.
» The Dually halter does not have a breaking point and this is intentional. It was done to discourage the user from leaving the horse unattended while he is wearing it.
» Never do anything that could restrict the horse's air intake.

Fitting

The Dually halter should be fitted so that it is comfortable in all areas of the head and throat-latch. It should be fairly snug, but not tight. The nose-schooling rope attachment should rest on the bony bridge of the nose, not so low as to compress the airways. It has three separate adjustment buckles. The crownpiece buckle adjusts the total length of the halter. The buckle on the upper nosepiece should adjust the size of the halter on the circumference of the horse's head immediately below the prominent cheekbones. And the buckle under the chin increases your adjustment capabilities at the level of the nose-schooling rope. You should use all of these buckles to achieve a comfortable position. The ring at the bottom of the halter under your horse's chin is for tying, and for leading the horse when not actually schooling him.

Schooling

When schooling with the Dually, you should use a longer than normal lead rope of at least 20 feet (approx. 7 meters) to enable you to operate at a safe distance from the horse.

I prefer to work with the Dually in a round pen of approximately 50 feet (16 meters) in diameter. It is advisable to have a safe perimeter fence more than 6 feet high (approx. 2 meters) surrounding your training area.

You should snap the lead into one of the schooling rings (those attached to the nose rope). It is not critical which ring you use, but it is important to use only one at a time. I often school with the nearside ring for a time, then change to school from the offside ring to achieve a balanced response from my horse.

You should work to create circumstances so as to intrinsically school the horse not to resist the Dually halter. When your horse resists the Dually, it becomes smaller and less comfortable, and when he cooperates, the Dually gives immediate reward by expanding, and becoming quite comfortable.

7.1 The correct way to fit the Dually halter to the horse.

The Handler's Goals:

1. Your horse should be calm and respond to your directions with a low adrenaline level.
2. Your horse should agree to walk with you, his nose near your shoulder.
3. Your horse should respect your space. He should not bump you with his head or shoulder, and should not walk so close that he endangers your feet or legs.
4. Should you choose to stop suddenly, your horse should willingly halt without tightening the lead.
5. Your horse should back-up when you ask. This should be accomplished willingly and with very little effort from the handler.

See figures 7.3–7.5 on next page.

You should encourage the horse to walk with his nose at your shoulder by gripping the lead and *pulling* backward when the horse is too far forward. It is best to allow the horse to bump into the Dually before you pull. He will then regard it as his error and he will accept this

7.2 Correct fit of the noseband and placement of the lead for schooling with the Dually.

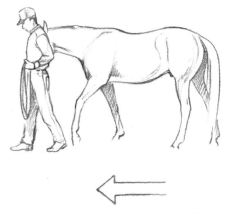

7.3 The handler's correct position is at the horse's head and at all times parallel.

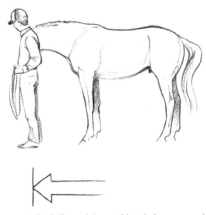

7.4 Correct "halt" position of both horse and handler.

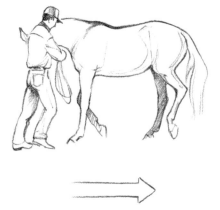

7.5 Correct "backing" position while schooling with the Dually.

self-administered discipline. You should always *pull* the Dually halter, not jerk it. On the other hand, if your horse fails to walk forward sufficiently, then grip the lead and walk briskly forward directing the horse to advance his position so his nose comes close to your shoulder.

You should move about the round pen quickly once the horse has his nose in the proper position. The next step is to walk briskly, then stop abruptly. Most of the time a horse will go forward for a few steps instead of stopping with you. Your leading hand should grip the line and firmly school the horse back into the desired position.

The next step is to walk straight forward again, expecting the horse to follow with his nose at your shoulder. Should he fail to do so, the lead rope squeezes and shrinks the Dually, drawing the horse forward into the desired position again. This activity should continue until you can walk briskly anywhere you choose, stop at will, and restart with the horse's nose remaining at you shoulder.

Having accomplished the procedures described above, you are now prepared to add the back-up to the scenario. I find it effective to walk quickly and halt abruptly, facing the same direction as my horse. At this point, I back myself up passing close to the horse's

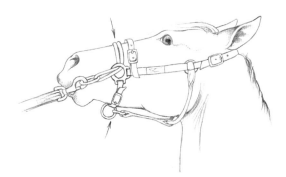

7.6 The Dually in action, tightening across the nose. Note that the lead is snapped into the "training" ring.

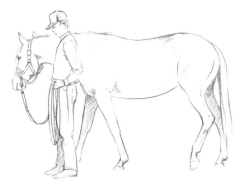

7.7 The horse has moved into a position that requires the handler to "school back."

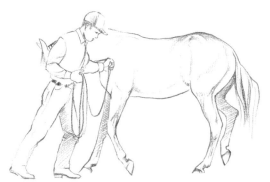

7.8 Schooling back is one of the most important maneuvers in the education of your horse.

shoulder. When I reach the horse's front leg, I grip the lead rope and school the horse with 3 or 4 backward steps in unison with mine. I again walk forward briskly for 15 to 20 steps, and repeat the process. I do this until my horse will back-up with me without requiring tension on the lead. The horse should execute these movements synchronizing his motion with mine. I want him to mirror my body motions to trigger his responses without the need for pressure on the halter. These movements should be accomplished with 2 to 3 feet (approx. 1 meter) of lead line between the hand and the halter.

7.9 Bird's-eye view, showing the length of rope between the handler and the Dually.

If, at this point, I have accomplished these procedures effectively, I should have a horse who is relaxed. He should be walking with his head fairly low. He should, with some regularity, lick his lips and chew, which tells me that his adrenaline level is down and that he is volunteering. I like to be able to stop at any point during this level of work and rub my horse's ears and all around his neck and head without him acting nervous or reticent. Experience has shown that if I get it right, I will often have a horse that yawns periodically. I have found this to be a positive sign of cooperation.

7.10 The handler gives a reward for positive actions.

The post Join-Up work with the Dually halter should proceed until you achieve strong signs of willingness and relaxation. Then, you can move on to accomplish other goals. The Dually halter will help a horse load into a trailer, walk into a starting gate (starting stalls), walk through water, stand for mounting or any other handling problems. It should be noted that the Dually is very effective for schooling a horse to stand for the farrier or the veterinarian. The Dually is an effective tool for long lining using both rings, or even riding with the reins attached to the training rings, creating a type of side pull. It is also an extremely good tool for schooling horses to be shown in hand. While there are many more uses too numerous to list here, the Dually will help you in nearly all areas of forming a partnership with your horse. Overcoming phobias is easily accomplished when your horse is firmly in the learning mode. Remember, adrenaline level up, learning down; adrenaline level down, learning up.

There is another step that I use when preparing a horse to load into a trailer or enter a starting gate. Immediately after the back-up, I will rush forward to separate myself from the horse by 10 to 15 feet (approx. 3 to 5 meters). I then turn to face the horse, and make firm contact with the halter by pulling the lead. It is my goal to have the horse willingly advance until his nose is near my chest. I then reward him, rubbing him for 20 to 30 seconds between the eyes. As I pull him forward, I am careful not to look him in the eye, but observe him with peripheral vision, while looking in the direction of his knees. It is important to accomplish this procedure allowing the horse to travel the 10 to 15 feet toward me without being pulled. If the horse resists the halter while you are some distance in front of him, it is best to maintain pressure. Move slightly on an angle right or left so that the horse is pulled to one side or the other. When your horse releases the

tension and comes forward, only take the slack he gives you; do not keep pulling. Should your horse travel only a part of the distance, you should back up to reestablish the tension and repeat the procedure. When your horse willingly travels all the way to your chest, give a reward of rubbing.

While executing any of these procedures, it is critical to release all tension on the lead rope if your horse rears or flies backward. If you fail to do so, your horse could fall and sustain injury. If you are not confident that you clearly understand when to release the tension, you should enlist the assistance of a professional. This person should be experienced in the schooling of horses for ground manners. If he is competent, you will soon cause him to understand this procedure.

There is a use for the Dually halter that is clearly separate from the preceding explanation. You can also use it effectively as a bitless bridle. That is, you can ride a horse with the reins connected to each of the training rings. This bitless bridle is very effective when there is a practical reason not to ride the horse with a bit. It then approximates a side pull (see "Mouthing," p. 33). It should be noted that this procedure can also be used for dual long lining. The lines can be fastened to each of the schooling rings, then passed through the stirrups as you would long line normally. Simply use the Dually halter as a side pull or bitless bridle from the ground.

In all procedures concerning the Dually, it is important to remember to work without anger or violence. Losing one's temper can cause injury to horse and human. Stay calm, and be safe. If you believe that you and your horse are not entirely safe, you should stop, get information and proceed only when you are comfortable. The Dually halter can be a wondrous tool, but it is only as good as the hands that hold it.

I recommend that students work with several calm, non-remedial horses when first using the Dually halter. Proceed with horses who have problems only when you feel that you understand the full extent of the use of this tool. I suggest working with a minimum of 15 older trained and non-remedial horses before advancing to horses that have the potential to be dangerous.

The Dually halter is marketed by us and accompanied by an educational video specific to its use. The video is a very helpful tool.

Monty's Points

» It is best to do Join-Up before using the Dually halter.

» It is critical to adjust the Dually properly.

» Use an extra-long lead rope.

» Never tie your horse using the schooling rings.

» Never leave your horse unattended while he's wearing the Dually.

» There is never a reason to reduce the horse's air intake.

» A safe working area with good footing is essential.

» Follow recommended procedures of schooling.

» Work quietly, and keep your horse calm.

» Work with several quiet, non-remedial horses before using the Dually to school a problem horse.

» The Dually is only as good as the hands that hold it.

» Study the Dually halter video.

Loading Your Horse, Trailer or Truck

Just as with virtually every problem I meet, I recommend Join-Up for the non-loading horse. I feel that perhaps the non-loading horse benefits significantly from this process, and is far more likely to cooperate with trailer loading if he has consciously chosen to be with you rather than away from you. Join-Up acts to make it easier to get the horse to accept the Dually halter. After Join-Up, virtually every horse is more likely to accomplish the loading process with a lower pulse rate.

Loading your horse is integrally connected to the use of the Dually halter. You should read and clearly understand the preceding section before attempting to execute the procedures described below. First, it is important to concentrate on developing cooperation with your horse by using the Dually. Do not underestimate the power of schooling the horse to willingly back-up. It may not seem important to a handler wanting to load a horse, but backing-up will ultimately prove to be extremely important in this exercise. Often there is the need to back the horse to unload and that is a factor one must also consider. More important, however, the horse that willingly backs-up and comes forward is more likely to load willingly than the horse that is reluctant to back-up.

I recommend that you use gentle horses who handle easily to hone your skills in the use of the Dually. You should not belittle the importance of learning how to safely use the Dually before dealing with horses that are apt to be difficult. A complete understanding of the use of the Dually coupled with a trained set of muscle responses can only be acquired through practice.

Before loading any horse deemed to be difficult or not, you should take great care to provide an acceptable vehicle. In the selection of your vehicle, you should be diligent and place safety as a priority. The horse's comfort should be the second consideration. A horse that is uncomfortable will often act out eventually and jeopardize his safety.

I believe that it is critical to provide a trailer with substantial length, width, and height appropriate for the size of your animal. While I recommend more than the minimum, there should be at least three inches total of free space in every direction from the horse's body. In other words, if the horse's chest is touching the bar or manger in front of him, there should be six inches of free space behind him. If your horse is standing in the center of the area provided, there should be three inches of clearance in every direction. This is a rule of thumb, but it should be considered the minimum requirement.

I am a believer in transporting horses at a 45-degree angle to the roadway. The anatomy of the horse is much better suited to this form of travel than when his long axis is parallel to the roadway.

Transport equipment should always be in good repair. Surfaces to be trod on should be of a non-skid material. Make sure you have proper ventilation. The vehicle pulling the trailer should be appropriate for the task, and brakes should be sufficient to stop the entire rig without undue difficulty. There are vehicle regulations in place in most states and countries that need to be carefully observed.

A horse should be transported with well-constructed protective shipping boots that fit properly without reducing the circulation of the lower leg. I recommend a poll protector attached to the crown of the halter to reduce the potential for injury. I also like to tie the horse in the trailer so that his head cannot reach the floor between his front legs. This lessens the potential for a neck injury when the trailer brakes. Give the horse some hay to munch on during travel time. I believe in stopping at approximately four-hour intervals. Also stop

where the horse can be unloaded on safe footing, offered some water, and a little exercise. Wherever possible, provide the horse with water brought from home. The use of flavored electrolytes while still at home will accustom your horse to a particular taste, allowing you to make acceptable water from another area by adding the same taste.

I am a firm believer in partial partitions in the trailer. There should be a minimum of 30 inches (approx. 76 cm) free space between the bottom of the partition and the floor of the trailer. The injuries that occur to horses because of the absence of this space far outnumber any injuries that occur because of this space. I further support the need for padded, smooth surfaces throughout the interior of your truck or trailer, free of any protrusions.

The method by which the horse transitions from the ground to the floor of the vehicle is critically important to the safety of the horse during loading and unloading. If a trailer is used and a typical ramp gate attached, then the ramp angle should be as shallow as possible, and there should be great attention paid to the traction provided by the surface of the ramp. If it is a step-up trailer, you should attempt to provide the lowest possible distance from the ground to the floor of the trailer. If the trailer is inappropriately high, then seek out a sloping area where the trailer can be parked to reduce the distance the horse is required to negotiate entering and exiting the trailer.

Once an acceptable vehicle of transportation has been selected, place the vehicle in an area where the footing is appropriate for loading. This means that it should be a friable soil surface such as sand with a minimum of two inches of cushion. Shavings or other show ring type surfaces are okay if they provide sufficient cushion (crumbly soil) and traction. I suggest that the trailer or truck be parked in such a fashion so as to create wings alongside the loading ramp. You can use a wall or fence for one side of the vehicle and portable panels or a disconnected gate used as a wing on the other side. I also suggest that the use of an appropriate wall or fence behind the horse will help greatly in the loading process. This is easily provided by backing into the corner while inside a building or field. If you have panels for each side of the ramp and behind the horse, essentially this is the best of all possible worlds. This is the method I most often use in loading demonstrations. One can use the corner of an enclosure with appropriate fencing if that is desirable.

After you achieve complete cooperation schooling with the Dually, you can progress to the next step, which is to approach the truck or trailer. Once in the enclosure, just behind the ramp, begin to work the horse in a forward-and-back routine, that is, two steps forward, two steps back. This is called a "rocking horse" motion by students of mine. During this procedure, you should make no attempt to load the horse until the forward-and-back motion of the animal can be evoked readily by body communication alone. You should face the horse, standing in front of the animal and looking down toward the area of the horse's chest. You should be able to step forward toward the horse's shoulder, and the horse should back-up readily with no tension on the lead. You should then be able to reverse yourself, and the horse should readily move forward with no tension on the lead, following your body motion.

Once this back-and-forth communication can be comfortably achieved with no exertion of pressure on the lead, turn and walk into the

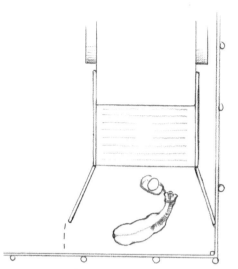

7.11 The appropriate configuration for schooling a horse to load into a trailer.

PANEL
(CUT AWAY)

RAMP

7.12 Side view of the loading configuration.

vehicle and expect the horse to follow. In extreme cases, should the animal refuse to come forward, you can place tension on the Dually halter, and wait for the slightest motion forward by the horse. If forward motion is observed, be quick to reward it with a rub between the eyes. If the horse flies backward, release the pressure, allowing the horse to reach the obstacle placed to the rear of the horse. Once the reversing has ceased, you should begin the pressure again on the Dually halter and wait to observe forward motion.

7.13 All the elements of an ideal environment for loading: proper trailer, safe panels and good footing.

7.14 The horse shows resistance in approaching the trailer. The handler has protected him well with boots and a head protector.

7.15 Monty allows the horse to create pressure on the halter.

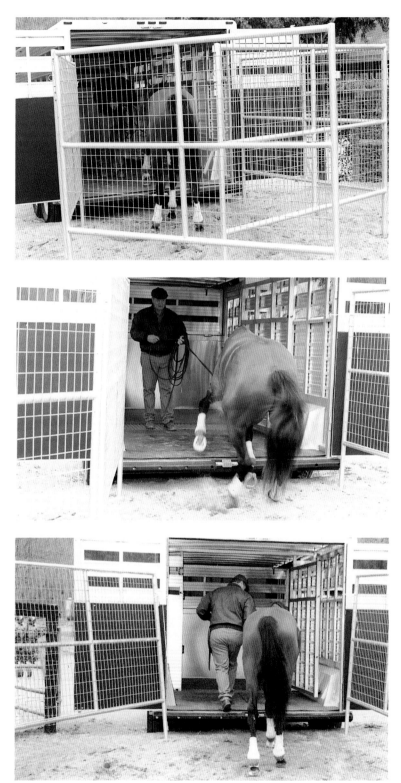

7.16 The escape route is closed off by bringing a section of fence (panels) around and to the back of the horse.

7.17 The horse has been schooled sufficiently that the panels can be opened up, and he steps into the trailer.

7.18 Finally confident that the trailer is not going to harm him, he manages to step into the trailer.

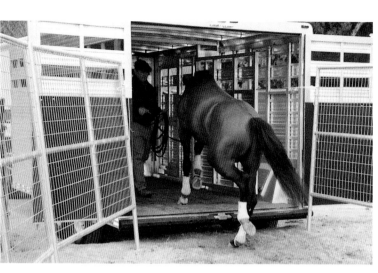

7.19 After having been loaded and unloaded several times, the horse begins to get the feel of going in and out.

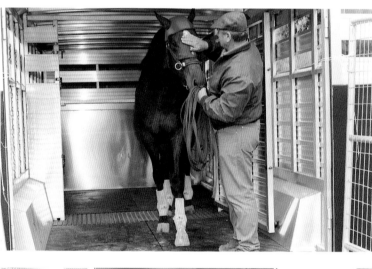

7.20 Monty gives the horse a reward for his efforts as a good student.

7.21 Now, Monty steps back with a long length of lead, allowing the horse to learn intrinsically.

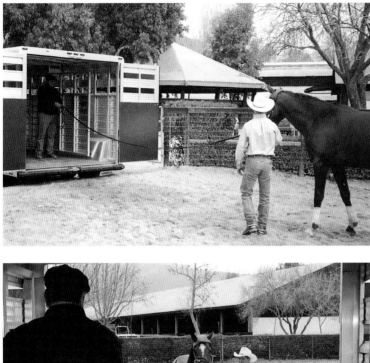

7.22 Having removed the panels, Jason holds the horse back away from the trailer. Monty walks to the front the trailer, allowing the horse to find his way and actually load himself.

7.23 A view from within the trailer.

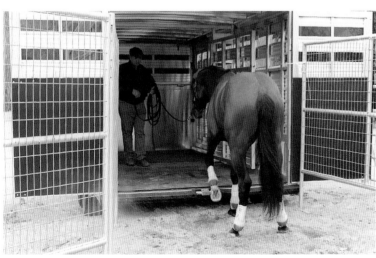

7.24 This time the horse loads himself, totally confident.

7.25 Note that Monty has now taken the lead off, and the horse is following Monty into the trailer voluntarily.

7.26 A close-up view of the horse looking at the trailer just as he steps close.

7.27 A totally relaxed horse, willing to trust that the trailer and Monty mean him no harm.

Chapter 7 / The Wonders of the Dually Halter

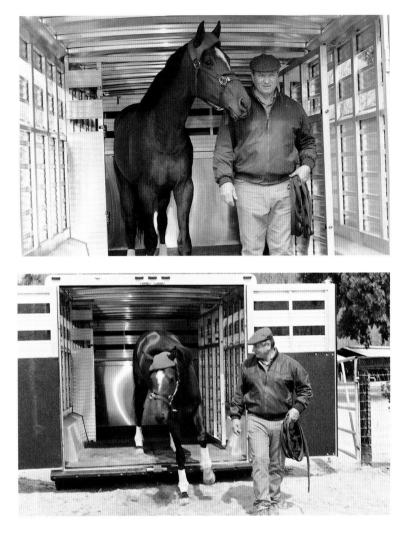

7.28 Graduation time. Both Monty and his student look out at the world, happy with the results of the lesson.

7.29 The horse exits the trailer after his positive experience of learning to deal with something that he no longer fears.

When the animal negotiates the ramp and enters the trailer, you should consider his work just beginning. The horse should be taken off the trailer and reloaded 10 to 15 times before making any changes. Once the horse is negotiating the loading process with adrenaline down and in complete comfort, you can begin to remove the influence of the wings and walls. You can also move the vehicle to lessen the effect of the assistance provided by these objects. You should continue the process until the horse loads with ease in a vehicle that is freestanding and without wings of any sort.

I believe that these loading procedures should take place on a day when there is no need for travel. Waiting until you must travel usually allows insufficient time to execute these procedures without anxiety. Each procedure described in this chapter should be conducted in a calm, cool and tranquil fashion. It should be your goal to achieve willing loading with the adrenaline level of the horse as low as possible. The horse should walk quietly with his head low, and exhibit licking and chewing, which denotes relaxation.

If you follow these procedures to the letter, the results are usually incredibly good. You can create a loader that you can send into the trailer on his own with very little effort. I often accept a horse for a demonstration that has been extremely difficult to load for years, and he generally negotiates the loading process within a minute or two of the time that I actually ask him to load. Take the time, keep the adrenaline level low and always regard safety as the number-one priority. And remember, *never tie your horse in a trailer while the back gate or ramp is open.*

Monty's Points

» **Thoroughly study and understand Chapter 4, "Join-Up."**

» **Accomplish Join-Up with your horse.**

» **Thoroughly study and understand the use of the Dually halter.**

» **Use gentle, easy-to-handle horses to train yourself in the use of the Dually halter.**

» **Study the "Load-Up" video.**

» **Place safety at the top of your priority list.**

» **Make sure your vehicle is in good repair.**

» **Ensure safe footing for loading.**

» **Use a poll protector to reduce potential for injury.**

» **Use appropriate shipping boots.**

» **Provide wings or structures as illustrated herein.**

» **Pick a day without the necessity for transport.**

» **Work without stress and excitement.**

» **Follow loading procedures to the letter.**

» **Take time to repeat the process until the horse easily accepts loading.**

» **Load without wings or structure.**

» **Never tie your horse in a trailer while the back gate or ramp is open.**

Walking Through Water

It is important to never make a demand of the horse, only *request.* I would like to investigate the things we request of young horses that might frighten them. These can include walking over a bridge, logs, into the water, and by frightening objects. Traditionally, you might have simply ridden the young horse to a scary object and insisted that the horse negotiate the obstacle just because you demanded it. Whips and spurs have been commonly employed in these procedures. But, once you begin to dictate to the horse, demanding obedience or causing pain, you will most likely have to employ strong-arm tactics throughout the life of the horse. I believe that if you can begin early in the horse's life to communicate and negotiate, requesting rather than demanding, you will instill an attitude of cooperation that will serve you well. In this regard, I think one of the most effective lessons for your student is to be schooled to walk through water.

It is essential that any horse can be relied upon to negotiate obstacles without endangering his rider. I am not just talking about trail or ranch horses, but all horses should be safe when dealing with potentially frightening obstacles without undue fear or panic. In this book, I have chosen to describe negotiating a water hazard. It will help you while training the young horse if you have the following equipment:

1. A Dually halter.
2. An older saddle horse who is perfectly comfortable walking through water.
3. Two competent riders.
4. An acceptable water obstacle, either manufactured or natural, that doesn't have a stony or exceedingly marshy bottom.
5. Two poles (jump poles), minimum 12 feet (approx. 4 meters) in length, and about 4 inches (approx. 10 cm) in diameter.
6. One sheet of plastic or a tarpaulin, minimum 8 feet wide (approx. 2.5 meters) and 12 to 15 feet (approx. 4 to 5 meters) long.

I recommend that you begin this exercise by schooling from the ground with the Dually halter, making sure that the horse is attentive and moves willingly forward and backward, synchronizing with you and listening to your requests with adrenaline down. Review the section on schooling your horse with the Dually halter, and then work to achieve the same degree of responsiveness while leading your student horse from your saddle horse.

7.30 The correct way to lead your horse from an experienced saddle horse.

Once you have a responsive student from the back of the saddle horse, you can move to the next step, which is to lead from the saddle horse over poles lying on the ground.

When you have clear cooperation over the poles, spread your plastic or tarpaulin and border it on either side with the poles. Ride over the poles and across the plastic. If your student refuses the plastic at first, you should roll it up and repeatedly walk over it, gradually unrolling it until your horse will walk over it fully spread between the poles.

Having accomplished all the necessary schooling with the Dually and negotiated the poles and the plastic, you are ready to attempt to cross the water. Do not try to lead your horse into the water from the ground; it can be very dangerous. Lead your student from the back of your saddle horse, attempting to have your student follow you and your mount through the water. Many will respond quickly. If your horse refuses to lead forward and into the water, school by riding your saddle horse into the shoulder of your student and back him in circles at the edge of the water. Eventually, you will have his hind feet in the water and you can ride into his shoulder, turning his forelegs into the water. Be generous with your praise and congratulations by rubbing your student on the neck during moments of cooperation.

Once you have achieved the position of having the student horse with all four feet in the water, you can lead on through. Immediately repeat the process several times until the horse negotiates the water obstacle comfortably. If further resistance is met and you are concerned with safety, add a step of wet or muddy ground between the plastic obstacle and the water obstacle. This usually instills confidence in your student and gives you a better chance to negotiate the water.

When your student is following the saddle

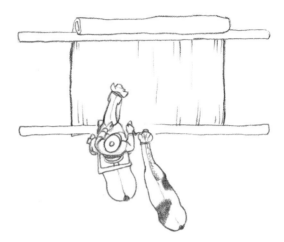

7.31 Approaching a "water obstacle" constructed of plastic or tarpaulin and wooden poles.

7.32 If the horse refuses to lead forward and into the water, school as shown in the diagram.

horse through the water with a calm attitude, tack him up and repeat the process while he is wearing the saddle and bridle with the Dually halter under the bridle. After this, you can add a rider and begin to lead through the water from the saddle horse. Once your student is negotiating the water with the rider, detach

       Chapter 7 / The Wonders of the Dually Halter

the lead and allow the student and rider to follow the saddle horse. As a final step, your student should negotiate the water obstacle with the rider up and no other horse present.

Monty's Points

» **Provide the Dually halter and follow the procedures for its use outlined in this chapter.**

» **Accompany with a safe saddle horse.**

» **School with the Dually halter from the saddle horse.**

» **Lead from the saddle horse over poles.**

» **Lead from the saddle horse over plastic.**

» **Lead from the saddle horse through water.**

» **Lead with tack.**

» **Lead with a rider.**

» **Follow the saddle horse.**

» **Ride through water without another horse present.**

Your Horse and the Farrier

Any person preparing a horse to be trimmed or shod by the farrier should take this responsibility seriously. I have seen extremely wild and fractious horses that require a week or more to be prepared for the farrier's visit. During this training period the sessions might take up to an hour a day. Half-hour sessions twice a day are not a bad idea.

In every country I have visited, I have found that some people believe that the farrier can educate the horse himself when it comes to standing and behaving while the footwork is done. This is an unacceptable mind-set. A farrier is a professional and should be treated as such. His expertise is to care for your horse's feet, not to train him. While it is true that some farriers are also good horsemen and quite capable of doing the training, most horse owners do not plan to pay the farrier for training services. The farrier often feels that he is being taken advantage of and should not be required to take the time necessary to train. This can result in short tempers, and horses dealt with in an inappropriate way. While farriers are generally physically fit, muscular and capable of administering harsh treatment, should something like this occur, the blame should rest with the people securing their services, and not the farrier.

Starting to prepare your horse to meet the farrier should preferably be done just after weaning, but you might inherit an older horse that has not had this education. So I'm outlining the following procedure for yearlings and older horses.

I would suggest that your student be introduced to the round pen and go through one, two or three Join-Ups on successive days. Once Join-Up has been achieved and your horse is perfectly willing to follow you with his adrenaline down and volunteers to stay with you comfortably, I suggest that you put your student though two or three daily sessions with the Dually halter.

Once that has been accomplished, you are well on your way to having your horse stand comfortably while you pick up and deal with his feet. To begin the farrier-schooling process, you should first rub your horse over, or spray him, with insect repellent. He finds it disconcerting if he has to stand on three legs and can't stomp one to remove an insect. Once the repellent is applied, you can begin to pick each foot up repeatedly. If, at this juncture, your horse is perfectly willing to give you one foot at a time and stand on the other three while you tap on the lifted foot and run a rasp over it, you are probably ready to give your farrier a call. If your student is reluctant, offers to kick, or refuses to allow you to tap or rasp the lifted foot, I suggest that you fabricate an "artificial arm," which I'll discuss later.

At this point, the good horseman should reflect on why a horse might react in this fashion. Each of us should quickly remember that the flight animal relies upon his legs to carry him to flee for survival. We should immediately understand that acting out violently toward the horse does nothing but convince him that we are predators and out to cause him harm. Delivering pain to your student is absolutely inappropriate.

To make an artificial arm like the one I use to train horses that are difficult for the farrier, you will need the following items:

1. An old rake or broom handle, cut 3 feet (approx. 1 meter) long, or a hardwood cane with a straight-handle grip, not curved grip.
2. One heavy-duty work glove.
3. One sleeve of a discarded sweatshirt or heavy work shirt.
4. One roll of electrical, gaffer or duct tape.

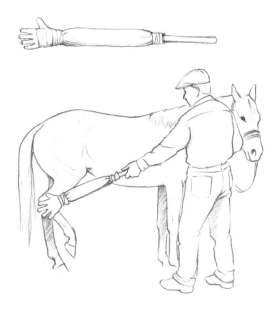

7.33 How the arm should look (above), and how a handler uses it to desensitize the horse to touch in hard-to-reach areas.

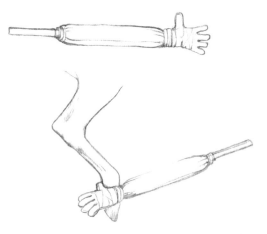

7.34 With a stiff thumb added, the hind pastern can be lifted easily.

Place the glove over one end of the pole and fill it with straw or shavings. Slide the sleeve into place so that the cuff can be taped at the wrist portion of the work glove. Fill the sleeve with sponge, straw or shavings, and tape the upper end of the sleeve to secure the material inside. You should have approximately one foot (30 cm) of uncovered pole for easy handling.

I'm finding it fun for me, at this stage in my life, that innovative students, encouraged to keep open minds, are making some very interesting discoveries. Kelly Marks is the director of the original Monty Roberts courses in England. She brought Ian Vandenberghe to be an instructor in my concepts. Ian came up with an idea that is very helpful, particularly for small, female trainers. He concluded that if the arm had a stiff thumb on it, the handler could, at the appropriate moment, slide the thumb down behind the rear leg, stopping at the pastern. Using the padded thumb, the handler could actually lift the hind leg without placing her own arm in jeopardy. I was on tour in England when I received a very difficult horse, with a strong desire to kick. The English team brought me Ian's improved arm and I found it very effective.

If your equine student wants to kick the artificial arm, do not discourage him. Return the arm to the position that bothered the horse until the horse accepts it anywhere you want to put it. Begin using the arm by massaging the body, shoulders and hips of the horse before proceeding to his legs. You can even rub the belly, and up between the hind legs. Spend considerable time in the area of the flank, as it will be often touched by the farrier's shoulder. Bad habits can get started if the horse is still sensitive in the flank

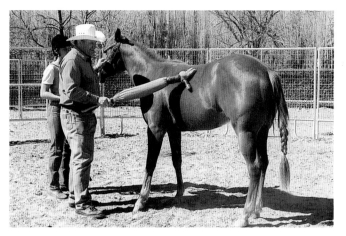

7.35 Desensitizing a horse using the artificial arm.

7.36 Here Monty uses the arm to touch the hind legs safely.

7.37 Lifting a hind leg is easily and safely accomplished with the use of the artificial arm.

area before the leg-lifting procedures begin. Use the arm to massage all four legs until the horse is perfectly happy dealing with the procedure.

If you are dealing with an extremely flighty or dangerous horse, you may consider using an assistant so that one person can control the head while the other uses the arm. Remember, if the horse acts out or pulls his leg away from you, drop the leg immediately and then school with the Dually halter. This will not be necessary with most horses that are raised domestically, but it could be an advantage with mustangs or horses raised with little human contact. Be alert and watch for improvement, and when you get it, remove the arm from that position at once and go to the other side of the horse to continue working. Your student will regard this as reward for not kicking, and is likely to quickly improve.

With your student cooperating fully when you pick up all four feet and tap and rasp, ask your farrier if he has an old pair of farrier's chaps that he can lend you, if you don't own a pair yourself. You need your horse to allow you to work on all four legs while you are wearing loose-fitting chaps, which may frighten him and present a problem when the farrier visits. Most horses become accustomed to chaps within five to ten minutes without a much difficulty.

On the day the farrier arrives, your student should have the person who has been working with him present for his first farrier procedure. You should choose a place for this work that the horse is familiar with and one where you have accomplished a large part of your schooling. It should be a safe enclosure with good

7.38 Introduce the young horse to the rasp and farrier's chaps prior to the arrival of the farrier.

lighting so that the farrier can see the feet clearly. Good footing should be provided, and a firm, level surface should be available so that the farrier can judge the action of the feet as the horse walks away from, and back toward, the farrier. You should have the Dually halter on your student, and move through the procedure slowly so that he accepts the activity while staying calm and relaxed. Advise your farrier that you believe it is a good idea to pick the feet up and put them down a few times before working on the foot just to accustom the horse to the activity. It is also a good idea if the farrier picks up the foreleg briefly just before picking up the rear leg on that same side, to help prepare the horse for work on the hind foot. If you find that you have done nsufficient work to prepare your horse for the farrier, then stop the procedure at once and allow additional time for further schooling before reintroducing him to the farrier.

Following these procedures, your farrier is likely to be a much happier member of your team than if he would be if required to deal with an unprepared horse. And just as important, your horse will be a much happier individual, likely to enjoy a lifetime of comfort with the farrier.

Judging the Farrier's Work

Anyone who owns a horse should read material written by notable farriers to better understand the importance of foot care. The old saying "No foot, no horse" is certainly valid. An owner should take the responsibility of being as informed as possible when it comes to this critical part of the horse's anatomy. The informed owner will judge the farrier's work by the angle, shape and health of the foot he helps to create, and not by the amount of material he removes.

I remember, as a child, my father telling me that he had never been to a dentist and that he hated the thought of ever having to go. I remember my first visit vividly. I was totally unprepared, scared to death, and hated every minute of it. By the time our children made their first visit to the dentist, times had changed dramatically, and our family dentist was willing to take the time for a mock visit, where an assistant explained to the children the value of dentistry, and educated them about the great lengths taken to keep it pain free. Consequently, our children have never feared the dentist, and our family has enjoyed a much improved dental environment than from my childhood. This is precisely the message that I believe to be applicable when preparing your horse to deal with the farrier.

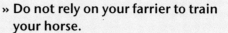

Monty's Points

» Do not rely on your farrier to train your horse.

» Do good Join-Ups on successive days.

» School with the Dually.

» Use insect repellent.

» Fabricate an "artificial arm" if your horse is uncooperative.

» Follow the "arm" procedure.

» School wearing farrier's chaps or other similar leggings.

» Provide a safe environment.

» Good lighting is crucial.

» Provide an effective place for your farrier to observe your horse as he travels.

» If you find you have not prepared sufficiently, send your farrier away and repeat the process.

» Keep the process painless.

Your Horse and the Veterinarian

To prepare your horse for the veterinarian is an important part of your total training program. An ill or injured horse that becomes obstreperous when the veterinarian visits can easily be big trouble. To help your horse accept such a visit, I suggest that you review the last section on "Your Horse and the Farrier." I recommend that you follow the same procedures when preparing your horse for a medical visit.

During the Dually sessions, it is important to stress that your horse should stand willingly. A horse unwilling to stand equals a bad patient. Once willing cooperation is achieved with the Dually halter, the handler should use the artificial arm on all parts of his equine student.

Besides the work outlined in "Your Horse and the Farrier," I suggest, wherever possible, you should provide examination (or treatment) "stocks." Some horsemen would call this an "examination chute," but it is, in fact, an enclosure that confines the horse for veterinary procedures or examinations.

I prefer not to recommend specific types of stocks because they are available in many different variations. In addition, these enclosures evolve constantly, and improved designs turn up with regularity. I prefer to recommend that you seek the advice of an equine professional on what is available to you in your community. You might seek the advice of the nearest school of veterinary medicine. Normally, the staff of these institutions is well aware of the available stocks in any given location. I do, however, recommend the type that has a belt over your horse at the withers to discourage an attempt to leap out.

If it is possible for you to justify having this tool, it is certainly worthwhile. Horsemen that I am familiar with often say to me that they can't imagine being without one once they are accustomed to using it with their horses. A good set of stocks is as important from a safety standpoint as it is from the convenience point of view. Dental work, worming, wound treatment, caslick procedures, and even grooming can be done very safely in a good set of stocks.

If possible, the knowing horseman will practice the procedures I've outlined here before the time they are needed. You should never wait until the day you call the veterinarian to attempt to get a horse to cooperate. These techniques should be practiced and well in place before the time when compliance with them is critical.

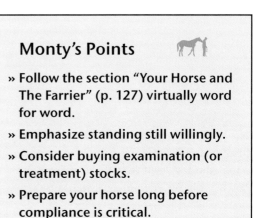

Monty's Points

» Follow the section "Your Horse and The Farrier" (p. 127) virtually word for word.

» Emphasize standing still willingly.

» Consider buying examination (or treatment) stocks.

» Prepare your horse long before compliance is critical.

The Difficult-To-Mount Horse

As with virtually every other remedial problem, I recommend that you do Join-Up with the horse before initiating work on the problem here. Once Join-Up is accomplished with a relaxed horse following the handler comfortably, you are ready to go on. Properly done, Join-Up will cause the horse to want to be with you rather than to want to go away.

With Join-Up accomplished, I recommend that you school the horse to the Dually halter. Accomplish each step outlined in that section, and follow the recommendations to the letter. I recommend practicing on a gentle, easy-to-handle horse before dealing with a difficult one.

You can then begin to work with the problem of the horse that refuses to stand still for the rider to mount. A horse such as this is often dangerous to the rider, and to himself. There are many reasons why this behavior develops. An injury to the back may, even when cured, cause it. The memory of the pain will often manifest itself with this bad behavior. And a badly fitting saddle can certainly cause a horse to be difficult to mount.

A student often says, "But Mr. Roberts, when I put my foot in the stirrup, the horse takes off!" This is not an uncommon problem—I have dealt with many horses that have developed this habit. Take care to pad your saddle sufficiently so that your animal's back is not traumatized by the mounting process. Snap into the training ring of the Dually halter a lead of approximately 10 to 20 feet (5 to 6 meters) in length. Walk up to your horse as if there is no problem. Lift your leg and point your foot toward the stirrup. Invite your horse to walk away. Let him complete several steps if he wants, and then school with the Dually halter. Repeat this process several times on any given day.

The Dually can be properly fitted beneath the bridle so that you have the use of the reins after you have mounted. Do not act out violently. Allow your horse to commit the error and then let the training halter do the work for you. If one uses the Dually halter properly, this problem is likely to be resolved in three or four schooling sessions.

For the extremely difficult horse, you can use an additional handler on the ground so that the Dually can be handled by a person other than the one mounting. You might use this technique until the problem has lessened to the point that it is safe for one handler alone.

Monty's Points

» First, do Join-Up.

» School with the Dually halter.

» Use appropriate saddle pad or pads, making sure the saddle fits properly.

» Be sure your horse's back is sound.

» Work as though there is no problem.

» Allow the horse to make a mistake.

» Place the Dually beneath the bridle.

» Do not act abruptly.

» For extremely difficult horses, use a second handler.

Chapter 8

Tools of
the Trade

The Foal Handler

The Foal Handler is extremely useful for getting foals to move into trailers, enclosures or across property, with or without their mothers. It is a safe method of handling the foal, allowing the handler complete control.

The Foal Handler is a length of one-inch-thick cotton rope joined in a configuration that makes a figure-eight. The length of this rope is determined by the size of the foal. The point where the rope comes together becomes a natural handle. The figure-eight can be adjusted to fit the intended foal. The two loops made by the figure-eight format are slightly different in size. Place the smaller loop over the foal's head and fit it comfortably just in front of the shoulders. Use the larger loop to encircle the hindquarters of the foal. The size should allow for the rope to fit comfortably just below the large hip muscle. The two loops should be adjusted so that the intersection of the figure-eight sits slightly behind the withers. It is useful to apply plastic or cloth tape to cover about 8 inches (20 cm) at the intersection of the circles. This effectively becomes a hand-grip.

Make sure the mare and foal are in a safe enclosure with good footing. Some foals may be frightened, and take a bit of time to accept the Foal Handler. It is important to keep them safe during this acclimation period. I advise that a halter is first placed on the foal. Once haltered, put the Foal Handler on by sliding the smaller loop over the head of the foal and then drop the larger loop around the hindquarters. The hand-grip area should lie on his back just behind the withers. Make sure that the foal is comfortable with the rope in place. Holding the center-grip area, apply a little pressure to the chest of the foal. The foal will most likely move away from the slight pressure. Relax the rope and congratulate the foal. Use this method to achieve forward movement by putting slight pressure on the rear of the Foal Handler. The foal is likely to respond quickly. Reward immediately.

You can school the foal until he responds with calm cooperation to the cues of the rope. This way, the foal will begin to understand the training method, that is, to reward positive behavior with rest or release of pressure, and to make it difficult for him to act out negatively.

8.1 Monty is holding a foal rope prior to placing it on the foal.

8.4 Here Monty is schooling the foal to walk alongside.

8.2 Here Monty has placed the large loop over the hips of the foal.

8.5 To school to back-up, Monty applies a slight pressure with the hand grip on the front loop.

8.3 With foal rope in place, a little pressure from behind starts to move him forward.

8.6 The foal backs up comfortably after a little practice.

An Additional Tip

For the foal who is a "master" in evasive moves, work with a helper who can very quietly and calmly ease the mare in a quarter arc around the foal. She is still close by, off to the side, and out of the way.

Since the Foal Handler is going to be used against the sensitive skin of young horses, it is critical to maintain it properly because it will tend to rub areas of contact. If used on several foals, the rope can become a carrier that causes a skin fungus. It is my recommendation that you dip each of your Foal Handler ropes in a strong anti-fungal disinfectant at the conclusion of each day, hanging it in a well-ventilated area to dry overnight. Your veterinarian can advise you as to the best disinfecting preparation available.

8.7 A foal who is a master of evasion.

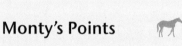

Monty's Points

» Adjust and use the Foal Handler precisely according to recommendations.

» Make sure that all movements around the foal are quiet, methodical, and synchronized.

» School until the foal is comfortable with the request for movement.

» Do not jerk, shout, pull, or otherwise raise the adrenaline level in the foal.

» It is critical to maintain the Foal Handler with proper cleaning as suggested.

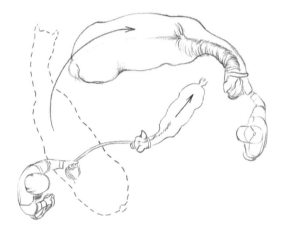

8.8 With an attendant moving the mare in an arc, the foal is in a safe position.

The Horse That Bucks

In this section, I am going to deal with the habitual bucker, not the horse who bucks a few times in the "starting process." I am going to examine why horses buck, how to cure them of this problem, and how to prevent it from recurring. Many people come to me with horses that have become buckers. I include buckers in my demonstrations because of the danger of this vice and the number of horses with this problem. Where remedial horses are concerned, I personally believe from experience worldwide that bucking, along with horses that are difficult for the farrier, are neck-and-neck for second place only to horses that are difficult to load into the trailer.

The fact that I am including this remedial problem in this book does not mean, for one minute, that I am suggesting you use these techniques personally unless you are young, athletic, and a very accomplished rider. It is important to study these concepts and to understand the value of using them without violence. You will need to educate yourself before enlisting the help of a qualified professional. When you set out to help your horse overcome the desire to buck, you should do an in-depth investigation of the qualifications of the professional you choose, rather than just turning your horse over to the first name given to you.

Anyone dealing with a bucker should first have the horse's back checked to be sure that there is no pain in that area. If there is a problem with an ill-fitting saddle, it is likely to trigger a survival response from the horse. Should your horse respond by bucking either with the saddle or rider on more than two or three occasions, you should consult a veterinarian or competent therapist. Obviously, if there is a physical problem, it should be eliminated before proceeding.

If physical pain is not detected, I then recommend you investigate your saddle, saddle pad and girth, to be sure that they are free of any pain-causing features. When you have eliminated the potential for a physical problem and found your equipment to be acceptable, you can proceed on the premise that your horse has a psychological reason for not accepting the saddle and rider.

Remember that the horse is only acting out of a desire to survive so we can justifiably surmise that the horse is thinking to himself, "There is something on my back that is going to kill me. I have to get rid of it."

At this point, you need to come to the realization that a horse in his natural environment desires to enjoy a tranquil existence. A horse is not particularly happy to be bucking. It is hard work for him. Most rodeo stock contractors will agree that one of the most difficult tasks is to keep a horse bucking. A very low percentage of bucking horses continue to perform adequately over an extended time. This is the reason that consistent bucking horses that perform at a high level are worth tens of thousands of dollars.

Bucking is often a display of pent-up energy, and there is no need to punish a horse for having high spirits. When I start horses in the round pen about 65 percent of them buck with their first saddle. This is a natural reaction to what they consider to be a predator that has suddenly become attached to their back. If I send them back out around the pen and allow them to think the problem through, they will, with very few exceptions, calm down and Join-Up with me. Clearly, they prefer to return to me, their new safety zone, rather than remain isolated and in flight. Very few horses started by my methods ever buck with their first rider and probably less than 5 percent will round their backs and attempt to buck. There will be a strong tendency for this reaction to not become a habit by using good horsemanship.

The remedial bucker can be, and generally is, extremely dangerous. It should be noted that there are thousands of people permanently injured or disfigured by remedial buckers. It is also a fact that tens of thousands of horses have been put to their death because they became habitual buckers and could not be ridden.

The Buck Stopper

It is with these facts in mind and my desire to save horses and prevent injuries that I have developed the following techniques. I recommend the use of a tool called the Buck Stopper. I have been using this aid for over 50 years, and I can state categorically that I have never injured a horse using this technique. Severe buckers that have tested the Buck Stopper for two or three consecutive days will sometimes exhibit a pink line on their upper gums. But it disappears in a couple of days and I have never known it to be of any lasting consequence.

The Buck Stopper is inert until the horse begins to buck, and allows the horse to discipline himself. If the horse travels with his head in a natural position, he will respond to the rider as if the Buck Stopper did not exist. It will not affect him unless he attempts to put his head down toward the ground. The effective bucking horse often executes this activity with his head right between his front feet. Often the effective bucker will lunge forward, high in the air, with his head in a relatively natural position, saving his tendency to bury his head near the ground for that moment when his front feet impact the surface. During this process the rider tends to sit straight up while the horse is lunging high, but then is jerked by the reins onto the top of the horse's neck or head. Injuries to the rider's face, neck and head are seen frequently. The rider will often be cast forward onto the ground in front of the horse. The next jump of the animal is likely to be a very dangerous one for the fallen rider.

Serious injuries and even death have occurred when the bucking horse jumps on the rider that has been bucked clear, and is otherwise healthy until the plunging feet of the horse come crashing down with tons of pressure per square inch. In view of the dire consequences that horses and people can suffer because of remedial bucking, the use of the Buck Stopper is without any question appropriate and reasonable.

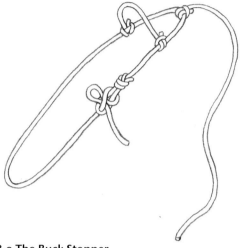

8.9 The Buck Stopper, a simple but effective tool.

What Makes a Bucker?

Whenever I am dealing with a remedial problem, I find it entertaining and informative to consider what I might do if my intention was to train the horse to do the thing I consider remedial. If the horse exhibits a particular behavioral pattern and feels he has gained something, he is likely to repeat the behavior. If the horse tries a particular pattern and finds it to be a nonproductive exercise, he is likely to cease the behavior. Let us investigate a make-believe scenario that often occurs, thereby creating a remedial bucker.

Let's say we have a young horse ridden for a few months, who has been cooperating with his rider and learning his lessons well. The horseman gets too busy or, for whatever reason, fails to ride the horse for a few days, allowing his energy level to significantly increase. With very little concern, our horseman tacks up in the usual fashion, and mounts, expecting a pleasant ride. The young horse explodes. He bucks much as he might have done had he been released in a field to play. Our rider, however, is caught off guard and bucked off, suffering, if not physical injury, certainly injury to his pride. "He has never done that before," the rider might say. "He has been as good as gold. I guess he will need a severe lesson regarding bucking."

A horse bucks, and during the course of this action, he unloads his rider. This, in the Language of Equus, is reward. It provides incentive to repeat the experience—thus he is apt to do it again. If he is treated harshly, it is likely that he will log in his brain that when he bucks, he is either going to get a reward or a beating. His tendency will be to buck harder. After four or five sessions of this behavior, our horseman will have a remedial bucker on his hands.

There have been many books written on how to whip the bucker and with what type of whip. I recall reading books that gave credit to young riders who could whip a horse on every jump. One book, I remember, said that you needed to whip them down between the ears while allowing the tip of the whip to strike them on the nose. It said that this would stun the horse into submission and stop him from bucking. *The Problem Horse* by R.S. Summerhays (S.R. Smith, 1940) states, "Personally, immediately after a bucking bout, I always hit a horse a couple of good ones down the shoulder...."

Unquestionably, the most proficient buckers come from parts of the world where the whip is typically used to deal with bucking. I have worked in many of these locations where most horses used in operations that employ harsh techniques buck until they are 14 years old. It is quite typical to hear the expression, "Watch him, he might be a little cranky." This means he is likely to buck you off. I have seen horses as old as 12 years of age that would work for four or five hours, then break in two and buck you off effortlessly, for no discernible reason.

It should be the goal of any horseman to *reduce* adrenaline during an episode of bad behavior, and the whip will do nothing but *elevate* adrenaline. The trainer who believes it works to whip a horse during bucking fails to realize that, in the horse's mind, this simply adds to his consternation rather than causing him to find a good reason to stop.

A horse that gets a reputation as a bucker will, most likely, cause concern and nervousness in his rider. An uncertain rider will exacerbate the problem causing the bucker to be more likely to perform. These horses are often sent to an auction sale and wind up in the hands of unsuspecting owners. They will often receive more harsh treatment that only expands their reputation. Eventually the only buyer at the auction is the guy with the truck headed to the slaughterhouse.

Having outlined all these circumstances, it should be noted that the bucker who has been whipped is unpredictable. He is more like a street fighter than a professional champion. This tends to make him more dangerous than the predictable professional bucking horse. The horse that has been whipped is acting out with anger when he bucks and is far more likely to hurt his rider than the horse who is trained to buck without the use of pain.

Now, in the intent of understanding more about the remedial bucker, let us investigate how horses are trained to buck and encouraged to sustain that tendency over a prolonged period. What would you do to train a good bucking horse for rodeo competition? In the interest of getting this information I have talked with some leading bucking-horse producers in North America. The following is a collection of their thoughts on the most appropriate methods of producing a bucking horse.

How To Train
a Horse To Buck

It is suggested that you start with a healthy, strong horse possessing athletic body conformation. Some successful bucking horses are crosses between a Thoroughbred and a draft breed. This will often get you size, strength and athleticism. It does not matter whether the horse is raised domestically or in open country, as long as they want to buck.

With a good prospect in hand, put your horse in a bucking chute and place on his back an official Professional Rodeo Cowboy's Association (PRCA) saddle. Cinch it down snugly, but have it equipped with breakaway releases on both the front and back cinches. Keep your horse calm and allow him to observe the situation without any antagonistic behavior on your part. Open the gate and allow your horse to exit the chute of his own volition. Do not apply pressure or create pain, as you want him to have fun with this experience.

If your student is inclined to buck, he will jump and kick high in an attempt to dislodge the saddle. Allow this to continue for no more than two jumps and then pull the release rope and allow him to buck it off. Let him settle in the arena and find his way to the catch pen, passing through the stripping chute. Repeat this process once a day for about three or four days, gradually increasing the length of time before you trip the saddle and allow him to buck it off. Therein lies his reward. Experts suggest no more than about five jumps on any of those procedures.

If your student is talented, he will gradually jump higher and try more aggressively to rid himself of the equipment. Give him a few days off at this point, and then repeat the process. It is best to make sure that he is sound and free of any pain, as this will only serve to reduce his desire to buck well.

After four or five more series with three or four days rest between, you can begin to con-sider adding his first human passenger. It is good to start with a rider who knows these procedures and is young, sound and athletic. This rider should be able to jump out of the saddle while the horse is still bucking at his strongest. Instruct the rider to stay with the horse for no more than four or five jumps, and then to get out of the saddle as safely as possible. The flank cinch should be stripped away from the horse as quickly as possible after the rider has ejected.

With the horse free of the rider you should help him to find the stripping chute as soon as possible. On each trip he has made through the arena he should have passed through the stripping chute to access the catch pen. Get the equipment off him as quickly as possible.

As before, allow four to six days between these exercises, with at least five or six of these controlled schooling sessions before any rider attempts to stay on him for the full eight seconds. It is at this time that you should assess your horse's potential to be a professional bucker. It is quite possible that by now he has shown tendencies to want to stop bucking. If so, you could put him into training as a saddle horse, using the procedures recommended to stop a horse from bucking, rather than those recommended to create a bucker.

If the horse shows promise, and is bucking with great enthusiasm at the conclusion of the controlled schooling sessions, you should look for riders who are learning the art of riding bucking horses. They are generally less apt to stay on, allowing the horse a further opportunity to take the upper hand in his quest to rid himself of anything on his back. Some of the best stock contractors will seek out a college rodeo environment, and the horse will remain bucking there for six months to a year before professional riders experience his talents.

Throughout this period of education, the bucking horse should be fed well, have his feet trimmed and experience several day's rest between each session. He should be allowed to have moderate exercise in a reasonably large area. It is recommended that you use a rider and a saddle horse to encourage your bucker to canter a mile or so a day. If with the use of these preceding techniques a predictable bucking horse can be created, then we can consider opposite techniques to stop down the tendency to buck.

The most obvious circumstance that encourages the professional bucking horse is the reward he gets for bucking off the equipment, or the rider. The knowledgeable trainer is obligated then to create an environment where it is highly unlikely that the horse will be rewarded in this fashion. It just so happens that it is also much safer to train your horse without being bucked off.

Curing the Bucking Horse

Let us return now to the world which regards bucking as a fault. While it is interesting to investigate the creation of a bucker, it is an area few of my readers would engage in. Now that we know how to train the professional bucking horse, let us investigate the procedures necessary for discouraging this dangerous activity.

I feel strongly that whenever you are dealing with a remedial problem you need to put yourself in a position where you can smile. When the horse acts out exhibiting his remedial behavior, if you cannot remain calm and comfortable, you have not created the proper environment.

Safety is paramount. You need the correct equipment and the appropriate surround-

ings to deal with the remedial bucker. I believe that a strong round pen is essential for schooling the remedial bucker. I recommend that it be approximately 50 feet (approx. 16 meters) in diameter, and have a solid wall, no less than 7 feet (approx. 2 meters) in height. It is essential that the footing be safe, non-skid, and with at least an inch and half of cushion on top of the base. You will need the Dually halter, a surcingle with a breast collar, a small saddle with an English-style girth, or a good rough stock Western saddle, if the rider prefers one. You will also need a life-size, human-looking dummy, and many hours of experience attaching this equipment to the horse. The Buck Stopper is also an

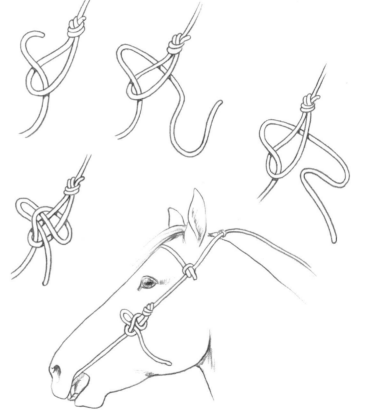

8.10 The knot used to tie the Buck Stopper, and final placement on the head of the horse.

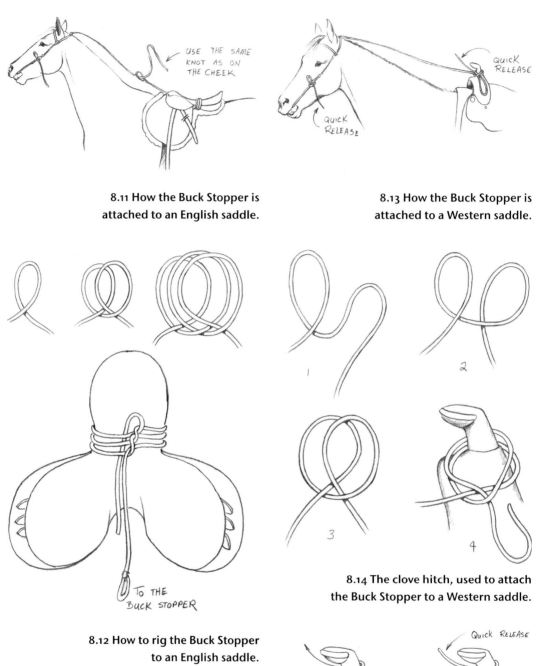

8.11 How the Buck Stopper is attached to an English saddle.

8.13 How the Buck Stopper is attached to a Western saddle.

8.12 How to rig the Buck Stopper to an English saddle.

8.14 The clove hitch, used to attach the Buck Stopper to a Western saddle.

8.15 Closeup of the clove hitch attached to the saddle horn, tied for a quick release.

important part of this list, with an appropriate bit or hacka-more for guiding the horse, and English-style stirrup leather to secure the stirrups at the side of your horse.

As with virtually every situation, I suggest you begin with Join-Up. If necessary, allow yourself a few days with 30- or 40-minute sessions so that the four goals, Join-Up, follow-up, the vulnerable areas and picking up the feet, are accomplished with comfort and ease. With that com-pleted, and if you are well-trained and competent in using the listed equipment, you can proceed to deal with your remedial bucker. Do not continue with this training pro-gram if you have any doubts about your level of compe-tence.

Bring your student into the round pen and again com-plete the four goals outlined above, Join-Up, follow-up, touching the vulnerable areas and picking up the feet. Then, take your student to the center of the round pen and put the Buck Stopper on him.

Place the surcingle on the back of your horse and at-tach the Buck Stopper line. Follow safe procedures to girth up the surcingle and then allow your student the freedom of the round pen to buck if he chooses. Allow your horse to canter freely until all attempts to buck have subsided. It is a good idea at this point to long line your horse in the recommended fashion using the side rings on the surcingle as a guide for the lines. With the Buck Stopper in place you can school your horse to become quite proficient at long lining. The Buck Stopper will not inter-fere with this process. Often, the feel of the long lines around the flanks and gaskins of the horse and along his sides will evoke bucking, and this will just be a further opportunity for your horse to learn.

With safe procedures, use Join-Up again and remove the surcingle, placing the small English-style saddle on your horse. Attach the Buck Stopper and ask your student to canter in both directions of the round pen with the saddle and Buck Stopper in place. If your horse does not stop bucking in a few laps in both directions, you may want to repeat the procedure with the English saddle on another day. However, if he is comfortable and the Buck Stopper is working effectively, most horses will stop bucking in less than one minute.

If your student settles and canters with the English saddle on, then anchor the stirrups down (see Chapter 4 for instructions). Then, I recommend you long line again so you can further train him to respond to the bit while allowing the stirrups to be active and visible along his sides.

With stirrups anchored against your horse's sides, and the girth adequately drawn up, you can

8.16 Attach the Buck Stopper to the surcingle before buckling. Then, if the horse bucks, all will pull away.

8.17 Put the saddle on over the surcingle, then remove the surcingle.

consider employing your mannequin rider. Using safe procedures, fix the dummy on the English saddle. This will generally evoke aggressive bucking by the remedial horse. Do not consider this a bad thing because the horse will be experiencing the Buck Stopper, which discourages the desire to buck. If you find it difficult to place your mannequin rider on the horse, you may wish to use a rolled-up blanket first. Tie small ropes around it in three different places so that you can attach it to the top of the saddle and in each stirrup. Work with this blanket until your horse is comfortable as you throw it on and pull it off. This will serve as an effective forerunner to using the mannequin.

8.18 A dummy being bounced up and down to accustom the horse to his presence.

I recommend taking the safe way and using the dummy for several days before you go on to using a rider. To get the horse used to the presence of the dummy, bounce it up and down beside the horse before bellying it over the horse. Again, long lining can be very useful during this process. It should be noted that you never long line with a human rider aboard, but long lining with a dummy can elevate trust within your horse to accept guidance from the human form riding on his back. Long lining with the dummy could evoke more bucking and thus more schooling as the Buck Stopper is only effective when bucking occurs. You can use the Dually halter while long lining by snapping a line into each of the schooling rings. This will work on the horse much as a side pull does, and is normally quite effective. A snaffle bit can be employed at this point if you prefer.

8.19 Let the horse feel the weight of the dummy by bellying over.

When your student is perfectly comfortable allowing the dummy to mount and ride on a daily basis without resorting to bucking, then and only then should you consider the live rider. If your rider prefers a stock saddle, spend an extra day or two accustoming the horse to the stock saddle and dummy so that there are no surprises to your horse when the rider mounts. If you choose to use a double-rigged

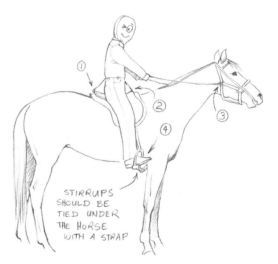

8.20 How the dummy is attached to the saddle: (1) to the cantle rope; (2) to pommel rope; (3) arms to the halter; (4) boots to the stirrups.

8.21 Allow the horse to deal with the dummy before putting a human rider aboard.

Western saddle (a saddle that has a flank cinch), use the flank cinch with the dummy for several sessions before progressing to the live rider.

When the rider mounts the horse, I believe it is best to leg him straight into the saddle, rather than belly over the remedial bucker. Remember that the dummy has mounted many times and has been laid over the horse in various areas, and bounced up and down on the ground. Unsnap the line from the horse's headgear when your rider is secure in the saddle. This will lessen the potential for tangling the rider in the line should the horse act out before you have an opportunity to detach the line.

Be certain that the Buck Stopper is in place during each and every one of these schooling sessions because it is essential that the horse learns early and well that everytime he bucks he will discipline himself by bumping into the Buck Stopper.

I believe that the Buck Stopper should be used for a minimum of 2 to 3 weeks on most buckers, and then should be replaced by a mock Buck Stopper. I suggest that a remedial bucker be ridden for the first 30 days or so alongside a well-trained saddle horse—one familiar to the bucker, if possible—and by a

competent rider. Should your equine student choose to act out, there is value in a steady influence and having another person to respond in any potential emergency.

8.22 A "mock" Buck Stopper.

With the use of the Buck Stopper, I have helped hundreds of horses to change their behavioral patterns and stop their habit of bucking in short order. I have achieved success with these techniques in an extremely high percentage of cases, but one can never be too careful. Always show the remedial bucker great respect. and never fail to recognize the potential for extreme danger when dealing with these animals. Use good sense and extreme caution at every juncture when dealing with this problem.

Monty's Points

» Eliminate physical pain.

» Eliminate painful equipment.

» Amateur and inexperienced riders should *not* attempt to work with a bucker.

» Use a safe environment.

» Make sure your equipment is in perfect order.

» School with safe and adequate footing and fencing.

» Never strike a bucking horse.

» Err on the side of caution.

» For safety's sake, do not skip any of the prescribed procedures.

The Head-Shy Horse

Before launching into a description of the techniques that I use when dealing with a head-shy horse, I believe that it is important to identify what the head-shy condition is, and describe its characteristics. I would estimate that nine out of ten head-shy horses are simply frightened animals. They are horses abused by humans. Often, this is caused by simply striking the horse in the region of the head with the human hand. Whips, ropes, and twitch poles are often weapons with which to make a head-shy horse. Any horse expressing the head-shy condition is likely to shy and lift the head abruptly when there is any quick movement by a handler. Touching his ears and/or his nose is often impossible. To deal with this phenomenon successfully, you must establish trust between the horse and handler.

I have found that 90 percent of head-shy horses are man-made, and while this is generally the condition I work with, it is also important to define the naturally occurring causes of this phenomenon in the other 10 percent. Before a trainer begins to work with a head-shy horse, it is a good idea to first investigate the potential for physical problems. It is possible that the horse is experiencing pain, which could easily be the root cause. Physical factors that can cause it may include dental problems, lice, ticks, or other external parasites around the cranial area. It is possible that a skin fungus or other irritations might produce pain sufficient to cause head-shyness. I have worked with many horses that had sustained an injury in their past and as a result of the necessary doctoring developed serious problems. A halter allowed to fit too tightly can also create pain that induces this condition.

No horse is born head-shy, but he is by instinct protective of this area. Should you abuse this part of his anatomy, it is almost certain that the horse will quickly experience a phobic fear of any motion about the head. The horse that is head-shy makes life difficult for himself and most of those around him. Once resistant to work around the head, he can be difficult to catch, clip, bridle or handle in general. This behavioral problem is quickly exacerbated by impatient handling, and if pain is experienced by the horse, the problem may develop into a phobia. Hitting a horse anywhere is unacceptable, but hitting it on the head is abuse of the worse kind.

Eventually a head-shy horse can become very dangerous to handle. He can violently swing his head to evade perceived danger, or rear up and strike out to protect himself. It is important to rebuild trust with this frightened or phobic horse, and the best way to accomplish this is to complete Join-Up. By communicating in the horse's language, you can build and repair trust. *Trust is the key to everything I do around horses.* When I have my equine student comfortable being with me and following me in the round pen in a relaxed fashion, I put the Dually halter on him and fit it properly.

The horse needs to know that you are not going to inflict pain. Spend time touching his head, but when he lets you into that area, walk away. By touching the horse on the forehead and then walking away, you are gesturing that you are not predatory or potentially dangerous. Repeat this simple gesture and observe the response from the horse. After a while, even the most phobic animal will begin to realize that you mean him no harm. Watch for signs that the horse's anxiety is subsiding. As the adrenaline goes down, the horse will relax and drop his head a little. He will also have a calm eye, and should not be sweating. Seize this opportunity, and when he is comfortable, rub his muzzle and then his face between the eyes and on the jaws, if possible. While rubbing with your fingers, use your forearm in an attempt to stroke up over the ears or poll. If your horse is resistant, go back-up to the nearest comfort zone and rub again for prolonged periods.

Again, the most important aspect of my work is the building of trust. It does not matter how long it takes to build that trust. No time limit should be placed on this work. You will not speed it up anyway. The horse will ultimately decide the length of time required to gain his trust. Remember, it is usually true that "slow is fast and fast is slow."

Continue to work with the horse until you can end any given session on a positive note. Each time the horse expresses anxiety by elevating the head in fear, walk away and allow your body weight to activate the Dually halter to encourage the horse to come to you. Again, initiate the rubbing and try to expand the area of acceptance until you can rub the entire head. Repeat this procedure day after day until the phobic behavior has been replaced with a calm trust.

Once you have established that you mean no harm to the horse, and he is comfortable with you rubbing your hands all over his head and ears, then start bridling and unbridling him. Plan your schedule so that you can put the bridle on and take it off many times before a riding session. It is really important that the horse learns that being bridled and touched around the head and ears is not associated with anything unpleasant. If you repeat this process, you will repair trust.

If you have a horse that is phobicly frightened of the clippers, do not use a twitch. Do not tie or force him to submit to the noise and feel of the machine. Instead, take the horse down the road of acceptance. This may take longer, but in the end you will have a horse that is not a problem to clip. The whole process can be undertaken calmly and more efficiently by spending quality time initially.

It matters little whether the problem stems from mistreatment, a physical malady, or simply a wild horse expressing a suspicious nature.

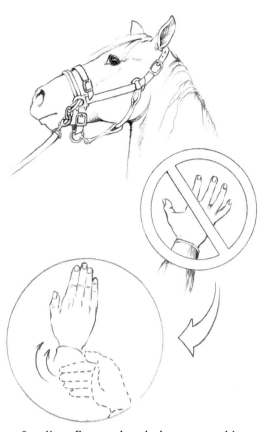

8.23 Keep fingers closed when approaching a head-shy horse, moving with a passive hand (see insert) to a position in which you can rub the horse.

8.24 A typical reaction from a head-shy horse.

You will encounter the odd horse here or there that is just so wild he will not allow you near his head. However, this is quite rare.

One of the most effective means of producing a horse that is trusting of a human is foal imprinting (see "Foal Imprinting," p.181). Dr. Robert Miller has brought to the horse industry a science that is exceedingly effective when it comes to creating trust in horses, and most particularly around the area of the head. Many horsemen, however, inherit horses when the window of opportunity is closed for foal imprinting. For our purposes here, I will deal with the subject as though the head-shy condition was brought to the horseman in an adult horse.

8.25 A typical Join-Up with a horse that has been abused, and who is looking for a friend.

Head-Shy Horse Equipment List
- A hair dryer
- Water and a sponge
- A long lead line
- A fenced or safe enclosure or a box stall
- An assistant
- A Dually halter

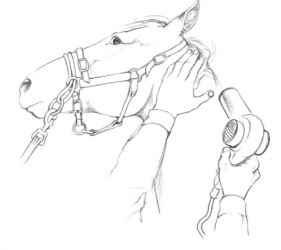

8.26 Hold the hair dryer away from the horse, and gradually bring the air flow nearer.

The Method

I first achieve Join-Up and am very diligent about rewarding the horse by touching whatever part of his body I can. If I can rub between the eyes, I will certainly do that. If it's only the shoulder or the neck I can touch, it will suffice. Once a solid Join-Up has been accomplished and trust established, I will school my student to the Dually halter.

Having these two procedures thoroughly understood by my student calmly and willingly, I will then begin to school the horse to

being washed down with a garden hose. I prefer the use of a spray nozzle set for a fine mist, wetting the horse all over, but most importantly I wet the head and neck. I then lead my horse into the round pen, or a safe enclosure, with good footing. I use a hair dryer on an extension cord. I recommend that the next phase of work include an assistant so that a safe environment can be created. One of you holds the horse while the other handles the hair dryer. Choose an assistant that is capable.

Holding the hair dryer away from the horse,

Chapter 8 / Tools of the Trade

8.27 Monty demonstrates the horse's phobic reaction to having his head touched.

8.29 The horse now allows Monty to touch the ears and get closer with the hair dryer.

8.28 Jason and Monty slowly approach the head-shy horse with a hair dryer, working first on the neck.

8.30 The horse is no longer head-shy, totally comfortable while allowing Monty to touch him all over.

turn it on so that the air flows away from him. Gradually, bring the flow of air around to touch him, first on the hindquarters, and then along the side to the shoulder. Work with the flow of air and the motor sound to begin to condition the horse to accept both stimuli. I bring my opposite hand into play by placing it in the flow of air and rubbing the wet hair, moving up the neck with the hair dryer.

Never do too much, too soon. I go slowly, and give my student time to accept the air flow over the ears and down the face before I progress to clippers or other work. Once the horse accepts the motor sound and the air flow, and my hand massaging the area around his head, the balance of this lesson is academic.

It may take several days to allay the horse's concerns, but if I persist it will only be a matter of time before I can handle the horse's ears, muzzle, and around the eyes without any sign of resistance. I find that this procedure causes the horse to accept many daily occurrences that normally stimulate fear—spray bottles for insect repellent, clipping the ears, or other sounds and sights occurring in the horse's environment.

Properly followed, these procedures will allow the horse to learn intrinsically. I take whatever time is necessary to allow the horse to accept, to whatever degree I choose, these handling procedures. I have literally caused horses to be willing to walk up to me and lower their heads to allow me to put a finger in each of their ears. I can massage the inner areas of the ears with horses acting as though it was a wonderful experience. The response is much as you would expect from massage or scratching an itchy spot on your back. Also, using these procedures, I have caused horses to allow me to reach into their mouth and grasp their tongue and hold it out one side while inspecting their teeth, or even while having them floated.

Monty's Points

» Be properly equipped.
» Check for physical maladies.
» Use Join-Up.
» Use the Dually halter.
» Work in safe surroundings.
» Follow procedures precisely for the use of the hair dryer.
» Allow for intrinsic learning— use no force.

The Rearer

I have dealt with literally hundreds of horses that rear. In Germany, France, the United Kingdom, and all over North America horses have responded well to the procedures I am outlining here.

No amateur—trainer or rider—should ever deal with the rearing horse. The principles outlined in this section are for the *professional only.* An owner or amateur equestrian experiencing rearing with a horse can ask a qualified professional to review this chapter before he or she works with the horse.

Before undertaking the challenge of curing the problem of rearing, the responsible horseman will have examinations done to learn if this problem has a physical cause. A good dental exam might reveal that the horse has a bad tooth or gum abscess that is aggravating the animal to the extent that it rears, simply acting out against the pain. Sometimes, it is discovered that there is pain emanating from the atlas joint or a cervical vertebra near that part of the anatomy. While you should always consider that physical pain might be involved, most of the time trainers find that rearing is caused by humans. If the problem is physical, then a responsible trainer will alleviate that condition first, before dealing with the rearing itself.

When a human being causes the problem of rearing, he most often does so subconsciously, and without ill intent. A rider asks the horse to go forward, but if the advance is too fast or abruptly, without thinking, he takes up the reins to slow the horse's forward progress. If the horse has a sensitive mouth, he will often feel that he has no place to go. The thought pro-cess of the horse might be, "He asked me to go forward, and then he punished my mouth."

This horse will often see rearing up as the answer to this dilemma. Upon rearing, this horse will often feel the rider become immediately defensive and tense up significantly. The horse likes this as he feels a sense of control. The horse is being "trained" that by rearing he controls the rider. Few circumstances are more effective for teaching the horse to rear than this one. The answer, of course, is to release any pressure on the reins, sending him forward immediately. He should be encouraged to move forward free of any restraint. The rider should then stroke the horse and congratulate him, allowing him to negotiate forward motion, if it is safe to do so.

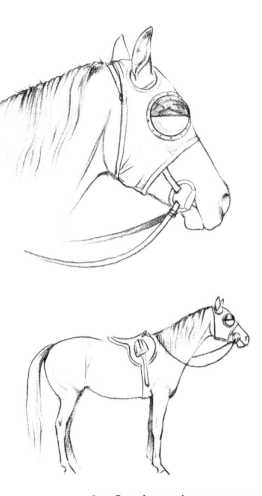

> **Rearer Equipment List**
> A round pen
> Dually halter
> Pair of long lines
> Saddle (English or Western) and pad
> Stirrup leather
> Bridle
> Blinkers with plastic see-through dome
>   goggles, the top part taped off

8.31 Goggles used to overcome rearing in remedial horses.

The remedial horse that has developed the habit of rearing is a very dangerous animal, both to himself and his rider. Fortunately, rearing does not always result in the horse falling over, and most of the time the horse regains his footing. When a fall does occur, it is often catastrophic. At best, saddles and equipment can be damaged. Much worse are the dozens of horses that I know about that have been humanely destroyed because of injuries sustained from rearing over. But both of those two pale when compared to the human injuries and deaths that occur.

I have read many books dealing with the rearing horse and some techniques I have read about are apt to shock the modern equestrian. One book I remember seriously suggested that you should take a discarded lightbulb, drill a hole near the base, and fill it with warm water.

When your horse rears, the "advice" continued, hit him on the top of the head with the lightbulb. It will break with a pop, the author suggested, and the warm water will cause your horse to think that it is blood. The author further states that the horse will be too frightened ever to rear again.

Another author, S. Sidney, recommends, "You may spur but not whip a horse while rearing" (*Illustrated Book of the Horse*. Wiltshire Book Company, 1875). He also goes on to recommend a harsher bit be used.

My father's book advised, "When you first start to ride him take a good heavy quirt or a piece of hose about 18 inches [45 cm] long with a loop in it for your wrist. When starting, if he rears up, be very careful that you do not pull him over backward. Loosen the reins, put your left hand on the saddle horn and hit him on the top of the neck right up between the ears as hard as you can" (Marvin E. Roberts, *Horse and Horseman Training*. Privately published, 1957).

I remember another book that suggested that the rider use ropes to create a running "W." When the horse rears, pull his front feet up to his chest. When he attempts to return to his normal stance, he will come crashing to the ground hitting his knees and muzzle. The intention was that this would teach the horse that rearing results in great pain to the knees and muzzle.

I also read a book published in the U.K. that suggested that the young athletic rider could pull the horse over backward each time he reared, and eject himself from the horse so as to not to be trapped beneath him. If the horse survived eight to ten of these episodes, it stated, he was likely to form a distaste for rearing. Another American author added to this scenario by saying that an athletic rider could jump off the back as the horse reared over, keeping the reins very tight and holding the horse on the ground. An attendant could then rush in and cover the horse with a tarpaulin. In the dark, it stated, the horse would not try to regain his feet and you could tie his legs to the horn of a Western saddle, reaching under the tarpaulin to do it. Leave the horse on the ground for the better part of a day and as you pass by throughout the day, jump up and down on the tarpaulin. The author suggested that the horse would be so frightened after that point in time that he would never rear again.

All these techniques remind me of old film footage of men trying to execute flight. Now that we know how to fly, we think they look ridiculous! Those early procedures to break

rearers are, I think, barbaric and ineffective. Many people were injured following the advice of those teachers and often the horses were sent to slaughter, labeled as dangerous.

It is important to again remember that when dealing with a remedial problem the qualified trainer should always put himself in a position where he is comfortable, safe and can smile.

Goggles

After Join-Up and several sessions of schooling with the Dually halter, I believe it is appropriate to introduce your horse to a piece of equipment that I call goggles. They are available from good tack shops and equestrian catalogs. Goggles come in two different forms, plastic and made of wire screen. I will first describe the plastic goggles.

This piece of equipment consists of a hood-like piece of cloth resembling racing blinkers. Instead of the cups that restrict rear vision, it is equipped with two half-round plastic bubbles that fit over the horse's eyes. The dome-shaped plastic covering was originally intended to keep objects from hitting the horse's eyes when he traveled in an open trailer. I advise you to drill several holes (¼ inch or .6 cm) along the bottom margin of each of these plastic domes to allow for air circulation. This prevents fogging the plastic, which will obscure the horse's vision.

The second type of goggles is made in Australia and called a "pacifier." It can be ordered from certain tack shops, but is not easy to purchase in the U.S. The pacifier has a similar appearance to the goggles, but the domes are made of a high-tensile wire screen and resemble tea strainers. This piece of equipment was developed for racing on turf where divots fly up.

To use either of these two pieces of equipment for the horse that rears, you need a roll of electrical tape or duct tape. Whether you use the plastic or the wire screen goggles, the idea is to tape over the top half of the goggles, shutting off the horse's ability to see above. A horse does not like to go where he cannot see. This technique only blocks his vision from the upper half of the dome, enabling him to see all that is necessary to remain safe for practically all riding activities. By using this technique, I have had a high success rate helping hundreds of rearers.

Procedure

As usual, I recommend a solid Join-Up and several sessions to achieve complete cooperation with the Dually. Once both lessons have been accomplished, I suggest you begin to actually work with the problems of remedial rearing in a secure enclosure with safe footing (see p. 31).

I suggest that it is good practice to first accustom your student to the goggles. Then, take a few days without a rider, until your horse can travel comfortably, wearing the goggles with the top half of the domes taped over. You could loose-school, or line-drive in a round pen, or lead your horse from the back of a saddle horse to be sure that he is comfortable wearing this equipment. Do it at a walk, trot and canter.

When he has accepted the goggles under these conditions, you can proceed to tack up and ride. I recommend saddling with the goggles in place. It does not matter which style of tack you use as it is unrelated to the use of the goggles. With saddle pad, saddle and bridle all in place, loose-school in a round pen requesting walk, trot and canter before mounting.

Extensively long line the remedial rearing horse wearing a saddle or surcingle—I suggest six or eight days, and a half-hour a day is appropriate. During this procedure, you should have your student willing to turn left and right with ease, and stay relaxed as he is directed to pass through the center of the round pen executing figure-eights in comfort. You should use the les-

son of backing-up on the long lines several times during each session. Backing-up, under control, will eventually be a great asset when it comes to curing the problem of rearing.

With this equipment in place, and your horse long lining comfortably, you are now prepared to attach your human-like dummy rider (see p.144). With your simulated rider in place, you should allow the horse to walk, trot and canter in the round pen until he is comfortable carrying the dummy. Next, you should attach the long lines again and repeat the long lining process, just as was done without the dummy. Remember, backing-up is an essential part of this schooling.

I recommend a few days of long lining with the dummy in place before the live rider mounts up. *Never, ever put long lines on your horse with a live rider up.* The consequences can be dire. I will not go into the long list of potentially catastrophic consequences this could cause, but suffice it to say, it is not an appropriate procedure under any conditions. The use of the long lines with the dummy up can help you to convince the horse that going forward, and not rearing up, is easier to accomplish than rearing with a rider.

Put a live rider on your student only when each procedure has been accomplished to the extent that it is done with great ease, comfort and low adrenaline levels. When selecting a rider, be sure that you choose someone who has ridden dangerous horses before.

Your rider should be advised that there is no intention to cause this animal pain, and that for the first two or three rides he should not even pick up the reins. Riding should be accomplished in the round pen with an attendant always present. The attendant can stand in the center to encourage the horse if needed. It is helpful if you can employ the assistance of a rider on a well-trained saddle horse to act as a stabilizing influence and to give your student another horse to follow.

I recommend that you remain in the round pen until you have spent a minimum of two half-hour sessions with the horse showing no tendency to rear. Once accomplished, the rider can go outside the round pen, preferably with the saddle horse out in front. He should ride only in areas where the footing is good and the environment is safe. No tarmac or hard surfaces are appropriate for the remedial rearer at this stage.

Once the horse is being ridden comfortably outside the round pen, be sure that he's allowed to move forward in a relaxed fashion. Do not ask your rider to achieve a "head set" until the horse is very comfortable being ridden forward. I find that rearing is caused by riders who demand an extreme "tuck." The dressage discipline has a particular affinity for horses that travel with the neck bowed and the chin tucked in. If great care is not taken during the training process when achieving this position, the horse may resent the demands made on him and express his displeasure by rearing. There are other disciplines, too, where this potential is evident. Western reining, Tennessee Walkers and other gaited horse disciplines might experience this discomfort.

When dealing with the remedial rearer it is wise to allow the horse the freedom to walk, trot and canter with the head and neck in as natural position as possible. This procedure should continue for a sustained period appropriate to the depth of the rearing problem. I recommend that riders follow this more relaxed mode of riding until the horse negotiates all gaits easily, stops comfortably and backs-up without resentment.

Should your student stop and refuse to go forward, you may consider taping off more of the goggles, leaving only the lower front quarter of the domes open to his vision. The use of the Giddy-Up rope can be helpful at this point (see p.157–158).

Take the time to school the remedial rearer to accomplish a variety of tasks while curbing his tendency to rear. Review my section on schooling a horse to walk through water (p.125). There you will find several procedures that, when well accomplished, will help you in dealing with the remedial rearer. When you can cause your student to investigate frightening objects and quietly decide to pass through or over them, you are helping your horse's thought processes to the extent that he can deal with the potential for danger without acting out by rearing.

After a month or two of rearing-free training, you can begin to remove the tape by cutting about ⅛ inch off the lowest portion. Repeat this process two or three times a week, until the tape is completely removed. If there is any hint of rearing during the removal process, you should add back a sufficient amount of tape to reestablish good behavior. The process can be repeated later until all of the tape is removed and rearing does not recur. The act of rearing is a lot of work for the horse, and it is not something he finds fun to do. He simply does not rear for no reason. The knowing horseman will thoroughly investigate and eventually pinpoint the circumstances causing the problem.

Once the horse's vision has been restored to an unimpeded state, the rider must take care not to send mixed signals. If he asks the horse to go forward, he must allow it to happen without so much as touching the reins. As I said earlier, many riders ask a horse to move forward and then, inadvertently, pull the reins as they feel the forward motion is too abrupt or fast. This is a bad habit. It is also important that you never require more work than is appropriate for your horse. An exhausted horse tends to revert to the type of remedial behavior that was previously effective in controlling his human partner.

Monty's Points

» Investigate the possibility of physical problems.

» Achieve a solid Join-Up.

» Backing-up is an essential part of this schooling.

» Remember, when dealing with a remedial problem you should be in a position where you are comfortable, safe and can smile.

» Your rider should be advised that there is no intention of causing the horse pain.

» Never put long lines on your horse with a live rider up.

» Follow the goggle-wearing procedures precisely.

» Ride without sending mixed signals.

Hoof Rings

I was introduced to hoof (kicking) rings in the 1980s, and have been impressed with their effectiveness. We call them "kicking" rings because they discourage a horse from kicking in the box stall.

Hoof rings (or kicking or massage rings) are an invention that I have recommended all over the world because they have proved extremely beneficial. I first learned about them from a trainer who had a stallion that kicked so much he couldn't keep shoes on. Someone told the trainer about kicking rings and his problem was over. The stallion only kicked two or three more times, and then placidly wore a pair of these "bracelets" on his rear pasterns from that point onward.

The first time I crossed paths with a race-

horse expressing this behavior, I directed that a pair of rings be made for him. I kept the horse on Flag Is Up for six months or so, and then returned him to his trainer on the racetrack in Southern California. I explained to the trainer how helpful the rings were and he continued their use. Within a month or so, I received a call from the trainer inquiring about the supplement I had given the horse to improve the condition of his rear feet. I answered that he only got the normal feed, but I asked about the condition of the front feet. His answer was that the front feet were the same as they had been earlier.

I discovered, through experimentation, that wearing these rings massages the coronary bands to such an extent that the increased circulation of the blood in the hoof encourages healthy growth and a thicker wall. I have, subsequently, used rings on all four pasterns of horses that have never kicked. The total improvement in the health of the foot is often dramatic.

How the Rings Prevent Kicking

Properly fitted, a kicking ring is worn in such a fashion so when the horse kicks, the ring moves up close to his fetlock joint as his hoof thrusts backward. When the hoof comes to a stop, the ring is thrust onto the coronary band, producing a feeling, I suppose, much like bumping your shin on the bedpost in the middle of the night. I have never found a horse yet that would continue to kick with a properly fitted set of rings. It is one of those remedial problems that has an instant solution. The premise fits comfortably into my concepts in that it allows the horse to teach himself. Once you get the equipment set up, there is no human intervening in the learning process.

With the addition of this procedure also improving the health of the horse's foot, you have the quintessential win–win situation. We have all heard the old saying, "No hoof, no

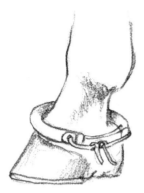  

8.32 Hoof (also known as kicking) rings, fit on the coronary band just above the hoof.

8.33 Measure here to allow the rings to fit onto the pastern.

8.34 How the rings work when the horse kicks.

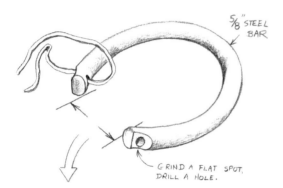

8.35 How the rings are made and where the hole should be drilled to attach the ties.

horse." Well, the use of these rings addresses this issue in a most exemplary fashion. You obviously remove the rings for riding and when you turn the horse loose in a field.

One of the well-known cures for flaky or dry hooves when I was young was to obtain lamb bones, usually the leg or cannon bones. We would then clean and polish them until they were white, put Reducine on them and massage the coronary band of our horses by the hour. It worked well, but it was very labor intensive. Kicking rings do the same thing with far less effort.

Before you put the rings on the horse, make sure that he is quiet and will allow you to pick up his feet and responds to your commands. I suggest that you first school your horse with the Dually halter. Work with the horse to move forward and backward. Should he try to barge past you, let him run into the pressure of the Dually. Your horse will soon learn that he can release the pressure by staying close and moving with you.

When the horse is ready, quiet and attentive, get your farrier or assistant to slide the rings onto the pasterns one at a time. This should be done with the Dually on and with the horse in full control. The rings should rest on the coronary band at the upper margin of the hoof. As the horse moves, a ring automatically massages the coronary band, stimulating blood flow to the area and promoting faster and healthier hoof growth.

How They Are Made

The rings are made from black, iron-bar stock, ⅝ inch (approx. 15 mm) in diameter, shaped like a horse shoe. They fit on the pasterns, sitting on the coronary band just above the hoof—the intention is for them to massage the coronary band. It is acceptable to place them on all four legs. They should be adjusted so that the openings just rub against the pasterns at the narrowest spot just below the fetlock joint. You should turn them and drop them straight down onto the coronet. Allow the horse to carry them around.

Warning: Do not stand behind your horse once these kicking rings have been placed on the pasterns. If they are not positioned correctly, it is quite possible that the horse could kick them off. A flying iron ring could do much damage. I recommend that you put these on the horse in a safe, restricted area.

If you find that your horse dislodges the rings, it is possible to solve this problem with a small addition. Have your farrier or iron worker weld small eyelets to the tip ends on each side of the rings. You can use leather shoestrings or thongs to tie across the openings. This will keep the rings in place.

Monty's Points

» Kicking rings are used to discourage kicking.

» Kicking rings promote healthy hoof growth.

» Follow exact procedures to construct the kicking rings.

» School the horse with the Dually halter.

» Have assistance when first putting the rings on.

» Do not turn out a horse with rings on.

» Avoid standing behind a horse that is unaccustomed to the kicking rings.

» Use a leather thong to secure rings if they tend to dislodge.

Balking

Refusing to go forward is called balking, napping, or jibing. It occurs largely because of pain caused by athletic injury, wear and tear, an accident or misfitting tack or harness. In the days when driving and working horses in harness was the order of the day, balking was commonplace. A misfitting collar was often the culprit. This piece of equipment was the main contact point as the horse pulled his load. Significant pain could quickly produce a balking draft horse.

Before dealing with balking through techniques I describe here, you should take great care to eliminate the potential for physical pain as the cause of the undesirable behavior. It should be noted that the problem may have been fostered through physical pain that is no longer present. The pain, however, could have been the catalyst to the development of the remedial problem. Once the trainer has concluded that the horse is currently free of physical ailments, he can go on with the training procedures outlined in this section.

It is a common problem among racehorses. With valuable purses available, demands are made on these horses, even if they are less than completely sound. In the quest for higher levels of performance, whips and other pain-producing tools are often used. Causing pain is likely to eventually create resentment, producing horses that have good reason to refuse to go forward.

Almost every balker that I am asked to work with turns out to be a horse that resists backing-up. For some reason, many horsemen seem to think that schooling a horse to back-up will cause him to be a balker. Nothing could be further from the truth.

As with loading, reverse is a direction that we should own in a partnership with our horses. The horse that is not trained to back-up willingly may use it against us when he

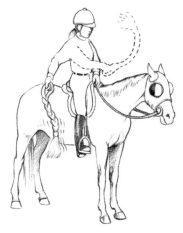

8.36 How the Giddy-Up rope is used.

chooses. The horse that will back comfortably and willingly, either from the ground or while you are riding, is far less likely to be a balker than a horse not trained to back-up.

Method of Schooling

One method I have devised is to first place ordinary blinkers on the horse so that he can't see behind. This is the type of blinker that closes off the rear half of the horse's visual plane. As I have said before, a horse has a difficult time going into a place he cannot see. With the blinkers on, the door is open in front of the horse, but he is discouraged from moving backward. So, riding a horse with blinkers will sometimes be sufficient to discourage balking.

If the blinkers are not sufficient to create a generous mover, I suggest the use of the Giddy-Up rope. This rope is made from cotton fibers braided into a thick rope. At one end is a tassel, and at the other, a loop that fits over the wrist. The rope can be swung in an arc in front of the rider, meeting the horse just behind the rider's legs. Due to the nature of the material and the type of braiding, the rope cannot cause pain. The rider should swing the Giddy-Up rope left and right across the midline of the horse in a rapid back-and-forth motion. With the blinkers in place, the rider should be patient and continue this motion, increasing its intensity, while waiting for the horse to take any free steps forward.

The rider should be diligent and watch for a positive response. The instant forward motion is achieved, the rider should cease to swing the Giddy-Up rope, and stroke the neck of the horse in congratulation. The rider might use clucking or chirping sounds during the use of the Giddy-Up rope to add to its effectiveness. By sending both visual and auditory cues, you are likely to achieve the desired result.

It is extremely important for any horseman to be reasonable in his demands where workload is concerned; you must never demand from a horse to the extent that you discourage his generosity. There is virtually no way to clearly outline here what is reasonable or unreasonable. It is, however, important that horse owners seek advice of professionals about the extent of the workload. There are horses who can handle a heavy workload, and then there are those who are a great deal more fragile. We must be diligent to watch for the signs of discontent when making demands on the energy reserves of our horses.

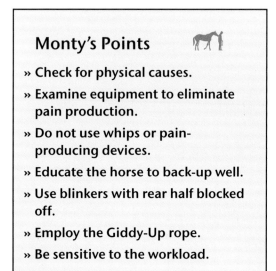

Monty's Points

» **Check for physical causes.**
» **Examine equipment to eliminate pain production.**
» **Do not use whips or pain-producing devices.**
» **Educate the horse to back-up well.**
» **Use blinkers with rear half blocked off.**
» **Employ the Giddy-Up rope.**
» **Be sensitive to the workload.**

Chapter 9

The Into-Pressure Syndrome

Into-Pressure

"Into-pressure" refers to a phenomenon that when any pressure is applied to the horse, he has an instinctive tendency to move *into* that pressure. This information gives us some clues about how to deal with a horse to gain his co-operation. The into-pressure reaction is a reflex deeply ingrained by the horse's millions of years of existence.

The horse's anatomy is designed by nature so that it is strong, fast and agile. The heart and lungs are encased in the protective rib cage, which allows for some flexibility while effectively protecting the vital organs. To be fast, the horse possesses strong hindquarters with the largest muscles of the body attached to the pelvic girdle and designed to drive the hind legs for maximum propulsion. To effectively drive the body forward, there is the need for a space between the ribs and the large skeletal apparatus that drives the hind legs. This space is covered by a thin layer of muscle and skin. It is one of the most vulnerable parts of the horse's anatomy.

To protect this area and have it remain lightweight and flexible, nature has interlaced it with a very large ganglion of sensitive nerves. Horsemen call this part of the horse the flanks. Anyone who has ever dealt with horses knows that this area is extremely sensitive. As I have explained before, nature has seen fit to design a response to stimuli in this area by causing the animal to press into any pressure applied there. As we all know, most of the nerve responses of the human body are designed to repel from pressure and pain. If we touch a hot stove, we pull our hand away. If we bang our hips on the margin of a door opening, we will walk further from it the next time we pass through. However, when a horse bangs his hip on the margin of the door opening, the next time he may lean closer to it and bang it even harder. We humans might think this is stupid, but we should realize that it is a response the horse has learned over many millennia.

The early horse was about the size of a Cocker Spaniel dog, weighing 30 to 40 pounds. This tiny grazer was then preyed upon by a multitude of carnivores. During this period, there were many flying predators of great size and strength, large enough to swoop down and literally carry a horse away. This resulted in the horse having great fear of overhead objects. (See figures 9.3–9.5.)

9.1 The horse has the tendency to move into pressure on the right side.

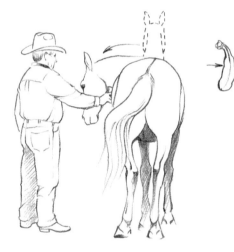

9.2 Then, when pressure is applied on the left side, the horse moves to the left.

The cat and dog are the primary predators of the flesh of the horse. I believe that the canine influence has to do with the natural development of the horse as an into-pressure animal. An attack from dogs will generally focus on that soft portion between the hind leg and the rib cage. Should the horse simply blast away when the dog bites down, there is the strong possibility that the dog can grip tightly with his jaws, and use the momentum of the horse to rip the thin layers of tissue in that area. A horse with his intestines exposed by an opening in the peritoneal wall is as good as dead. The dog can trot alongside his prey, and just wait for the inevitable result.

Nature, through survival of the fittest, has provided for this shortcoming by allowing for the culling of those who run away from pressure, while rewarding those who would stop and press into it. Survival is far more likely when the horse leans abruptly toward the biting dog, and then kicks fiercely to drive him away. One can test this, taking care to avoid the kick zone, by pressing a finger into the flank of an untrained horse. The horse will move into that pressure, not away.

This phenomenon is present in nearly all parts of the horse's anatomy, while it is most obvious in the rear and fore flanks. It is also true that certain parts of the human anatomy respond in a similar fashion. The human mouth, without any question, operates on an into-pressure basis. It seems to me that nature provided this response so that we would not starve during all those centuries before dentists were available. It is clearly displayed by the human infant who will choose to bite on a firm object when teething. If we did not possess this tendency, we would refuse food during episodes of mouth pain, and such a situation would be life-threatening.

I have explained my findings regarding into-pressure where horses are concerned so that you can understand and deal with it in an appropriate manner. It is true that we can *train* horses to move away from pressure. The sidepass movement is a perfect example of an exercise where a horse is trained to move away from the leg of a rider. It is just as true, however, that in the early days of schooling to achieve this, the horse will act instinctively and go *into* the pressure of the rider's leg. Nearly all parts of the horse's body will require training to move away from the pressure.

Chapter 9 / The Into-Pressure Syndrome

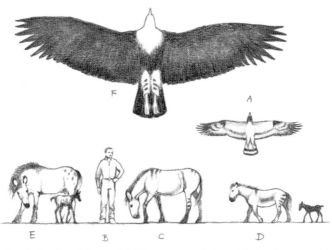

9.3 A comparison chart of animal sizes: (A) Miocene predatory bird, wingspan 7–8 feet; (B) human (C) *Pliohippus*, 12 hands; (D) Miocene *Merychippus*, 8 hands, with foal; (E) *Equus caballus* (first true horse), 12 hands; (F) *Argentavis*, wingspan approx 19 feet.

Use Distractibility, Not Aggression

Recently, an example was brought to me of a horse that would bite the feet of his rider. He would literally pin his ears, bend his neck and try to savage the foot of the rider with his teeth. I was told by the former trainer that his method of discouraging this behavior had been to kick the horse in the lips with the foot that was being attacked. He went on to tell me that the problem became much worse over a period of about two months. I simply directed the rider to use his *opposite* foot on the ribs of the horse each time he was attacked. Within five or six episodes, this horse would initiate his attempt to bite the foot of the rider, but then straighten his neck up to look at the other side of his body. Distractibility is the ally of the trainer.

Attacking the point of aggression is an open invitation to warfare. Should a trainer decide to forcibly discipline a horse directly at the area of aggression, the horse will consider this as an antagonistic act. The point of aggression, for

9.4 Primitive three-toed horses flee an overhead predator.

instance, would be the mouth of a biting horse, the front foot of a striking horse, or the hind leg of kicker. The nature of equus is triggered to fight back. The very problem the trainer had hoped to eliminate, he succeeds in exacer-

9.5 The horse survives by pressing into the canine predators and kicking.

bating. Knowledgeable horsemen have come to understand that distracting a horse, rather than being aggressive, is far more effective.

Hitting or spurring the horse on the right side of his neck or body to get him to turn left, or vice-versa, falls into the same category of equine psychology. It is normally not very effective and can create many serious problems. To hit a horse on top of the head for rearing is equally ineffective, and causing pain to the area of the horse's nose as he attempts to bite you is unacceptable horsemanship. As outlined earlier, I suggest that whipping the racehorse is a breach of these principles also. He will eventually resent the whipping, and actually run slower (p.101).

Timber

Timber was sent to me because he refused to load into a trailer. He is joined in this particular aversion by thousands of horses around the world. Timber had evidently been loaded into a trailer with a low roof, which frightened him. This caused him to thrust his head upward and sustain an injury to the top of his skull. This had effectively set Timber on a course of going into the pressure he perceived as coming from

the roof of the trailer. The owners explained to me that it had been more than two years since they acquired Timber and that his phobia was well in place when he first arrived on their property. It so happens that the stall door in their barn had a beam over it that allowed about 8 feet (approx. 2.5 meters) clearance. There was no way to convince Timber that he should pass through that door. Their stable was set up with corrals attached to the barn, which allowed in and out movement. There was a gate into the corrals from the outside. The construction of the gate was such that there was a 2-inch pipe over the corral gate about 10 feet (approx. 3 meters) above the ground. They could convince Timber to go through that gate, but only after several minutes of coaxing. When he agreed to pass through the gate, either going in or out of the pen, it was a blast at full gallop, with his head raised as high as possible actually trying to bash into the horizontal pipe. The owners learned to live with this, but had to feed and water Timber in the corral as there was no way he would pass through the door into the stall. He remained in the corral through two years of weather, either storms or heat, depending on the season.

To consider loading Timber into a trailer was a joke. He would not go near a trailer or pass under the roofline of my round pen. The roof of the trailer was like a magnet for the into-pressure urges of Timber. The into-pressure phenomenon expressed by this horse was of the strongest magnitude. Survival of the fittest had taught Timber to go into the potential for pain in an attempt to survive.

My next step was to use the piece of equipment that I had developed for rearing horses described earlier on page 151. But in Timber's case, the "rearing goggles" were used to take away the sight of the overhead object. When they were in place, Timber walked through his stable door without hesitation.

Each time I removed the goggles, Timber

Chapter 9 / The Into-Pressure Syndrome

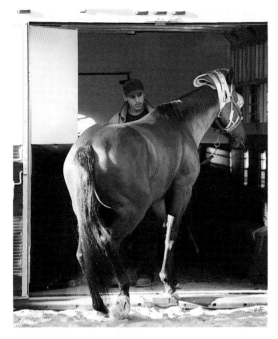

9.6 Timber enters the trailer with extensive head protection.

9.7 A relaxed Timber steps out of the trailer. Note how his upper vision is blocked.

refused to walk into his stall. It should be noted that he would attempt to contact an overhead beam nearly 8 feet (approx. 2.5 meters) above the floor. While virtually impossible, Timber would set himself and thrust his head upward and literally reach in an attempt to meet the wood beam. My next goal, as I could see it, was to cause Timber to be comfortable with objects above his head when he could actually see them. To accomplish this I decided to fix a ceiling in his stall made of a nylon mesh similar to that used by garden nurseries to shade their plants. I arranged this ceiling so that its height could be adjusted. I began at the 9-foot level (approx. 3 meters) and gradually lowered it about an inch (2.5 cm) a day until it literally rubbed his ears as he walked around the stall with his head at normal height. Timber would often startle and try to bash into it. The nature of the material would allow it to stretch, thereby thwarting Timber's attempts to meet a solid object. I found this to be an effective way of desensitizing a horse that is terrified of objects above him.

Training the Horse To Move Off Pressure

One of the primary goals in training a horse to move off-pressure involves moving the horse away from the pressure of a rider's leg. I have found it to be effective to ride the horse into a corner. It should be a 90-degree corner of a wall or a fence. I stop the horse with his head an inch or so from the corner. I then press one of my legs against his side. If he comes *into* the leg, I continue with the pressure. If the horse goes into my leg sufficiently to take me all the way to the fence, I continue to bump that side with my leg until I can get him to move *off* the leg. At the instant I get a positive response, I take the pressure away, give the horse a stroke on the neck, and sit totally relaxed for at least ten seconds. I repeat the process with my other leg and very shortly my horse will understand that moving off my leg gets him rewards, which are cessation of pressure and a period of relaxation. Normally, in a very short time, I can walk my horse into the corner and move his entire body with ease in either direction. Once I have accomplished this routine in a corner, then I begin to make the same request in the center of the riding ring expecting favorable results. Do not hesitate to return to the corner if you are not making satisfactory progress.

I do not believe it is necessary to use spurs early in this training procedure. The softer you can be to gain the desired results, the better. Should you wish to use spurs later, you should remember that they are for communication only, not to inflict pain. The spur should be looked upon as an instrument that puts your contact point closer to the horse for better communication. To ensure that I never cause pain, my spurs are covered with rubber, but the leg without spurs is far better in the early stages of schooling.

Into-pressure is a response that the horseman needs to deal with when educating a horse to accept communication sent through the reins and the bit. There are many ways to initiate the process of requesting your horse to yield to the bit or the hackamore. The primary objective is to create an environment where the horse drops his chin away from the bridle or headgear, and lowers his neck. At this point, it is your obligation to reward the horse by releasing any pressure on the reins. You can again ride into the corner, pick up the reins and drive the horse slightly forward with your legs moving him into the headgear. When he yields to the pressure, reward him with a release.

The elements of into-pressure can be initiated even before riding by bitting the horse up with side reins. It is advisable to have elastic in the reins so that the horse intrinsically learns through first applying pressure to himself, and then achieving release of that pressure by dropping his head away from the headgear.

You should be aware that the softer you can be with the demands of your hands, the lighter the mouth you are likely to create. If you insist on using harsh and heavy-handed techniques, the horse is likely to require that level of pressure throughout his life.

Starting Gates

Even if you have no connection with racing, you can still benefit greatly from this section, because these principles are applicable to equine behavior in all disciplines, including leisure riding.

I have worked extensively with horses that have problems with starting gates (also known as starting stalls). I travel to all parts of the world to work with racehorses that have become negative at the starting gate because their inherent nature is misunderstood and because of the subsequent use of force meted out by track workers. It is far more difficult to deal with horses that have taken the law into their own hands than it is to deal with the young and unspoiled.

For decades now, most equestrians involved in this process have used extrinsic training. I define extrinsic training as the attempt to force knowledge on the student. It is external to the brain of the student. Intrinsic training lets the brain of the student learn from within. This allows the student to draw into the brain information voluntarily. This is a far more effective way of learning than when information is forced upon you from external sources. In fact, most horses will be broken to comply with the demands made of them. Some, however, will resent this harsh treatment and become phobicly resistant to the starting gate. These are the ones I am asked to reform.

When a racehorse first enters the starting gate, feeling the sidewalls intruding into the area of his flanks, his natural reaction is to lean into what he perceives to be a life-threatening situation. Often the jockey or handler will whip the horse in an attempt to punish him for this behavior. This simply serves to convince the horse that the starting gate is a dangerous place to be. He might think there is a big cat in there with claws and teeth or a flying predator. Following this experience, the horse's tendency is to resist loading into the gates at any cost. Man's tendency is to then force him by various means. He might use whips, twitches, lip chains, or a combination of these things in an attempt to demand compliance. Trying to force a horse is usually unsuccessful, and goes against every tenet of my concepts. The larger the horse, the more likely the gates will feel intrusive.

9.8 Nine men could not push or pull Lomitas into the starting gate once he identified it as a terrifying monster. Those men were fighting an evolutionary response to pain, fear and possible death. The race was run without him and he was banned from racing worldwide.

There are two types of problems in this area. One is caused by incorrect schooling, which usually includes fear and pain, and the other problem is caused by the fact that the horse is innately an into-pressure animal. I will deal with the former first.

Dealing with the Remedial Horse

Traditionally, in the extrinsic method of training, a horse is put into a starting gate with a few others he is going to compete against. Next, a button is pushed which causes the gates to fly open, thereby freeing the horses to run forward. Often, the trainer encourages the horse by hitting him on the hips or the hocks the moment the gates are released. The jockey might use both vocal and physical "persuasion" to press the horse forward into immediate flight.

To train a horse intrinsically, I have revised the first experience. The horse should be qui-

etly walked into his gate, placing him next to one or two more experienced horses. When the gates are opened, everyone remains silent. The older horses leave immediately, while the younger, inexperienced one might dwell, not knowing what is expected of him. He will usually watch the other horses as they leave and generally follow, even if quite tentatively. The riders on the older horses will have been instructed to just canter at a slow pace. Once the young horse is 50 feet (approx. 16 meters) or so clear of the gate, then, and only then, should his rider begin to encourage him to go forward at a higher rate of speed. The young horse will see the older ones and perceive them as competition. He will begin to run faster and his rider will press him past the slow-moving horses, causing him to think that he is the victor. The next time the young horse is taken to the starting gate, he is likely to view it as fun. As he enters the gate, his mind will probably be thinking *forward*, remembering the competition, and be ready to go again.

The horse trained extrinsically will probably be reluctant to go into the gate. Once he is forced, the horse trained in this manner will be nervous and unruly. His mind is likely to be thinking backwards. He is likely to concentrate on his hip or hocks, where the whips were applied previously. It is at this point horses will often tend to incriminate the footrails and will develop a phobia against them. The intrinsically motivated horse is happy to go into the gate and looks forward to competing. During the second session, he still finds his rider remaining quiet. When the gates spring open, this young horse reacts more quickly, and passes the older horses earlier than he did the first time. I find that three or four of these educational sessions will produce a racing prospect that is far more effective at the starting gate than the extrinsically motivated individual.

9.9 The protection afforded by the blanket, from a side view.

In 1991, I was called to Germany to deal with a three-year-old Thoroughbred. Lomitas was a beautifully conformed, well-bred chestnut that had earned the title, "Champion Two-Year-Old in Germany" in 1990. Due to circumstances not entirely known to me, Lomitas had obviously concluded that starting gates were a dangerous place to be, and he was willing to fight tenaciously against entering them. Nine men were unable to achieve loading through force. I met him, did Join-Up with him and convinced him through communication and trust that there was no reason to fear the starting gate. Lomitas was the 1991 Horse of the Year in Germany, and the highest-rated horse ever produced in that country through his performances and earnings.

9.10 Monty, with Simon Stokes up, schooling a young horse to the starting stalls with the blanket.

The Monty Roberts Blanket

In 1992, I designed a piece of equipment to help the horse by protecting his vulnerable

9.11 Attachment of the blanket to the starting gate, as Monty watches a horse being schooled.

9.12 The side (running) rail that often is the cause of the problem.

9.13 The training gates at Bremen, Germany, racecourse. Simon Stokes is up, with Monty schooling from the ground. Note that the gates do not have a running rail.

areas. It is a double-carpeted blanket that fits behind the saddle and drapes over the hips down to the hocks. The primary objective was to cushion the effect of rails that run along the inside walls of the starting gates. These are protrusions found in all gates designed to protect the feet and the legs of the jockeys. The blanket protects the sensitive sides of the horse from the annoying stimulation of the rails. A ring is attached to the rear of the blanket into which a rope is snapped. This allows an attendant to pull the blanket off as the horse leaves the gates.

I was educated to the need for and efficiency of the blanket by Prince of Darkness, a very large and athletic Thoroughbred colt. Trained by Sir Mark Prescott of ewmarket, England, Prince of Darkness could be a perfect gentleman, or a killer on a moment's notice. He considered the starting stalls to be small and frightening, inducing claustrophobia. He would fight like a tiger to protect himself from the invasive walls. When I was observant enough to protect him with the blanket, he became a winning racehorse. There was never any need for force.

I always complete Join-Up with the horse first, and once trust has been established, I school with the blanket, taking the horse through the stalls with the gates open. Depending on the severity of the problem, this can take from one day to several months. I make every effort to end each session on a positive note, leaving the horse time to consider the advantage of this added protection the next time he enters the gate. Horses of this type should wear the blanket through each schooling and on race days. It is counterproductive to allow the phobic horse to rediscover the rails he considers abusive. I do not advise that the blanket is discarded once the horse is working well and leaving the gates normally. Remove the protection, and the horse might return to the previous condition and refuse to enter. Once properly schooled, minimal effort is required to continue this process, and I feel that it is well worth it.

Blushing ET

Blushing ET was brought to Flag Is Up Farms in November of 1997. He was a beautiful, athletic, chestnut Thoroughbred who had been banned from the track due to a violent phobia against starting gates, and a deep-seated distrust of humans. I was sure that I would be able to get him back to Santa Anita for the start of the racing season on December 26. When I began to work with him, I realized that I was dealing with a new dimension in troubled horses.

Blushing ET dived at me with teeth bared when I went to put the protective blanket on him. The first few days were devoted to securing the blanket and getting him to enter an enclosed area. Getting him into the gate itself was absolutely out of the question. Despite daily visits to the gates with his work rider, Blushing ET showed no improvement. In the stable he was kind, agreeable, and allowed himself to be groomed, bandaged and blanketed. Anywhere near the gates, he became dangerous. If we put anything like long lines around his hocks, he exploded. I was convinced it was the side-rails that had started this phobic behavior; however, I was astonished that using the blanket, and hours of work had not produced the hoped-for effect.

One evening, I was watching a football game on television, when I realized I barely knew who was playing. My mind was fixed on Blushing ET. I decided to tackle the problem. I enlisted some help and drove to the round pen. I saddled up my Quarter Horse, Dually, checked the reins back to the saddle, and left him standing in his stall. To this day I do not know why I did that—perhaps subconsciously I knew I might need Dually's help.

I then saddled Blushing ET, but left the stable blanket on. I did this to lessen the effect of the long lines near his hip and stifle. Once in the round pen, he was just as violent as he had been without the stable blanket. As I worked, his anger increased. Teeth bared and ears back, he flew at me. My assistants opened the pen door letting me out. The more I thought about it, the more I realized that the abuse he had received because of trainers' attempts to cope with his natural aversion to the starting gates had only compounded his phobia. The harder they whipped him, the more terrified he became. I tried another tack and tied bits of cloth onto the stirrups so that they dangled along his sides. His behavior worsened. The cloths were soon ripped to shreds by his violent kicking. Every time I faced him with the long lines, he became violent, almost nailing me with his deadly feet. I decided it was time to enlist the help of Dually.

I rode Dually into the round pen, and from his back, carefully attached a long line to Blushing ET's halter, and began to drive him with one line. The kicking continued with extreme violence. When the long line was put over the hips and allowed to drop to the hock, he kicked, bit and struck out with his feet, twice making strong attacks on Dually. Each time I jumped Dually forward, I would throw my arms up to avoid the charge of a very angry Blushing ET.

I continued astride Dually, and very gradually, Blushing ET began to learn to stop kicking. When he got quiet, I took off the long line, thus rewarding him for his good behavior. With his adrenaline gradually going down, he could assimilate the information I was giving him that the line was not a whip, and was not going to cause him pain. That evening marked a turning point in my work with him. We continued with the routine at the gates with considerable improvement. However, he was still so phobic about them that he rushed to get through as quickly as possible, and was still a very dangerous horse to handle. Up to this point in my relationship with Blushing ET, every episode proved dramatically that he was bent on going into what he perceived to be dangerous pressure. He would then make every attempt to kill the attacker—long lines, side rails and even me. It didn't matter.

Necessity being the mother of invention, Blushing ET provided me with the information I needed to come up with a new device, and thus a solution to slowing him down upon leaving the gate. I call it "the hallway." It works on two principles. Repetition is the heart and soul of learning and herd animals find comfort from moving in circles. From overhead, this device looks like a miniature racetrack. An oval with two short straight-aways and two small turns, the whole device is no more than 100 feet (approx. 35 meters) from start to finish. The track is defined by 7-feet-high panels (approx. 2.5 meters) and the horse enters the oval through one such detach-able panel. The riderless horse is led, typically counterclockwise, around the track. At one point on the oval stands the inner stall of a starting gate; the outer stalls sit outside the hallway. The gate is left open and the horse walks through the gate and continues around the hallway and back through the gate again. While the protective blanket was still critically needed, Blushing ET taught me the value of this new training device in adjusting his out-look on the starting gate.

We spent hours there. Days passed. I even-tually added a saddle, then long lines and finally a rider. Progress was slow, but it was progress. Blushing ET finally did get back on the track and became a high-level winner. Working through Blushing ET's phobia about starting gates was like attending an "equine university" for me. The hallway has the chance to become a tremendous asset to the racing industry.

I have now successfully used the starting-

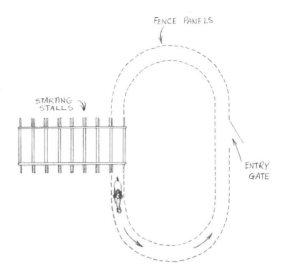

9.14 Diagram of what Monty calls "the hallway."

gate blanket on over 100 horses throughout the world. I did not patent this invention and I have encouraged people to have them made for their own use. Thousands of horses have benefitted from using the blanket, continuing careers that, without it, most likely would have been cut short. It should be said that the Du-ally halter was an extremely valuable tool with all horses that I have trained at the starting gate. It is effective when used in the same fashion as described in the section "Loading," p. 115).

It is my hope that this chapter on into-pressure will serve to inform trainers the world over of a phenomenon rarely discussed before. I believe that it is among the most important facts I have used to my advantage throughout my career. Failure to understand this character-istic is likely to result in the use of techniques that are counterproductive when educating our horses. The examples that I have given are only a few of the areas where into-pressure affects the relationship of humans and horses. The reader should use these suggestions to explore issues critical to the various disciplines.

The Pull-Back Horse

Virtually everyone who has owned a horse has, at some time, experienced an episode where the horse pulls back while tied. Early in the horse's training, if he pulls back and everything is strong enough to withstand the pressure without breaking, your horse will generally imprint in his brain that pulling back is not good.

Should your horse pull back and cause something to break free in the process, you are likely to have a phobia set in where the horse feels compelled to pull and break anything he is tied with. Two or three of these episodes will virtually assure you of a pull-back horse. The into-pressure phenomenon takes over in this case, and you can watch your horse glaze over, eyes tending to roll high in his head, and then with utter determination he will pull with all his might.

The phobic pull-back horse can break what a normal horse could not come close to breaking. He will crouch his body low and strain with all four legs in the ground to pull with every ounce of his power. If something breaks at this point, it is very likely that he will shoot over backward and often injure himself seriously. When this occurs, it simply exacerbates the problem as it further convinces the horse that he has to break his tie.

Pulling back can obviously occur any time the horse is tied; however, certain activities are more likely than others to evoke it. When the horse is standing tied with comfortable, proper-fitting equipment in a quiet location, the potential for pulling back would be at the lower end of the spectrum. The condition that is most likely to promote it is when the handler opens the rear portion of a trailer before untying the horse. This is a red-letter mistake. The confinement, footing and sound all combine to create an extremely dangerous environment for your horse. In general, horses that fly out of the trailer can easily produce injuries to people or animals outside as well as to themselves. In addition to untying the horse before opening the trailer, never *tie* a horse without securely closing the door behind him first.

Bridling or saddling the horse while tied increases the potential for pulling back. I am often presented with horses at my demonstrations that are frightened about being bridled or saddled. Many times this stems from an incident of pulling back while these procedures were attempted, so I recommend that when bridling and saddling your horse, you control him with your hands rather than tying him.

Horses that pull back are often brought to me at Flag Is Up Farms. I think it is most productive to explain to you exactly what I recommend and allow you to approximate my procedures as close as your facility will allow. I suggest that the person who executes the procedures be a professional trainer, or an extremely competent horse handler.

Procedure

I have a solid, smooth wall, eight feet high (approx. 3.5 meters) and 24 feet (approx. 8 meters) in length. There is a 14-inch (approx. 31 cm) power pole set in concrete just behind and in the center of the wall. It has a tie ring on a long bolt that goes through the wall and the power pole. When you view the wall from the horse's side, it is smooth and featureless, except for the ring dead in the center and about 7 feet (approx. 2 meters) off the ground. My wall is made of wood jacketed with smooth steel, and is free of any protrusions.

When I prepare to school a pull-back, I place a tie in the ring that is about 3 feet long (approx. 1 meter). I then use two 14-foot (approx. 4 meters) panels that are about 5 feet (approx. 1.5 meters) tall. They have 6

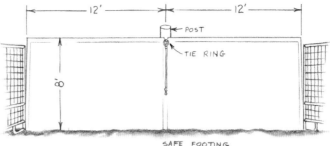

9.15 The wall, and where the bungee is attached.

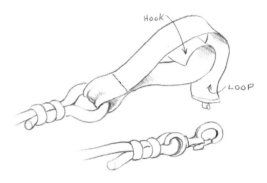

9.16 The bungee and the snap.

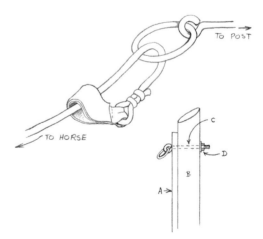

9.17 The post to which the bungee is to be attached. (A) wall; (B) post; (C) rod with eye in one end, threaded on the other end; (D) washer and nut.

horizontal bars and are constructed of very strong material. I fix a panel to each end of my solid wall. I put a steel fencepost in the ground just outside each panel at the point where it makes an intersection with my wall. I then move the two outer ends of the panels toward each other until they are 16 feet (approx. 5 meters) apart. At that point, I put a 16-foot panel in position so that it joins the two panels together. I then set two more steel posts to secure the intersections of those panels. This creates a "D"-shaped enclosure, with my large wall being the flat portion of the "D," and three portable panels creating the semicircle portion.

The wall and panel configuration can vary, as long as it is safe. This arrangement lets me uncouple the panels at a junction and lead my horse into the D-shaped enclosure wearing a high-quality, unbreakable halter. With caution, I fix the tie to the halter and exit quickly along the wall, climbing over one of the panels. It is critical that whoever attaches the tie can physically move quickly and smoothly out of harm's way. A horse that pulls back, and then jumps forward, can cause serious injury.

The tie I use is very important in this procedure. I suggest a commercially produced stretch tie. A 3-foot (approx. 1 meter) length will stretch to about 10 to 12 feet (approx. 3 to 4 meters) before it gives your horse anything solid to pull on. At that point, your horse's hindquarters are up against the panel, restricting him from pulling back any further. Usually, the horse will freeze in the pulling position, and the elasticized tie simply keeps pulling until he yields. A few days of this will usually produce a horse that no longer pulls. I suggest that you continue to tie the horse up exclusively with an elasticized tie for a year or so. It is important to tether only to substantial objects more than 5 feet (approx. 1.5 meters) above the ground. I have experienced a high level of success using this procedure, and I strongly recommend it for anyone who has a horse with this problem.

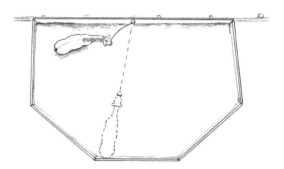

9.18 The "D" enclosure for schooling the pull-back horse. Five-panel configuration shown.

9.19 The horse is being led to the enclosure; note the doubled lead rope.

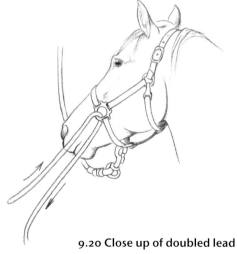

9.20 Close up of doubled lead rope—tie elastic in place.

9.21 Jason leads a pull-back horse to the wall.

9.22 Jason is careful to stay out of the way.

9.23 The horse is left to deal with his phobia in this safe enclosure.

9.24 The horse attempts to pull back, but finds that the rules have changed.

9.25 The horse becomes quiet after he realizes that he cannot break the tie.

The Cinch-Bound Syndrome

The behavior whereby horses act out against the girth or cinch being tightened is known in most of the English-speaking world as "cinch-bound" or "cinchy." It is the reaction of a super-sensitive horse to the stimulus induced by a snug girth or cinch. Every horse has a web-shaped network of nerves just behind each of his elbows. This network lies in the outer layers of tissue covering the rib cage in the lower anterior portion of the thoracic region. The response aspects of this nerve system are discussed in detail on pages 159–160.

The cinch-bound horse is likely to manifest his condition with one or more reactions from a significant list of responses. When the girth or cinch is drawn tight, the cinchy horse will stiffen his entire body. He will most often raise his back and round his body, crouching back over the rear legs. In the early stages of acting out, the cinchy horse will most often elevate his neck. The neck will become rigid, the eyes wide open and appear to look toward the area of the girth or cinch. If he is to take it further, the cinchy horse will usually move in reverse and often lose control of the hind legs, crouching lower and lower. In extreme cases, the cinchy horse will drop to the ground on his hindquarters and throw himself over backward. Many saddles have had their trees broken by a horse falling over backward, slamming the saddle to the ground under him. Obviously, the potential for injury to the horse is great.

If the cinchy horse is tied during a traumatic episode, he is likely to act out by pulling as hard as possible, usually breaking any kind of tie you use. If the equipment is strong enough to withstand his pulling, the horse will often fall against the tether, placing himself and the handler in a critically dangerous position. The horse who pulls, but is unable to break loose, will sometimes catch his balance and then lunge forward striking out with the front legs, again exposing himself and the handler to extreme danger.

I have seen a cinch-bound horse that will lower the back during a cinchy episode, raise the head and neck and sink his chest down near the ground, crouching back with his front feet remaining in their original position. This response would resemble the way we often see dogs stretch in the morning, yawning while they stretch back with their front feet well out in front. Unlike the relaxed dog, this horse will sometimes come forward out of this position with violent thrashing. This can be extremely dangerous to himself or a handler.

Then there is the cinch-bound horse that simply reacts violently against the girth by bucking like a professional in a rodeo. Often, this type of cinchy horse will express himself for 20 to 30 seconds, and then be fine for the rest of the day. I have also observed a horse who expresses the cinch-bound syndrome by traveling as though he was lame. Fiddle D'Or, a world champion I showed, was one of those individuals. If I was not careful to give him a bit of time to get accustomed to the cinch, Fiddle would walk off as if he was severely lame on the near foreleg. The unknowing observer would swear that he had a broken leg. If I immediately loosened his cinch, and gave him a few minutes to accustom himself to it by tightening more gradually, he would travel normally.

In studying the condition of cinch-bound, you would have to ask why this occurs in some horses, and not in others. While it is true that all horses have the nerve apparatus to produce the cinch-bound condition, some are more likely than others. I have had horsemen tell me that it follows genetic lines, and yet others dispute that theory. After a lifetime of observation, I have come to some conclusions, none of which I can defend with hard scientific evidence. The fact that I have started more than 12,000 horses, however, seems to provide me with some license to hypothesize.

When I snug up a cinch or girth for the first time on any animal, I have the opportunity to assess his potential response. Some horses will seem to have their skin on fire, so to speak, quivering in preparation to act out against the tightening band. Others will seem to accept it quietly and without significant sensitivity. It seems to me that over the years more fillies have been inclined to hypersensitivity than their male counterparts, although I can only remember one filly expressing this tendency with the first saddling in all my years of experience in starting babies.

While I seldom give color a place important in assessing behavioral traits, it is apparently true that the chestnut is usually more skin sensitive than the brown or black horse. Medication bottles often refer to chestnut-skin sensi-

tivity. Learned veterinarians have concluded that chestnuts will often blister when treated with the same substance that would simply cause the brown horse to sweat. I have also read veterinary reports that suggest chestnuts are more prone to epidermal allergies than darker-skinned horses.

Color aside, it seems to me that certain horses have a far more sensitive ganglion in the foreflanks region than others. I believe that the cinch-bound syndrome most often occurs following the first few saddlings. This would suggest that human error of one sort or another is generally involved.

I sincerely believe that the procedure of foal imprinting (see p. 181), properly done, will virtually eliminate the tendency for a horse to be cinch-bound. If a handler properly massages the foreflanks area, both with human hands and a soft length of rope as described in "Foal Imprinting," the tendency to act in a supersensitive manner is lessened appreciably. Some horses, it seems, just have their foreflank ganglia closer to the surface than do others. This is true whatever the color.

There is no substitute for steady, well-thought-out movements by the handler throughout the training process of any horse. The trainer in a hurry, who girths up rapidly, is inviting a horse to develop cinch-bound tendencies. A careless trainer who uses a dirty—sweaty and stiff—cinch or girth, increases the potential to cause pain to the sensitive foreflank area.

The knowing trainer should always be aware of the condition of his cinches and girths. He should take care to put pads with clean material on cinches and girths with a horse that shows sensitive tendencies. He should girth or cinch rather loosely at first, walk the horse for a minute or two and tighten appropriately. An ounce of prevention is worth a pound of cure. A trainer aware of the danger that a cinch-bound horse can cause will untie a horse before saddling. If saddled while tied, the cinch-bound will often pull back and add to their problems the pull-back phobia I discussed on pages 170–172.

Many people ask about what to do with a cinch-bound horse they have inherited from someone else. The following is my recommendation for dealing with the condition already in place. With your horse in a box stall of at least 12 by 12 feet (4 by 4 meters), put a substantial stable blanket on him, and fasten all of the belts and buckles. Over the blanket in the area of the heart-girth, place an elastic over-girth. I prefer the type with a breastcollar. These over-girths can be purchased at a good tackshop and are generally about 4 inches (10 cm) in width, and easily stretched by the human hand. Place the breastcollar appropriately, and buckle up the elastic over-girth so it is just touching the skin. Allow your horse a few minutes in the box stall to become accustomed to the over-girth, then tighten a notch or two so it begins to stretch the elastic material.

This girth is easily expandable and the horse usually does not react to it as violently as he would a less forgiving cinch or girth. You should continue to tighten periodically until you have stretched the girth to snugly encircle the heart-girth area of the horse. It is appropriate to allow him to carry this apparatus around the box stall for up to three or four hours. Usually, within two or three days of this treatment, your horse will accept the elastic over-girth without a cinch-bound response. When your horse is comfortable, you can go to the next step in the process.

Once your horse can take the light, elastic girth relatively snug from the outset of the day, you can remove the blanket and allow the girth to come directly against his skin. Usually, this will not be of great concern to your horse. When this is accepted, initiate a pattern of putting the elastic girth on about one-half hour before the time you intend to saddle your

horse. Most cinch-bound horses will then take the girth or cinch quite comfortably if you tighten gradually over a period of five to ten minutes. If your horse is more severely affected, simply extend the time of each of these procedures until your horse is comfortable. Most cinch-bound horses will be relatively free of this anxiety within a month or so if you are diligent about following these procedures to the letter.

Monty's Points

» Cinch-bound might be genetically influenced.

» Sensitive skin might play a role in causing a cinch-bound syndrome.

» Cinch-bound horses are usually caused by people.

» Handlers should use clean, appropriate equipment.

» Being in a hurry is often the cause of cinch-bound.

» Use a light, elastic over-girth.

» Follow the corrective procedures to the letter.

Chapter 10

Imprinting Good Behavior

Catching Horses

It is so important to remember that everything you do with a horse is training. Good human habits create good horses; bad human habits create bad horses.

I am often asked how I catch my horse. My answer is that I never catch my horse, I allow my horse to "catch me." I show how certain gestures and procedures can cause the horse to want to be with me. Therefore he comes to me, thus catching me. A handler who goes after the horse, demanding that the horse is caught, becomes exasperated throughout the process. Generally, after a long pursuit, when both horse and handler are exhausted, the horse is caught. The human is often angry by this time and places a halter roughly on the horse, treating him harshly and proving, "You do what I say or I'll hurt you." Following this negative message, why should the horse want to be caught again? View this common occurrence through the horse's eyes, and I guarantee you will observe the true measure of its foolishness. In addition, when the handler pursues his subject, he often looks the animal straight in the eye. This, in the Language of Equus, means "go away." Attempting to catch a horse in this fashion represents a mixed message of the

strongest nature and is considered to be giving the horse "bad instruction." Once the handler has taken the time to learn the horse's language, he will readily see the error of his ways.

If, when you go into the field to catch the horse, you use Join-Up techniques, you will virtually always find your task far less difficult. A knowledgeable horseman will achieve Join-Up before releasing a horse into a field, and thus seldom experience the difficulties of catching a horse.

To illustrate the principles that I employ, I often tell this story. A fellow had a five-acre field and in that field he had two horses. One was a bay and the other was a chestnut. He decided, one day, that he wanted to catch the bay horse. He entered the field and began the process of trying to catch and halter his bay

> *"Never catch your horse, let your horse catch you!"*
>
> —*Monty Roberts*

177

horse. About twenty minutes into the process, he realized that the chestnut horse was walking around the field following him, but there was no way that he could approach the bay horse.

After an hour or so, everyone was exhausted. And, for the last 15 minutes or so, he could not get the chestnut out of his way. Finally, he cornered his bay horse and managed to get him caught and haltered. Pulling him around, he "changed his name" a few times before taking him from the field.

A day or so later, the man decided to catch one of his horses again. Not wanting to go through the same process, he decided this time he would catch the chestnut. Would you believe that on this day the chestnut decided to act exactly as the bay had a couple of days before? He angrily repeated the process this time with the bay horse following him around and the chestnut refusing to be caught.

The moral of the story is, if you want to catch your horse, do not look him in the eye. Use the concepts of Join-Up and you do not catch your horse, you let your horse "catch" you.

Should field-catching problems persist, you can do Join-Up from a saddle horse in the field. This will allow the horseman to travel the necessary distance.

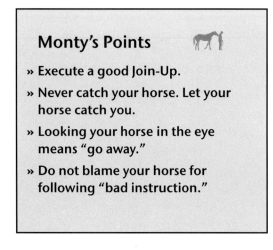

Monty's Points

» Execute a good Join-Up.

» Never catch your horse. Let your horse catch you.

» Looking your horse in the eye means "go away."

» Do not blame your horse for following "bad instruction."

The Barn-Sour Syndrome and Separation Anxiety

There are two categories of remedial behavior that I believe are so closely linked they should share a section. "Barn sour" could be called "home sour," or "property sour." These terms simply mean that the horse does not want to go away from home and, even if you are successful in achieving some distance from the horse's home, there is still a great desire on the horse's part to return as fast as possible.

Every question-and-answer session that I conduct includes someone asking, "How do I stop my horse from taking me back to the stable against my will?" She will go on to say that her horse will often refuse to go in a direction away from the stable and, if she persists, the horse is likely to act out negatively. Stopping and refusing to go forward (balking), rearing, bucking and kicking out are the most often mentioned actions of the offender.

These actions are often dangerous for both the rider and the horse. Most stables have hard surfaces surrounding the buildings because of their need for vehicular activity. Obstreperous behavior on a hard surface is one of the most undesirable behavioral traits we can experience. Rearing, for instance, on tarmac, concrete or cobblestone surfaces can result in injuries that run the gamut from minor to lethal.

The horse that rears and then loses his footing can go over backward and quite easily injure his spine, hips or skull. Practically every equestrian knows of someone who has had a broken leg or other serious injury from a horse rearing over. Wheeling around to return to the stable often results in a fall—rider, horse or both.

Ironically, these problems are generally the result of a rider inadvertently training his horse to unilaterally decide to return to the barn. I realize that most equestrians would prefer to believe they had not trained their horses to do this, but the fact is, most have done just that.

If you direct the horse straight back to the barn, ride inside, get off, remove the saddle and give the horse a good place to rest—complete with feed and water—you are training the horse to decide unilaterally that this is the best place for him to go. Before long, the horse will become sluggish leaving home yet swift to return, making his own decision to take you back to the barn where he feels the next step is to be comfortable.

A horse trainer will often advise you to use a more severe bit so that you can force the horse to comply with your wishes. He is likely to recommend you hit him hard with a whip to show him "who is boss." Usually, in a short time, the horse will grow to resent this treatment and will act out by rearing, bucking or refusing to go at all.

The inquiring rider will ask, "What do I do to cure this horse of these awful habits? Tell me how I can *make* him stop doing these things." "You probably cannot *make* him stop," I might answer. Note that most people use the word *make* in posing these questions. This implies the use of force. The process by which he learned to be barn sour was *intrinsic* (p.164), which is to say, you allowed him to show himself the benefits of the activity. When you ask what you could do to *make* him stop this behavior, you are suggesting *extrinsic* measures employed to correct the problem. I think you can quickly see that the extrinsic motivation will virtually never overcome the mistakes made by riding the horse straight back to the barn. The knowledgeable horse person will recognize at once that there is the need to deal with this horse to reduce his motivation to manifest this behavior.

My answer is to never ride your horse home. You can ride him nearly home, turn him around, and ride in the opposite direction, proceeding until your horse has settled.

Then, get off and lead him back to the barn. In this way, you are getting the horse's attention to stay with you and your activity until it has been completed, rather than the horse dictating to you. As you train a horse, you should always look to a procedure that expresses *bilateral* agreement between horse and rider.

When you just ride your horse back to the stable, enter the building and dismount, you are sending your horse a wrong message for your purposes. It sets well with the horse so his learning is deep. A knowledgeable equestrian will eventually conclude that, while his intent is pure, he often trains his horse to do exactly what he does not want.

Virtually every rider has come across a horse that travels reluctantly going away from home, and speeds up when he reaches the turning point. As the home turn is reached, it is common to find the barn-sour horse become "chargey," and anxious to complete the trip back to the barn. Do not get off and finish the ride until the horse has settled down into a proper walk, neither too fast nor too slow. The best way to complete this walk home is to keep going until the horse is willing to negotiate any direction the rider chooses. Then stop, back the horse up a pace or two, and dismount. Loosen the girth and give the horse a good rub on the forehead. In this way you are reinforcing that the horse has pleased you. It is often a good idea to spend a few moments just standing. When you are both ready, lead the horse home. If this procedure requires you to walk great distances back to your barn, then attempt, wherever possible, to ride on 45-degree angles to your home point so that you can ultimately dismount at a reasonable distance of 100 yards (approx. 100 meters) before walking to the barn.

Each time, dismount at a different spot and often go in a different direction, so as not to create another habit. This will mean that your horse is never quite sure when he will be rewarded, and is unlikely to ever race for home.

With a horse that is extremely barn sour, you should follow this next course of action. Coax your horse away from the barn by whatever means you can, short of dealing pain (see "Balking" and the Giddy-Up rope, pages 157–158). Ride the horse some distance from your property (more than 2 miles or approx. 3 kilometers) and leave the horse with a neighbor, friend or trainer. Then, ride a different horse home and exchange the boarding responsibilities. Do this a sufficient number of times until your horse appears settled and no longer difficult about leaving to your stable. Once you have noticeably improved the behavioral pattern, then begin the training techniques I described earlier, and return the horse to your own property.

If this condition is in any way connected with your horse being bonded (sometimes called "separation anxiety") to another horse, then increase the length of time the horses are separated on any given day. Your horses should not scream for one another or seem affected by separation.

As our population grows and we live closer to one another on land parcels of ever-decreasing size, our horses, too, are living in closer proximity. Equus, being a herd animal, is far more comfortable in a group than he is as an individual. This creates a pattern of behavior whereby a horse becomes extremely upset when separated from a "buddy."

Before deep bonding occurs, the knowing equestrian will be diligent and change the location of horses often enough to reduce this unwanted behavior. The "barn-sour" condition will often have its beginnings as "separation anxiety."

If you follow these procedures before there is a problem, it is unlikely that you will experience the barn-sour condition or separation anxiety. Once these problems are deep seated,

they are very difficult to cure. Be diligent about your habits when returning your horse to the stable. One lazy day or two can start a pattern of behavior that might be extremely undesirable.

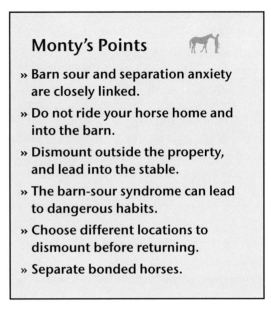

Monty's Points

» Barn sour and separation anxiety are closely linked.

» Do not ride your horse home and into the barn.

» Dismount outside the property, and lead into the stable.

» The barn-sour syndrome can lead to dangerous habits.

» Choose different locations to dismount before returning.

» Separate bonded horses.

The Shying Tendency

During my question-and-answer periods someone is likely to ask, "What do I do with my horse who shies constantly?" She will explain that when she rides her horse she is often frightened when her horse slams all four feet to the ground startled by some object in the distance. It is exasperating, she says, to find that there is a tiny plastic bag swinging from a bush or a squirrel playing in a tree. She might tell me that her horse is extremely frightened of bicycle riders, or cattle in a field. There is no end to stories that I hear about the silly little things that cause a horse to shy. Obviously, the horse that startles and takes flight is far more dangerous than the horse that startles but remains in place. Many people have been injured by the accident that occurs when the shying horse bolts, causing them to lose their balance and possibly fall.

All horses shy. Nature was careful to imprint a behavior pattern by which horses regard anything unfamiliar as dangerous. If horses were not afraid of things unfamiliar, they simply would not have survived the millions of years of their existence. Horses, being flight animals, are inherently prepared to flee anytime they feel they are potentially threatened. It is an effective way of avoiding capture by a hungry predator. The wiggle of a bush might mean the movement of a lion or a tiger. With horses, even the sky above can be frightening as their ancestors were much smaller and subject to attack by flying predators.

You should allow the horse the right to be shy. Once you have accepted for this to occur, you are better prepared to deal with it. Being tolerant, keeping your adrenaline down, stroking your horse and showing him the plastic bag is far better therapy than lashing out against your animal when he is frightened.

Besides increasing your understanding of the shying syndrome, you can use Join-Up as a great advantage in dealing with this phenomenon. If you take the time to do at least four to six good Join-Ups, the tendency to shy will usually be lessened dramatically. The horse that wants to be with you is far less likely to bolt and take flight when startled by some unfamiliar object.

A knowing trainer will help his horse to become familiar with those things that often cause the shying. Plastic bags placed on the wall of a stall or the fence in the corral will assist you in this area. Exposing your horse to those things that often cause him concern will tend to lessen his volatility when he does shy. You should remember that the well joined-up horse is happy to be with you, and less likely to be concerned with those things outside the sphere of influence created by your partnership.

Monty's Points

» **Shying is a natural phenomenon.**
» **You must be tolerant of the horse's natural tendencies.**
» **Join-Up can be your greatest ally when dealing with shying.**
» **The horse that wants to be with you is less likely to bolt when frightened.**

Foal Imprinting

This section is a version of foal imprinting introduced by Robert Miller, DVM, in his book, *Foal Imprinting*.

Imprinting is the act of introducing a young horse to the human at the time of birth. There is a window of opportunity, only open fully for about an hour after the foal is born. This is the optimal time for imprinting. It does not mean that you cannot imprint after that hour, but it is not as effective. You should maintain the good husbandry practices recommended for foaling (see p.184) and imprinting should commence only when you are entirely comfortable that the foal is being born under normal circumstances, and it is not interfering in any way with the mare bonding with the foal.

While I have been a student of Dr. Miller's foal-imprinting methods, I have allowed my experiences to modify the process. The "imprinter" should place himself on his knees at the dorsal (back) side of the foal, near the withers. He should take care when handling the foal to never get between the mare and foal.

I recommend that imprinting begin with the nose and the mouth. You should stroke inside the nostrils and mouth with gentle, smooth rapid motions. You will find that each foal will vary, but there is a point in time when the foal will accept the motion with obvious relaxation. The imprinter should massage each area in smooth but rapid motions at approximately two strokes per second. Dr. Miller has found that many areas will require 50 strokes before the foal relaxes. Do not hesitate to reach that number if necessary.

One should be diligent about massaging every portion of the head area, including the eyes and the ears. A finger should gently massage inside each ear until the foal relaxes. Massaging the full ear from the outside is also important.

With the head completed, you should then massage the entire neck and often this can be done before the hind legs are fully outside the mare. I like to use my hands wide open, one on each side of the neck, followed by a hand on the crest and a hand on the throat. When the foal is thoroughly relaxed following the head and neck massages, the imprinter can move on to the area of the shoulders. By this time, the hind legs are probably out of the mare. Allow as much time as possible for the umbilical cord to remain in place.

It is at this juncture that you should begin to do imprinting on the front legs. I begin to imprint the front legs by starting with the feet. You should pat them on the sole to initiate this process. Gently but firmly, grasp the fetlock joint while holding the foot still, and begin to pat the sole of the foot with the open palm of your hand. The rate of patting should be approximately 50 pats every 20 seconds. This process should be completed once for each foot. If the foal has not relaxed after the 50 repetitions are completed, then continue to pat. When the foal is relaxed, you can then go on to the next step.

After you have worked on the front feet, work your way up the legs rubbing first the fetlock joint, then the shinbone, knee, up to the forearm, and onto the shoulder and withers. The rubbing should be done at the same rate as the patting so that you allow about 20

seconds and 50 strokes for each of these different areas. If the foal does not relax in this time, continue rubbing the same areas.

Continue with the shoulders, over the withers and back of the foal. *Note: Do not do the sides of the foal. Leave them alone.* It is important that the sides of the foal remain sensitive because they are where the rider's legs will go. It is a good idea to leave all of nature's sensitivities in place between the girth area and flanks of the foal.

This brings you to the first extremely sensitive area to imprint—the area where the girth will eventually draw snug. A horse has a large, well-defined web of nerves here. You can dramatically improve the process of his accepting his first saddle with a good job of imprinting. You should take great care to massage both sides extensively, though you will need to complete the accessible side first, and then wait to roll the foal over to do the other side.

If at this point, the mare wants to stand, as often happens, you should allow this to occur. Remain relaxed and encourage the mare to approach the foal and lick him if she chooses. It is at this point that the placenta needs to be tied up so that the mare does not step on it. If necessary, you can leave the foal at this point, tie up the placenta, and treat the navel with an appropriate antiseptic.

Returning to the imprinting, you should continue to massage the back of the foal and continue rubbing down toward the hips, down the hind legs, rubbing around and under the tail and genitalia of the colt, or udder of the filly. The hind legs should be imprinted in the same fashion as recommended for the front legs. You then should roll the foal over to repeat the process on the areas you were unable to reach in the initial process. Normally, this amounts to the opposite shoulder and hip. Everything else should be reachable while the foal is in his original position.

When the whole body has been done in the

Chapter 10 / Imprinting Good Behavior

prescribed fashion, it should have taken about 10 minutes, no longer than 15. Then, bring out a hair dryer with a long, safe extension cord. The less cord you have in the stall, the safer it is. It is a good idea to move the foal to a point near the stall door before using the hair dryer. You use this to introduce the sound of a motor to the foal, and the warm air creates a comfortable association with that sound. Be sure that it does not get in the way of the mare and foal.

Test the heat on the back of your hand first. Then, holding it about 4 to 6 inches away from the foal, introduce it to the head of the foal, around the chin, nose, and up over the ears, then down the neck, and finally, cover the entire body. You do not have to *dry* the foal, and you must not take too long, only 5 to 7 minutes. A foal does not normally stand up for at least 15 minutes after he is born. Should you need to stop the foal from getting up, it may help to gently hold the head down and elevate one front leg for a moment. Under no circumstances do I ever recommend that you keep the foal on the ground for more than 20 to 25 minutes. Once the foal has been covered with the stroking warmth of the hair dryer, stand away from the foal and allow the mare to take over completely. It is important to always allow the mare to continue her natural desire to bond throughout this process. As I said earlier, *never position yourself between the mare and the foal*. If the mare is nervous or fractious, it is a good idea to have an attendant with a lead rope on the mare to ensure safety.

When the foal is standing, whether nursing or not, take a soft lead rope or a sash about 3 to 4 feet in length (approx. 1 meter) and wrap it around the foal where the girth will go. Then, gently squeeze and relax it, gathering it at the top of the foal. Repeat this gentle squeezing and relaxing at least 50 times, or until the foal is comfortable about this gentle compression on his girth area. Repeat this in the rear flank area. (Do not touch the area in the center of

the foal's sides.) Now I recommend that you leave the foal and mare alone, completing the normal husbandry procedures. This first imprinting, both lying and standing, should take no more than 35 to 40 minutes.

While learning these techniques, it is understandable that you may be slower at first, but do not extend the time you spend with the foal on the floor. It is most important to restrict that part to 20 to 25 minutes—no more.

At three days of age, a second imprinting can be achieved. The best time to do it is when the mare and foal come in from the field. You should greet the foal and when in the stall, try to imprint all the areas you completed originally, but remember it will be more difficult with an older foal who is standing. Pick the feet up one at a time, tapping the soles. If you find the foal lying down, carry on with the early procedures but only if the foal remains comfortable. The hair dryer can also be used in the same way. The second imprinting should take no longer than 30 minutes. After 7 to 10 days, you can do a third imprinting (probably standing), which should be a repeat of the first imprinting, but lasting only 15 to 20 minutes. The second and third imprinting are very important as they reinforce the work you did at birth. A fourth imprinting (probably standing) has some value, but is not necessary. Should you choose to execute a fourth, I recommend that it take place at 15 days of age.

The imprinting program should run as follows:

First imprinting: At moment of birth; 20 to 25 minutes lying down, and approximately 15 to 20 minutes standing up—a total of 40 minutes.

Second imprinting: Day Three, a repeat of day one (but maybe a little shorter—about 30 minutes).

Third imprinting: Days Seven to Ten—15 to 20 minutes.

Fourth imprinting: Day Fifteen—15 to 20 minutes, always repeating the procedures as prescribed.

Once Day Fifteen has passed, I like foals to grow up as naturally as possible. It is important to not dwell on the little problems you may come across. For example, if a foal dislikes having his feet trimmed, just get the job done as quickly and kindly as possible, and be relaxed about it. In my experience, the imprinted foal will cooperate a lot more quickly than the one that has not been imprinted.

If your foal is imprinted in the manner I have described, he will generally trust a human much more. And it would be unusual for him to buck with his first saddle. He will be easier to handle throughout his life and thus less apt to be injured or cause injury to others.

Note: At no time do I recommend you kiss or hug your foal, or remain with the mare and foal throughout the night. Over-imprinting has been responsible for unwarranted criticism of this procedure.

A horse always knows that you are a human and you should always be mindful of the fact that he is a horse. It is bad horsemanship to create a too "humanized" equine student.

The Growing-Up Months
At Birth

The foal should be imprinted within the first hour and he should not be expected to stay down for more than 25 minutes. The mare should be allowed to bond with the foal by having the foal within reach while someone is holding her. When you release the foal after imprinting, he should stand and suckle. It is very important that the foal gets the colostrum needed for life. All this must be done in addition to the normal husbandry procedures, such as treating the navel, weighing the placenta, clearing the amnion, wiping out nostrils, checking that the foal's breathing and pulse rates are normal and that he is anatomically correct. An enema is also routine, particularly for foals who have more difficulty passing the meconium (first stools).

Where possible, the mare and foal should be turned out in a small enclosure during Day One, and in a larger enclosure from Day Two. It is best to involve two people, one for the mare and one for the foal every time you move the pair. I recommend the use of the Foal Handler to help in guiding the foal.

Monty's Points

» The imprint window is open widest in the first hour.

» Imprinting can begin before the foal is fully born.

» Do not interfere with the mare and foal bonding.

» Follow the imprinting procedures precisely.

» Use a hair dryer to accustom the foal to motor noises.

» Use a soft sash to place around the girth area.

» Repeat the imprinting process at least twice after the original imprinting.

» Do not over-imprint.

Day Nine

It is possible the mare will be covered while on her foal heat. During the breeding, the foal should be attended to by his own assigned person. The properly imprinted foal is likely to stand and be cooperative while the mare is being examined and covered.

Day Ten to Weaning

Mares and foals should be turned out with their peers. Anyone helping with the handling of mares or foals at this critical time should be experienced and understand that there will be no violence in the process. The Foal Handler is of great assistance in moving mother and foal to and from stables or fields.

Feeding

"Creep feeding" is a way to feed the foal, protecting the food from full-sized horses. It should be available from about 10 days of age to ensure the achievement of a well-constructed nutritional program. Creep feeding is an accepted practice worldwide and most veterinarians will help you to design the proper facility. I recommend that foals of both sexes be allowed to run together until weaning. The more social interaction you can encourage during the rearing process, the more likely you are to raise a well-adjusted adult. Many farms allow both males and females to stay together outside until 10 or 11 months of age. I find no fault with this, but recommend close observation to intervene should dangerous behavior jeopardize the well-being of any of the individuals.

Care and Management

A good horseman should allow a young horse to begin his life as an independent individual without much intervention from people. If for any reason a foal needs to be brought into a stall, it should be done quietly. To be completely safe, the Foal Handler (p. 134) should be used. Necessary procedures such as those performed by the farrier and the veterinarian should be done at recommended intervals as set out by the professionals. These will vary according to your geographic area and environmental circumstances. Footcare, for instance, will change according to types of soil and conditions of moisture. It is also true that an individual foal may require footcare appropriate to his anatomical structure. Some foals require trimming every 10 days to two weeks for a particular problem, while others may be fine with a six-week interval. All procedures should be done as quietly and kindly as possible. If there is undue resistance, you must carefully assess the practices used, then follow my recommendations to create an environment in which the foal is cooperative. It is extremely important that a foal doesn't regard human contact as uncomfortable, frightening, or something he should resist. Anyone involved in the rearing of foals needs to be critically observant of the foal's physical well-being if he expects to be successful in this endeavor. It is, however, even more critical to become a keen observer of psychological well-being. A foal not well adjusted psychologically soon becomes physically impaired. A foal depressed, unhappy or angry eventually manifests physical symptoms associated with these psychological conditions.

Peptic ulcers have been found in as much as 85 percent of certain groups of young horses experiencing psychological stress. It does not really matter how sound your husbandry practices are, or how much money you spend on feed supplements if you have a psychologically traumatized foal. Angry, uncooperative foals experience injuries at a far greater rate than those that are content, and recuperating from these dramatically interferes with normal physical development.

To promote sound mental processes in your foals it is very important to create human presence without trauma. Ideally, a quiet, knowledgeable person should walk through the herd daily and touch each foal as he goes past. Touching young horses and walking away imprints them with the understanding that their human contact is not acting as a predator. Predators do not make contact and then go away. Occasionally, you should take the time to rub the foal over his head, neck, and body, pick up the feet, and then walk away. A foal experiencing this treatment will be far more likely to cooperate on the days the veterinarian and farrier arrive.

It is highly recommended that the same individual who has dealt with the foal is present during the visits of the professional practitioner. You should be familiar with the characteristics of the foal, and have a good understanding of their needs. It is also true that your presence will be a stabilizing effect. You should be quick to reschedule the work if negative behavior occurs. Many lifelong equine phobias have been created from one session of impatience. A few days of specific work to overcome a foal's concern will result in creating a happier foal, veterinarian, and farrier.

Weaning

There are many accepted methods of weaning the foal from his mother. The number of mares and foals involved will affect the procedure selected. I recommend weaning at five to six months of age. For this book, I describe the weaning procedure I use and most often recommend. Should it be necessary to use a different procedure, consult your veterinarian for appropriate advice. In our operation, foals are weaned in pairs of the same sex. Later, if they have to have any veterinary treatment or travel, they should be brought up and kept with their companion, if possible.

Once the foal has been weaned and no longer calls out for his mother, I recommend Join-Up sessions. Accomplishing Join-Up is a great way for your foal to enter that period of

his life when his mother is no longer a factor. Properly done, it will promote an understanding between weanling and human that will be beneficial lifelong. I recommend two or three Join-Up sessions on consecutive days. I have seen significant value in bitting and using a surcingle at this stage. They have proven to simplify the starting process later, and schooling with the Dually halter, together with these sessions of Join-Up, is particularly helpful. Be gentle and patient with foals as they are small and ultra-sensitive.

Doing too many Join-Up sessions at this stage is usually counterproductive. It is a little like often telling a child the same story; the foal will come to resent it and exhibit gestures of anger. Prudently accomplished, two or three Join-Up sessions will allow you to live by the concepts of Join-Up throughout the relationship with your horse.

Eleven Months to Starting

I like my babies to lead as natural a life as practical. But someone should go to the field and touch them daily. It is a good idea for a person to pick up and examine their feet from time to time, and rub their head, neck and body. Their experience with the veterinarian and farrier will be less stressful when these practices are included in the rearing plan. You should be diligent when selecting a farrier, and make sure he understands and agrees that you are rearing your horses without violence. Should the farrier have undue trouble with any of the babies, it is wise to stop the procedure. If you feel that the problem is significant, refer to the section "Your Horse and the Farrier" (p.127). While it was written with the adult horse in mind, the same principles apply.

Veterinary visits and procedures should follow the premise of non-confrontational handling, just as I have suggested for the farrier. Routine and minor veterinary care may be done while in the field. However, to ensure the safe handling of your youngster, bring him in for major work. I recommend to all of my students that they have a safe set of stocks (examination chute) available. These will often avoid injury to horse and human, and help to reduce psychological trauma.

During this span of time between weaning and the starting procedures, I recommend close personal observation of all veterinary and farrier activity. For this book, I do not intend to specify exactly what should be done, but I admonish the reader to be diligent in studying footcare and other routine veterinary visits considered appropriate at this stage in the life of your animal. In addition, I strongly suggest that you become educated about the nutritional needs of your horse and how those requirements relate to your geographic area.

Quarter Horses and Thoroughbreds are generally started to the saddle around 18 to 24 months of age, whereas Arabians and Warmbloods are more likely to be started at 24 to 36 months. It is a good idea to have a reputable equine dentist look at your horse's teeth before you start mouthing. If there are any problems and you still want to proceed with training, you can long line using the Dually halter until you are sure the mouth is in good condition.

Should you choose to use a few days to prepare your horse for the starting process, I recommend that you do Join-Up and use a surcingle with a breastcollar. The breastcollar will prevent your surcingle from sliding back into the horse's flank area. Once your youngster has accepted the surcingle, you may put a snaffle bit on should you chose to begin the mouthing process at this juncture (p.33).

My surcingle has a top ring, two wither rings and two side rings. I normally attach the reins in the two rings that sit on each side of the withers. This leaves the side rings free for my long lines. The side rings on my surcingle approximate an area where a rider's knees will

be. A few days of long lining with a surcingle on will normally significantly reduce the potential for trouble during the starting process.

The process of mouthing is simply an extension of the surcingle work that I have described. To execute good mouthing, I believe it is essential to place side reins with elastic on your equine student. I recommend fixing the side reins quite loosely at first, and taking two to three days to apply enough tension to tuck the horse's head. Once you have accomplished this, I recommend loose longeing with snug side reins. Your horse will teach himself, under these conditions, to yield to the bit and handle it with soft responses. Mouthing the young horse is a very important part of the training procedure. It can be done effectively before you get on, or shortly after riding has commenced.

Monty's Points

» **Use safe techniques.**
» **The Foal Handler is a valuable aid.**
» **Violence should never be a part of any procedure.**
» **Creep feeding advised.**
» **Psychological health is important, and affects physical health.**
» **Touch the foal daily, and then walk away.**
» **Wean at five to six months of age.**
» **Do two or three Join-Up sessions after weaning.**
» **Use normal husbandry practices.**
» **Use stocks (examination chute) for veterinary care.**
» **Mouth before the starting procedure.**

Chapter 11

Creating a Willing Performer

Respect for Sensitivity

The horse is affected by everything we do, for better or worse. Every move we make, the velocity and body language connected with it, is registered in his brain. Our putting constant pressure on the bit will dull the highly sensitive area of his mouth. If it was our intent to create a "hard-mouthed puller," this is how to accomplish it because a "puller" means a horse made insensitive in the mouth by constant pressure. A puller is simply going into-pressure (see p. 159) and consequently is one who refuses to respond to subtle cues from the hands. The tissues have been toughened and conditioned to the point that the horse pushes into them to resist cooperation. To create a light mouth, you must give signals with hands acting appropriately by using only the gentlest amount of pressure required. Once the desired response is achieved, you must be quick to release the pressure, which acts as the reward. Reward, through release of pressure, is probably the most critical factor in sustaining a light mouth.

I attended a clinic a couple of years ago in Santa Ynez, California, given by Sheila Varian of Arroyo Grande. Sheila is a well-known and well-respected Arabian breeder, but many people would agree that her greatest claim to fame is the production of a mare called Ronteza. Ronteza was a registered Arabian and the only one to win the open reined cow-horse competition at the Grand National in San Francisco, California, against all breeds.

After Ronteza, Sheila went on to produce many champion Arabians, both ridden and in hand. She has spent much of her career learning to develop light mouths and sensitive responses from her ridden horses. I remember Sheila dealing with a bay gelding, probably around ten years of age. She did not run and slide him, spin him around or work a cow, but she explained the equipment and the use of it to achieve optimum sensitivity. Sheila picked up the reins both from the ground and from her horse's back. She lifted them as if they had the strength of a human hair and touched his mouth with the bit as if his jaw was an eggshell. Her horse consistently dropped his chin at the appropriate time and responded beautifully to Sheila's slightest request.

I remember that Sheila described the feeling in the horse's mouth. She said that it felt like warm butter and that she brought the bit against the bars as though it was red hot and coming against the buttery tissues. As she demonstrated, I recall that her descriptions made sense to me, given the level of responsiveness that her horse was showing as she displayed her light touch.

I recall certain things that I have said in speeches made over the years. One of them was that reins should be tied to the bit with a two-pound test fishing line. I wonder how many riders would successfully complete a day's work without breaking them off. You might ask if it does not take a lot longer to train when you do not take charge with harsh commands. My answer is, "Yes, it does take longer, but not unreasonably longer, and who ever told you that creating a sensitive mouth should be an overnight project anyway?" It is my position that creating these sensitive responses is training of the highest order. Forcing a horse into compliance through pressure-filled commands is not training, but only accomplishing a desired result without concern for getting your horse to *want* to do it.

In later discussions with Sheila, she told me that she realized many trainers could achieve longer slides and faster spins in a short time with rougher techniques. It is also true, she went on to say, that the careers of nearly all of those horses are extremely short because they soon resent the repeated heavy-handed demands. Sheila told me that it was one of the joys of her life to create a horse that accomplished his work in complete comfort responding to the slightest of cues.

Monty's Points

» **Everything we do affects our horse.**

» **Reward is most critical.**

» **A good mouth feels like warm butter.**

» **Creating a sensitive mouth is not an overnight project.**

» **Creating a sensitive mouth is training of the highest order.**

Stopping Your Horse

At my demonstrations I spend between three and four hours interacting with people from the communities I visit. It really is amazing how similar the questions are, whether I am in Germany, New Zealand, Scotland, Texas or Massachusetts. The questions usually fall into a narrow range adding up to about fifty problems that horsemen explore repeatedly. They may have slight variations, but are of the same theme. One I find consistently in the top ten is "How do I stop my horse?" At this point, the person may launch into several oblique areas of inquiry. Sometimes, I am told that the horse has an extremely hard mouth and that the rider has unsuccessfully used tougher and tougher bits. Another example is that the horse is nervous, gets frightened at the canter, blasts off and is not responsive when asked to stop.

The answer is that you need to cause your horse to want to stop. The solution to stopping lies at the heart of what I have explored in this book. I believe we are not effective when we force our horses instead of intrinsically motivating them to accomplish the desired goals. If we want to speak French, we must study the necessary material to learn the language; the same holds true for stopping your horse.

It seems to me that many riders believe that if they pull the reins and say "Whoa!" the horse will stop. Often, this works and causes the rider to feel competent. It never ceases to amaze me how cooperative the horse can be. Many equestrians seem to believe that stopping is an attribute that horses were born with and that there is no reason to educate them in this regard. This, I have learned, is an unfair assumption. I believe that it is far more effective to take the time to communicate with the horse in a way to cause him to want to stop, rather than forcing him.

I will outline the procedures that I believe will help to educate a horse to stop. The first thing you might do is to clear your mind of the notion that it is necessary to put on some harsh instrument of tack to cause the horse to stop. As I have suggested often in this book, horses are into-pressure animals. When you use force for stopping your horse, eventually he may go *into* that force, refusing to stop. It is also true that pulling on the horse's mouth with an instrument of leverage, you will desensitize the very tissues that you depend upon for a willing and sensitive response. There is no question that the best "stopping" horses in the world stop with little or no pressure on the reins. Find a video of any reining championship to see incredible stops by horses who do so with slack in the reins.

11.1 Monty stopping Fame Pay Gold in a reined cow-horse competition. This pair won championships in reining, working cow-horse and in hand competition. Note the loose reins.

Once you understand that it is your responsibility to *educate* the horse to stop rather than *demand* compliance, you can begin to study the essential elements of intrinsic training where stopping is concerned. I believe that it is important for the horseman to realize that some of the best training for stops can be accomplished at the trot. If you can achieve a desire within the horse to stop immediately on cue from a trot, then your chance of accomplishing this in the canter goes up dramatically.

It took me many years to learn how important ground surfaces were in training the stop. If the ground is deep and heavy, it will strain ligaments and can turn ankles. Super hard ground will be equally counterproductive, but in a different way. The concussion of very hard ground will be painful, thus reducing the comfort of your horse during the execution of this maneuver. Anytime there is discomfort in the action you are attempting to train, it will detract from your endeavors.

For this book, I chose not to delve into the intricacies of the sliding stop that typifies the Western reining horse. It is my opinion that this area should be reserved for a specific book on that discipline. It is my hope to herein give the general population of equestrians around the world a knowledge of stopping the horse appropriate to a broad cross section of equine disciplines. Show jumping, dressage, polo, and Western disciplines all might benefit from the concepts I outline here, but without the specificity each discipline requires to comply with the style of stopping needed.

I will outline what I believe to be the most comfortable footing for your horse when schooling to stop. Refer to the section "Footing" (p.31), where my recommendations are quite similar with one exception. Wherever possible, try to reduce the amount of the

11.2 Monty on Johnny Tivio winning the Salinas cow-horse class. Johnny won four world championships.

it is beneficial to school your horse by trotting down the center of the long axis of the riding ring, straight across, and on diagonals. Your horse should find no particular pattern in the direction you choose to travel. When you have your horse comfortably handling these early procedures, just point him toward one of the fences and instead of making a turn when you get there, hold him so that you move straight toward it. From a trot your horse will obviously stop and not crash into the fence, or try to jump. At this juncture, you should take care to use the reins to prevent turning.

cushion of sand on top of the firm, level base to only about ½ to ¾ inch of loose, friable soil. This will allow your horse to come to a stop with a minimum of resistance from the soil, while giving him sufficient cushion to reduce impact.

I suggest that you begin to trot your horse at an extended trot comfortable for your horse and a bit slower than that speed at which he might step into a canter. It does not matter whether you are in an enclosure or an open area. It is best if you have fences or barriers that are more than 5 feet (approx. 1.5 meters) in height. These obstacles can be in various locations where the footing is right. Most equestrians use a typical riding ring, and I feel that it will be helpful to most readers of this book if I outline my comments in that context. If you choose to vary the context, it should not matter as long as the concepts are followed.

You may choose to trot on the perimeter of the riding ring at first, and I find no fault with this. However, as you progress in your training,

Should you choose to use the bit and bridle to cue a horse to stop, it should be executed with minimal pressure. This cue should be used only to steady the horse to stop and never as the primary piece of communication. Many world-class stopping horses do so with no pressure on the bit at all. Use good judgment to be sure that the obstacle is appropriate for the exercise.

Approaching the fence, the Western rider should sit deeper in the saddle, allow the legs to come slightly forward, press the bottoms of the stirrups and say the word " Whoa!" Many equestrians from other disciplines will use the term "quit riding" to define their cues to stop. While the horse is trotting, you are actively engaged in the forward motion. Your position should be forward in the saddle, with the upper body on a slightly forward angle from the waist up. Your knees and legs are clearly engaged in the forward motion. To execute the stop, sit down, move your legs slightly forward, and press on the stirrups. The word

"Whoa!" is simply to habituate your horse through sound as well as motion. This will broaden the conversation you are having with your horse when you tell him that you would like him to stop.

As the horse comes to a stop, allow him to relax for 30 seconds or so, stroking his neck in congratulation. Repeat this process until you reach a point at which you will feel your horse begin to stop as you sit down in the saddle and execute the cues while saying the word "Whoa!" You will soon realize that your horse is beginning to learn to stop from the cues and not from the fence in front of him.

It is at this point that you should begin to start the cues slightly further from the fence. If the horse carries on to the fence that is fine, but continue this process until you feel your horse taking the cues and stopping short of the obstacle. Be observant, and the first time you feel your horse stopping because of the cues, allow him to stop short of the fence, and you dismount. If this incident is late in your daily routine, you may decide to simply lead your horse back to the stable and call it a day. I suggest that this procedure, as I have described, is a great lesson no matter the discipline.

11.3 Monty on Night Mist at the Cow Palace in San Francisco. Night Mist won two world championships and won 31 working cow-horse events back to back.

11.4 Monty on Pepinics Dually. Dually won the National Reined Cow-Horse Association Triple Crown. Note the loose reins.

I feel that the horse trained in this fashion will spend the night considering that stopping is not a bad thing. The horse might be thinking, "When I stopped because my rider gave me cues, I got to go home, get a bath and go to my room with a good meal and fresh water." In a subsequent lesson, you might even sit down and cue your horse a considerable distance from the fence, giving him a chance to choose to stop or not. It is important that you make a great effort to decide when results are being achieved, thus creating the environment for rewarding your horse.

A good trainer might use a month to six weeks doing nothing but trotting during the schooling process for stopping. If there are other factors going on in the horse's training, you should accomplish them first, and then give the horse a chance to show how well he stops, ending the day on a positive note by dismounting immediately after a willing stop. One note of advice to help your horse is to school by using a fence or obstacle whereby your horse is facing away from his stable to increase his motivation to stop. It is a bit unfair to expect a willing stop from the novice horse when he is moving directly toward the stable until he is well-trained and accepts these concepts.

Once your horse is willing and generous with his stopping, you can proceed to the canter and simply repeat the entire process. As you might imagine, your horse will probably take much less time to become a willing stopper after learning the concepts at the trot. Picking up the reins during the stop is helpful, but only to steady the horse and give him a bit more support as he comes to a stop, rather than using them to demand a stop. I believe that it is helpful to rein back a step or two after some of your stops just to encourage full compliance in responding to bit and bridle.

With the above-described procedures well in place and executed willingly, the trainer of the Western horse might effectively move on to achieve sliding stops from a full gallop. These are maneuvers necessary for many competitions held within the Western disciplines. These techniques have been explored in many books specific to these activities. It is with that in mind that I decided to confine this chapter to those rudimentary elements of the stop that I consider to be applicable to virtually every discipline, from the leisure rider to the most accomplished trainer.

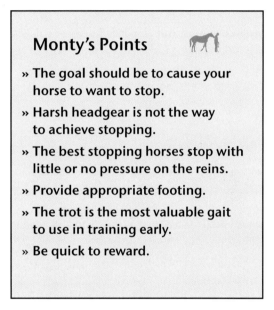

Monty's Points

» **The goal should be to cause your horse to want to stop.**

» **Harsh headgear is not the way to achieve stopping.**

» **The best stopping horses stop with little or no pressure on the reins.**

» **Provide appropriate footing.**

» **The trot is the most valuable gait to use in training early.**

» **Be quick to reward.**

Turning Your Horse

I want to explore in this section the points of good horsemanship that create a desire within the horse to turn properly on cue. Just as in stopping, the same admonitions apply to creating intrinsic (p.164) rather than extrinsic learning. The horse most willing to change direction left to right, and vice-versa, will be the horse trained without pain and pressure, not the horse struck or spurred to do turns. Just as in the section on stopping, I do not intend to discuss in detail some extreme spinning that can be seen with the Western reining and cutting horses. Nor do I intend to go deeply into the precise movements of the classical pirouette used in dressage. I intend to give the general information necessary to cause a horse to be responsive in turning left and right.

I believe that forward motion is the enemy of schooling a horse to turn. Each time I set out to accomplish exemplary turning, I want the horse to understand how to position his rear legs on the ground using them as a pivot point, and then walk around that pivot point with the front legs. It will become evident to your horse that if he is to execute these turns with fluidity, he must cross the front legs as he steps in a circle to propel the shoulders, neck and head in a circle around the pivot foot.

Once you have accomplished the pivoting, you can begin to ask the horse to turn while executing forward motion. I recommend, however, that your horse first becomes proficient with a form of turning by which one hind foot remains in contact with the ground at a single point throughout the turn. In the world of teaching the pivot turn, most of the top professionals create a pivot by which the inside rear foot drills a hole in the ground while the outside rear foot walks forward around it, creating a circle about one foot in diameter. For some reason, the way I train causes the horse to use the outside foot as a pivot point. He then backs the inside rear foot around the pivot foot, creating the circle.

I find little difference in the quality of the turn whether your horse uses the inside or outside rear as the pivot foot. The important thing is that one foot drills a hole. The forelegs step laterally, to create a circle 5 to 6 feet (approx. 1.5 meters) in diameter around the pivot point. The head and neck should remain relatively straight in front of the horse, curving slightly in the direction of the turn. The spine of the horse should also curve slightly toward the intended turn, but not excessively.

I like a low head set when a horse is turning, because it suggests that he is executing his turn without pressure on the bit. If a rider uses much pressure on the headgear, he will bring the horse's head up and add an element of demand to the exercise that I consider undesirable. The slightest pressure with the reins, left or right, should cause the horse to respond and willingly follow that cue if it remains in effect. It is a beautiful thing to see when a horse willingly responds to left and right cues, particularly when the request from the rider is so subtle it is virtually imperceptible.

To get this kind of response from your horse, I recommend that you begin your work on a good surface. The one I described in the stopping section is better than the deeper surface of the round pen. There is very little concussion in this exercise, therefore the horse has less material to push with his foot as he pivots. One should be diligent about using only level ground as it is very difficult to learn to turn when the surface is uneven.

To start the lesson, you should first give the horse a normal day's workout to burn off pent-up energy. Once the horse has settled and is responsive, stop. Allow your horse 10 or 15 seconds to settle and then (usually with a snaffle bit) pick up either the left or the right rein. Encourage your horse to yield to the bit in the appropriate direction. The unschooled horse will move forward as he begins to execute the turn. Leave your hands down, allowing him to make the mistake of going forward two or three steps, and then pull with both reins straight back to put your horse's rear legs near the original starting position.

Repeat the process in the opposite direction. Your student will probably make the same mistake again when you undertake the same disciplinary measures. Do not hit or spur the horse for any reason. What we are attempting to do with this lesson is to open a window through which the horse can pass. This window is located just outside the rider's inside leg. In other words, as you move your horse to the left, you are encouraging him to find that spot about four feet outside your left leg through which he should pass. As your student explores the directions available to him, he will choose one that includes forward motion.

It is less than natural for the horse to think about locking up the rear legs to create the pivot point. It is the obligation of the trainer to use positive reinforcement to cause the horse to find the open window. Once you have backed your horse away from his forward motion several dozen times (it may take a few training sessions), it is likely he will begin to catch himself as he moves forward, stop short and follow the bit in a circle for just a step or two. When he does, relax the reins and give him a stroke on the neck.

Using both directions equally, gradually require more steps until your horse will put down the pivot foot and walk 360 degrees around, willing and comfortably. This may take as many as 30 days of schooling. Once you have achieved this procedure, you can begin to increase the number of revolutions to two or three full circles in each direction. This may take place over an additional 30 to 60 days. During these early procedures, never ask your horse for speed. At this stage of the game, it is simply a matter of education and not one of style or complexity.

If you should choose to increase the efficiency of turning by requesting speed in the turn, you should do it primarily with your legs. Build the desire for speed equally on the outside and inside, but not at the same time. A few bumps of your outside foot might speed your horse, but is likely to move the horse's head to the outside of his turn and put his spine in a counter curve. To further explain this process, it refers to the bumping of the rib cage of your horse with your foot. I further recommend this be done first on one side and then the other, but not at the same time. It is necessary to then use equal pressure with your inside foot so that you bring the neck and spine into closer compliance with the direction that your horse is turning. I term this action "bicycling." That is to say, use one of your legs independently and then the other, much as you would do on a bicycle.

For this book, the elements of turning that I have described will cause your horse to be willing to rein left and right adequately for most disciplines. These same principles will apply as you increase the speed should actual spins or pirouettes be your goal.

It is not acceptable to hit or spur the horse on the right side to get him to turn left, and just as unacceptable to hit or spur him on the left side to turn right. This is extrinsic training and will eventually produce a resentful horse and bad turns.

If neck reining is wanted, you should continue these exercises until the horse is totally compliant and comfortable with his turns in either direction. At that point, simply put four fingers between the reins of the snaffle bit and hold them in one hand. Begin to turn your horse, flexing your wrist slightly to tighten the inside rein. Soon, you will realize that it is not necessary to tighten the inside rein and, as if you had waved a wand, your horse will be neck reining. The average horse will usually complete this transition in 60 to 90 days.

As with all the procedures that I recommend, there is no place for anger or violence. If you are dealing with an athletic horse, you will get exemplary turns by using these methods. Stay the course, believe in the concepts and smile. Results will come your way and it will happen while you and your horse are having fun.

Monty's Points

» Train without pain or force.

» Eliminate the desire to move forward while turning.

» Create a turn with a pivot point.

» Create a window through which your horse can pass.

» Be bilateral in all of your training.

» Provide the appropriate footing.

» Make sufficient time to achieve your goals.

» Stay the course and smile.

» The horse will learn while both of you are having fun.

Changing Leads

The walk is a four-beat gait. Each foot strikes the ground at a separate time becoming a part of the natural walk cadence. During the walk, the horse travels with his spine in a straight line from tail to head. The trot is a two-beat gait. This simply means that two of the feet strike the ground at the same time so that the cadence becomes the unmistakable clip-clop of the trot. While virtually every horse tends to possess a slight curve in his spine, the trot will normally be executed with the spine relatively straight.

The canter, including the gallop and run, is the gait I am going to concentrate on in this section. This third gait of the horse is recognized as a three-beat gait. It is during the execution of this movement that the legs on one side reach a greater distance than their corresponding counterparts. This is why this is known as "the lead." Given this information, I think it is fair to define the word "lead" where horses are concerned as "the action

by which the four-legged animal reaches a greater distance in each stride with one side of his body than he does with the other."

The very fact that this gait is bilaterally asymmetrical creates certain unique characteristics. If you visualize a human running, you quickly observe that there is bilateral symmetry. If you are sound and free of physical defects, you will do about the same thing with your left side as you do with the right. To explore further, visualize a kangaroo. He is constructed similarly to a human and yet he chooses not to split the legs, but to jump, using the two powerful hind limbs side by side. It is at once obvious that the kangaroo is also bilaterally symmetrical. In both examples, the spine remains relatively straight with the direction of travel.

But the horse's method of locomotion in the canter is not symmetrical. If, let us say, the horse is on the left lead front and rear, then the two right legs will tend to take a short half-step while the two left legs will reach significantly further to complete the stride. Conversely, this is true in mirror image if the horse is on the right lead. The fact that one side is acting far differently than the other creates a situation by which the spine of the horse is not typically held in a straight line. Generally, your horse has a short side and a long side and many equestrians feel that horses are born with this. It can be compared to us being left- or right-handed. For this study, I will deal with the short side–long side phenomenon only where the canter leads are concerned.

As you ask your horse to step into a canter, it is very difficult for him to initiate a lead on his short side. Let's say that you are walking along and you want your horse to initiate a canter. If you gather his nose slightly to the right and use your right leg against his side, it is extremely difficult to expect him to initiate a right lead. Drawing the nose slightly right and pressuring the right side will create a short side on the right, and a long side on the left. This, in effect, opens up the left side, and the horse's tendency will be to move off the leg and reach to lead with the left pair of legs. Obviously, if you meant for your horse to initiate the canter on the left lead, then you have executed the proper cues. You then could reverse these cues to initiate a right lead.

Once the lead is in place and the horse is in the third gait, you should shorten the leading side by drawing the nose slightly toward the leading legs and apply what we will call inside leg pressure. If you are executing a circle, this action will bring the horse's spine into compliance with the circumference of the circle that most equestrians agree is desirable. It is generally accepted that if the horse is circling left with a "short right side" while on the left lead, it acts against coordinated movement.

The circling horse is far more coordinated, powerful and responsive if he is traveling with his lead legs on the inside of the circle. A horse traveling with the lead legs to the outside of the circle is said to be in a "counter-canter." While it is advisable to train sufficient control in your horse to be able to execute a counter-canter, it is not considered the most efficient way for your horse to travel. The fact that your horse travels best when leading to the inside of the circle in the direction he is going creates the need for the horse-and-rider combination to be able to alter the leading legs while cantering.

Flying lead changes are an important part of virtually every athletic endeavor. While I realize that they have nothing to do with the trotting horses and many other unique disciplines, it is critical to most disciplines. Flying lead changes can mean the difference between success and failure in dressage, reining, working cow-horses, hunter hacks, English and Western pleasure, flat and jump racing and other activities. Flying changes are critical in determining whether a competition horse will win or lose.

Many people believe the racehorse simply leaves the starting gate and runs around an oval track, but the truth is that the horse who does not use both of his leads will be less likely to win than the one who does, and if he does not use them appropriately, he will probably lose. Racehorses on a typical track, to use their energies efficiently, must run their turns with the inside lead and their straight stretches with the outside lead. In today's keen competition, show jumpers that do not have an understanding of flying lead changes are distinctly disadvantaged.

One of the most important facets in creating an effective flying change is to be mindful

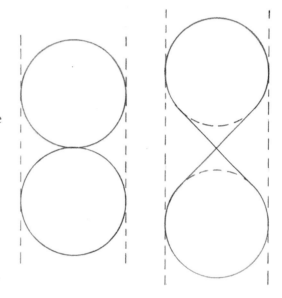

11.5 Two circles, side by side (left); two circles with slight separation, and an "X" to join them (right).

that this exercise is most efficiently executed when the spine is straight. Many equestrians believe that a flying change simply means to go from a circle in one direction to a circle in the other. A figure-eight is the typical format by which we test the horse's ability. If you think of the figure-eight as two circles side-by-

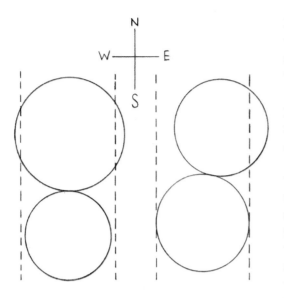

11.6 Two common errors: circles of different sizes (left), and circles not aligned (right).

side, you are apt to get into trouble. I suggest it is much more appropriate to place your circles with a slight separation between, and an X to join them.

It is important to study the proper geometry of the figure-eight before beginning to train your horse in this area. The circles must be geometrically sound; they should be the same size and lie in proper linear form and shape. It is a common fault to create one circle larger than the other, or to lay one circle slightly to the east or west of the other. Study these illustrations and avoid these common faults.

I am a strong proponent of schooling sessions that include many circles without flying changes at all. Where the figure-eight is concerned, I am not in favor of consecutive changes. I suggest cantering two or three circles, and then executing your flying change, doing two or three more circles in the opposite direction, and then executing another flying change. Consecutive changes can cause your horse to anticipate the creation of the new circle. This will encourage curving in the X instead of traveling a straight line. Should your

horse fail to change front and rear leads while traveling on the X, I suggest you stop on the straight line on the end of the X, and start on the correct new lead again.

In the early stages of flying lead training, you should use the figure-eight pattern, Training 8, that includes two equal circles lying on areas next to one another with approximately 15 to 20 feet (approx. 5 to 6 meters) between them. These circles are connected with an X centered between. The intersection of the X should fall on a spot that is equally distant from the two circles. The lines of the X should travel from the intersection to points on the circumference of the circle at its widest portion. For the purpose of this exercise, consider that all the illustrations are lying north and south. The Training 8 that I recommend should be the initial figure used to introduce the horse to this exercise.

The exercise of flying changes should only be done with a young horse when he is handling himself well while executing circles in both directions on the proper leads. This horse should step into the desired lead without hesitation at virtually every asking. He should stop on cue, stand relaxed and turn with the slightest request from the rider. Once your student can execute all these maneuvers with generosity and adrenaline down, you are ready to begin flying lead training.

Observe the illustration Training 8 (fig. 11.7). Imagine that you can already canter your horse on each of those circles comfortably, traveling on the inside lead, front and rear. Now, execute this action several times to orient your horse to the lay of the land. When you feel it is appropriate, begin to use the X as follows:

Start by traveling clockwise on the south, or bottom, circle and on the right lead. When you reach point number 1, guide your horse on that straight line pointing his nose at number 2. Gather your horse slightly with the right rein and crowd him slightly with your right

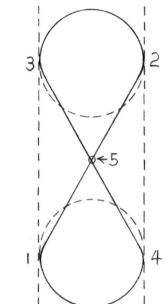

11.7 Training 8: circles showing the importance of lines of the "X" falling on a spot equidistant from the two circles.

leg. This will effectively create a long left side, and a short right side. You will open up the left, inviting him to reach with the left legs, thus changing his leads. As you pass the center point at point number 5, crowd harder with your right leg if the change has not been made. Should your horse remain on the right lead until you reach number 2, stop him there, let him settle, and begin the canter counterclockwise, on the left lead again. This will place you in a position to travel on the north circle as shown in the diagram.

To school your horse properly, it is essential that you are able to quickly recognize on which front lead your horse is traveling. You should practice identifying this every time you ride. Cast your gaze directly in front of the saddle horn or pommel. While looking at that point on the crest of your horse, think about what you see in your lateral vision. Watch for the shoulder movements because just as the front leading leg reaches further, so does the shoulder. This is not difficult, but is a skill that should be achieved to properly help your horse.

Once you have accomplished this, the rest of the world of flying lead changes is academic. It will become your goal to have your horse change his leads from the slightest leg signal. For instance, refer to figure 11.7 and set a goal to cause a flying change between points 1 and 2, precisely at point 5. I remember I set goals for my champion horse, Dually, by which I could make four changes between points 1 and 2. This exercise would help keep him honest, holding his straight line fully from point 1 to point 2, while executing multiples of straight-line flying lead changes. Practicing in this fashion insured that Dually would not change without my direction.

Dually became so sensitive to my leg aids that I could simply quiver a muscle in my left calf causing a change from left lead to right lead, and then repeat the process in the opposite direction. This exercise would accentuate the act of keeping his spine straight while executing the change. Eventually, Dually would travel on a straight line from one end of the arena to the other, changing on single strides. It should be noted that this level of training was not reached until he was around six years of age when he had a minimum of four years of education.

As your horse becomes accomplished at lead changes, your figure-eights can progress to resemble figure 11.8, called "Finished 8." In this illustration, you will see that the straight lines of the X have been shortened to bring your circles together and lay down a figure-eight that is more traditional in shape.

I have not yet discussed the importance of the flying lead change being complete, which is to say, that the front and rear legs must lead on the same side. A horse who is seen to lead with his rear leg, opposite to his front, is said to be "cross-led" or "disunited." This is a method of travel in other species. The bovine is a "cross-lead' animal, which is the primary reason that a horse can outrun a cow. I do not

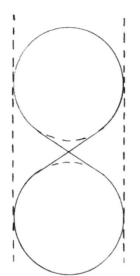

11.8 Finished 8: ideal circles for a figure-eight.

motion of your horse. The enjoyment we experience with our horses stems from achieving a better understanding of their thought processes and their idiosyncrasies. The canter of the horse is a unique method of locomotion, and once fully understood, partnership with your horse becomes easier in other facets as well. The rider who is unaware of the leads of his horse is merely a passenger, not a partner.

know why nature is set up this way, but cattle's third gait is not efficient. I would like to think it is so we can catch up to cattle with our horses and control them with our superior athletes. I doubt this is sound reasoning, but at least it is true!

In this section, each time I mentioned a flying change, I discussed the need for your horse to change at both ends. But when I described the act of identifying which lead your horse is on, I confined my comments to the front leg. My reasoning is that virtually every horse initiating the canter leads properly, front and rear. If your horse is cross-led, it feels as though you are in a vehicle with a rear flat tire. Your horse is out of synchronization. Be sensitive to the smoothness when he is leading properly, and the uncoordinated feeling when he is not.

Whether a professional or a casual rider, you can have a great deal of fun studying the

---

Monty's Points

» **The word "lead" is defined as the action by which the four-legged animal reaches a greater distance in each stride with one side of his body that he does with the other.**

» **Flying lead changes are an important part of virtually every athletic endeavor.**

» **Study the proper geometry of the figure-eight before beginning to train your horse in this area.**

» **Learn to identify which legs are leading.**

» **Study the principles of lead-changing.**

» **Attempt to finish training sessions on a positive note.**

» **Follow illustrated directions.**

» **Have fun learning about this unique form of locomotion.**

Chapter 11 / Creating the Willing Performer

Backing Your Horse (Reining Back)

In this section, I deal with two separate aspects of training the horse to move in reverse. The two aspects are non-remedial, and remedial. I first explain the methods I use with normal, young horses (non-remedial), which have had no particular problem, but simply need to learn what is expected of them when asked to back-up. In America, it is usually considered proper to say "backing your horse," while in other countries some use the term "rein back."

I have a very strong belief that a horse not properly trained to back is more apt to become reluctant to move forward than a horse educated appropriately. I feel that backing your horse on the first day of the starting process is very important. I always ask my equine students to take one step back on the long lines. I generally make this request at least twice in the first long lining session of Join-Up.

It is not important to me how precisely he executes this maneuver on the first day. I simply ask him to take one step back, and then I release the long lines as praise for his accomplishment. I repeat this process on a daily basis, gradually increasing my requests, until I have the young horse backing-up three or four steps, and doing it willingly.

When the horse is ridden, I also try to set it up so that the daily routine includes a few moments of backing-up two or three steps. This should be accomplished at three to four different times in each session, and I plan it so that I do the backing-up at the conclusion of what I consider to be a "paragraph" in the training routine. I like to reserve the backing-up for a time when it is appropriate to stop, stand and relax the horse. This might be between times when you work on the trot, stop, relax and then transition to working on the canter. I believe that the horse is well served

when the trainer regards the reverse as just as important as any other desired maneuver.

There are people in the world of horsemanship who seem to believe that training a horse to back-up in the early stages produces a horse that is likely to want to balk or nap. Nothing could be further from the truth. I believe that a horse not trained to back appropriately regards the reverse as his property, and not a maneuver held in a partnership with the rider. It is this horse that is likely to use the reverse against the rider when a request is made he is not entirely comfortable with.

I am often called to work with the "balkers" and the "nappers" of the world. I usually arrive to find a horse that is unwilling to back-up at the rider's request. This horse is likely to pin his ear and run backward when asked to execute a direction he doesn't want to go forward. I have backed-up each of the thousands of horses I have started from the first day, and I cannot identify a single horse that has become a "balker" or a "napper."

In dealing with the *remedial* balker, I will work with the backing-up maneuver from the very outset. The racehorse that refuses to willingly work on a racecourse will often be asked by me to back-up a greater distance in a given training session than he is asked to go forward. Once backing-up is accomplished easily, going forward is generally simpler to do. I never put pressure from behind on this type of horse to drive him forward. Remedial nappers have usually had more of that done than was ever appropriate. Attempts to force the horse forward with whips lie at the heart of the creation of a napper.

If the horse simply will not back, then remedial measures need to be put in place if you expect success. Sometimes, the non-backer will rear rather than back-up. I have seen horses that would "lock up," refusing to take a step backward, and then leap forward pawing the air with their front feet. Some I have worked with refuse to back, then lock their head on their chest and march forward as though they intended to pull your arms off.

I recall I was asked to work with a gray filly who was phobicly averse to backing-up. The owner told me that she would fall down before she would agree. I believed that the owner actually meant that the filly would flip over backward, a maneuver I never found to my liking. What I discovered was that the filly would "lock" her feet to the ground, and then as you requested the back-up, she would settle closer to the ground so that eventually her keel (chest or brisket) would touch the surface. If you continued to request the reverse, she would simply fall over on her side left to right. While this might be acceptable as a movie stunt of some sort, it was not desirable to me.

I have devised a system to work with reme-dial non-backers that has worked for me 100 percent of the time. It involves the Dually hal-ter and some lengths of panel fencing. As with every remedial horse, I first recommend Join-Up, and for this particular problem, I also rec-ommend schooling to the Dually halter. When executing the advice in Chapter 7 on the Du-ally halter, pay particular attention to the pro-cess of backing-up on the Dually. The remedial non-backer virtually always will accomplish reverse with you using the Dually from the ground.

With the elements of Join-Up and the Dually clearly accomplished, you should place the fence panels in an area where you normally ride. The footing (see p. 31) should be safe and appropriate. You should fix one end of the pan-els to a secure fence that delineates the arena or riding area. This panel should then traverse

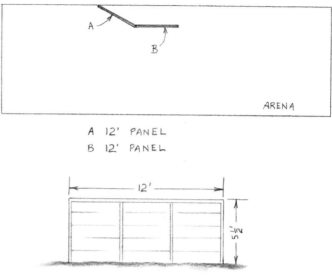

A 12' PANEL
B 12' PANEL

11.9 Ideal configuration for training a horse to back.

outward from the fence to approximately 40 inches (110 cm) from the arena enclosure. You can secure the panel with steel or wooden stakes driven into the ground and lashed to the panel.

With this in place, you have created a hall-way 40 inches (110 cm) in width at the widest, which then narrows to zero where the panel connects to the fence. The length of this panel should be a minimum of 12 feet (approx. 4 meters). This provides an opportunity for you to remain outside the panel while leading the horse into the narrow hallway using the Dually halter. You should pass the lead rope over the panel, and walk the horse as far forward as it is safe to do. The horse's shoulders will eventually find a spot that is too narrow for him so he will stop. You should allow the horse to relax a mo-ment or two, and then back him in the same fashion as was accomplished Chapter 7.

Once the horse is backed outside the hall-way, you can walk a circle or two and repeat the process. When this maneuver can be accomplished comfortably, you should add another panel. The second panel should maintain the approximate 40-inch (approx.

100-cm) hallway. You should repeat the process from before until the horse is quite comfortable backing-up the 20 feet or so (approx. 6 meters) of the newly created hallway.

When the horse is backing comfortably from the greater distance, you can consider riding the horse through the same set of procedures that he has accomplished from the ground. You should take care to remove the second panel and just start with a single panel. This encourages the horse to back-up more effectively. You should gradually increase the request made through the reins so that the horse accepts the cue to back-up from the rider, as opposed to the panels and the environment you have created.

I recommend that there should be nothing remarkable about the tack chosen for this procedure. I suggest that you use whatever equipment you would normally use when training this horse. I do not recommend harsh headgear as a short cut to effect backing-up. I believe it is a mistake to think extrinsically. Force should not be a chosen course of action with this or any other training procedure.

Once the single panel is accepted comfortably, the rider can replace the second panel and back the horse the greater distance. When this is accomplished, it is then appropriate to begin the process of asking the horse for a step or two back with no panel used. Take care not to demand from the horse, and if he is reluctant, then continue the use of the panel until you gain a cooperative attitude.

You should keep in mind that throughout the process of schooling to back-up, it is extremely important to congratulate your horse for positive actions. When he takes one step back in the early going, you should take the time to relax and rub his neck, letting him stand for a moment or two. Later, when it is appropriate to ask for several steps back, you should be ever mindful of congratulating him in that same fashion. A horse will understand the pattern of action and reward, so he will work hard to please you if you get the environment right.

If the recommendations of this section are carefully followed, I am certain that problems with backing-up will go away. I am just as certain that these procedures will create a willing performer for you whether it is going forward or reverse. I have used this technique with literally hundreds of horses. It is tried and proven. You should always take care to be safe, and this requires having the horse back comfortably while you are on the ground outside the hallway. You should ride only when the procedure is done comfortably from the ground.

Monty's Points

» **Backing-up the young horse does not *cause* a "balker."**

» **The horse that backs well is usually a more willing partner.**

» **Backing-up should be a daily routine.**

» **Remedial non-backers should do Join-Up.**

» **Use the Dually halter on remedial non-backers.**

» **Use fence panels to create a hallway.**

» **Work the horse in the hallway from the ground.**

» **Use the hallway when first backing-up while mounted.**

» **Use normal tack and equipment.**

» **Follow procedures carefully to remain safe.**

Chapter 12
Conformation

Conformation Defined

"Conformation" means the physical structure of an animal, the assessment of which critically hinges on the intended discipline. To describe a horse as having good conformation is to say that his physical structure is exemplary given its intended use.

For hundreds of years, conformation has been a subject of books on horses. It is imperative for anyone assessing a horse to have some knowledge of this subject. Your guide should be from reading and observation. The more time you spend around horses using your eyes, the more information you will find about good and bad conformation.

An ability to judge conformation is acquired through years of experience assessing animate structure. You can be trained in the sound principles of this, but there is no substitute for experiencing the actual performing qualities of good and bad structure.

Therefore conformation, including soundness, should be a guide to the athletic potential of a horse. The draft horse needs to be strong, wide and possess a low center of gravity. While draft horses that are tall and bred for certain tasks such as shows and parades are impressive, those that are wide and shorter of leg are usually the most efficient at pulling heavy objects.

A tall and narrow cutting horse will probably have a difficult time synchronizing his movements to the short-coupled cattle he is expected to control. This work requires coordination, agility, and a willingness to use enormous amounts of energy to change directions efficiently and quickly. This is more easily done when the horse is short-coupled and low set.

Much like a horse, the human long-distance runner is always lightly built and lean. There are two distinctly separate types of muscles within mammalian bodies. One is a slow-twitch muscle, and the other is a fast-twitch muscle. Both these types are powered by oxygen except one type of fast-twitch muscle, which is powered by a chemical reaction. It is this muscle that can grow into a greater mass thus creating the shape of the horse that becomes the sprinter. Therein lies the reasons for the human Olympic sprinter to more closely resemble a bodybuilder than he does a distance runner.

Comparing the Quarter Horse and the Thoroughbred is a similar exercise. The Thoroughbred has been bred to run fast over moderate distances of ground of 1 to 1½ miles (approx. 1,400 meters), while the Quarter Horse's conformation is more suitable for sprinting up to

¼ mile (approx. 200 meters). In human terms, the wrestler is apt to be blocky and heavily muscled, unlikely to ever make a long-distance runner. Conversely, the long- distance runner is highly unlikely to excel at wrestling.

When judging conformation with a certain task in mind, it is my opinion there are features relevant across the spectrum. The horse that is well balanced, possessing a symmetrical body type, is likely to be better at his task than the individual found wanting in these categories. No matter what discipline is planned for the horse, if he has balance and symmetry he is virtually always superior, other attributes being equal. Many years ago artist and sculptor Jack Swanson, CAA (Cowboy Artists of America, master artist), showed me a method by which he judged balance and symmetry. The illustration clearly delineates the anatomical features that the artist used to judge the conformation in these areas. Perfection demands that the triangle be equilateral. It would suggest that the baseline should be parallel to the ground and the apex should be directly over the center of the horse's back.

There are two large muscle groups that are part of the anatomy of any horse; one group forms the shoulders and the other the hips and rear quarters. It is the action of these two muscle groups that cause locomotion. The rear quarters are used almost exclusively to propel the body forward. There is actually very little pulling that takes place with the shoulder muscles. The shoulders are responsible for propelling the front legs forward as they are needed to meet the ground to keep the front portion of the animal from falling.

The two angles at the base of the triangle should be the same if the anatomy is to be perfectly symmetrical. It is at this point, however,

that the intended discipline begins to enter the picture. You are likely to see less acute angles on the sprinter or the animal whose discipline requires short, agile movements. The angles that are more sloping, creating a wider base, are generally reserved for those horses that require longer, more open movements as in the distance runner. I have observed over the past 50 years a distinct superiority in horses who have complementary sides of the triangle, whatever the activity. But, as with almost anything in life, there are exceptions to the rule. I have seen horses with a steep angle behind and a shallow angle in front who have performed well enough to become champions. We can never underestimate the value of an "elite heart," a horse possessing that extreme desire to please.

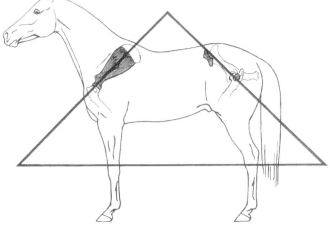

12.1 The perfect triangle for judging balance and symmetry in the conformation of a horse.

Conformation aside, I would predict better things for the horse that is trained by an extremely competent person than the one trained by an incompetent horseman, whatever the conformation. Conformation should be a significant measure of the horse's potential for success, but should never be the only criterion by which we judge him.

Non-Critical Elements of Conformation

There are parts of the horse's conformation that I consider to be critical aspects when judging the horse for a particular discipline. There are other facets of his anatomy I consider important to the complete picture, but not critical.

One of those features that I consider not critical is the eye of the horse. Once you have judged the eye to be sound and anatomically correct—workable if you will—then how the eye appears is one of those subjective measurements where beauty is in the eye of the beholder. I, personally, like to see the eye of a horse large, dark, and appearing to be kind and generous. I often say that I like to see the eye of a horse look like that of a doe. However, I have known many horses in my time who had a large, seemingly kind, generous eye, and yet their personalities were the opposite. Most equestrians hold the opinion that a small, beady eye is likely to be on an unkind horse, and that an eye exhibiting a lot of white is likely on a wild or spooky horse. I believe, after more than five decades of observation, that these beliefs are generally far more imagined than they are real. If all else were equal, I would probably choose the horse with the beautiful eye. However, I consider it less important than those anatomical features more specific to the intended discipline.

The head, while not critical to the performance of a horse, gives you a first impression that may overcome a horse's shortcomings in the eye of the conformation judge. I like a head that is short from top to bottom. It should be complementary and in proportion to the body of the horse. The very large draft horse should not have a tiny Arabian head. Nor should the Arabian have the head of the Percheron or an other draft breed.

I prefer a head with wide-set eyes, with its greatest width at the eye level. The ears should be equal in size and positioned to appear alert. Aesthetically, I am not fond of ears that are extremely large or listless in appearance. I like a horse with a sharp, mobile ear constantly following the path of the eyes to give the impression that the horse is alert and observant.

I admire a large nostril and a mouth whose corners, while relaxed, end near the center of the open portion of the horse's dental structure. It is important that a bit placed gently into the corners of the horse's mouth is then able to ride directly across the bars without interfering in any way with the teeth. I do not particularly like a large, droopy lower lip as I feel it gives the head an appearance of being dull and insensitive. I like to see a tidy muscle with a lower lip that sits firmly against the horse's upper lip.

It is important that the upper and lower incisors of the horse meet so that the table of each opposing tooth meets squarely with its counterpart. I consider overshot and undershot jaws to be unacceptable conformation faults. Most geneticists agree that aberrational mandible (jaw) construction is inherited.

I am vitally interested in the throatlatch of any horse that I assess. We are now coming into an area that to me borders on the critical. I like a throat to be small, but I like a great deal of distance between the mandible bones. Many people who study the respiratory tract of the horse feel that a wide passageway between the two mandible bones will increase the potential for a healthy breathing apparatus. I believe that a tidy and very small throatlatch presents you with less resistance when a horse is trained to be responsive to the bit and bridle. A horse that is flexible, clean and lean about the throatlatch is far more likely to be light-mouthed and responsive than is the horse that is thick and meaty in the throatlatch. Throughout most of my career, I have discovered that attempting to cause the horse that is very strong in the throatlatch to be light in his mouth is a rather futile exercise.

I, personally, like a very long, lean neck and I suppose that follows the lean features that I want in the throatlatch. The long, lean neck provides you with a flexible and responsive anatomical feature that connects your hands and the horse's mouth, which is his guidance system. The horse with a neck that is very bulky, extremely muscular and short is likely to be difficult to train to be nimble and responsive during the guiding process. The neck should exit the withers and shoulders relatively parallel to the ground and not come out extremely high and arching. Athleticism is best accomplished when the horse has his neck parallel to the ground. There are certainly disciplines where a high, arching neck is preferred—all breeders of the Morgan horse and the American Saddlebred find it desirable. In the past ten years, I have come to know and appreciate the Friesian breed. It is exceptional in two disciplines. Friesians can be wonderful riding horses, but they are most desirable in the driving disciplines. The Friesian horse proudly displays a high, arching neck that the breed originators considered a desirable feature, but while I appreciate the breed, I never saw a Friesian that would be successful in the disciplines with which I am most closely associated—cutting, reining and racing.

Any horseman who cares to become proficient in a wide spectrum of horsemanship should learn to appreciate all breeds in the world for what they do best. The older I become, the more I learn to find value in the wondrous array available to us. Features peculiar to their conformation should be considered when choosing an animal for a given purpose.

The shoulder clearly fits into the list of anatomical features that can be considered critical when it comes to judging a horse. Most horsemen will agree that the long, sloping shoulder is preferable to a shoulder that is upright. To be more objective about this feature would be to say that if you take a line down the spine of the scapula to the head of the humerus, a good angle to the perpendicular would be 45 degrees, and a shoulder as straight as 50 degrees is too upright. I have been a proponent all my life of sloping shoulders. I feel that when a horse's shoulder approaches a 45-degree angle, he generally possesses a greater potential for athleticism than the horse whose conformation has more acute angles.

Another aspect I place a high priority on is that the slope of the shoulder should be complementary to the angle of the proximal end of the ilium to the proximal head of the femur. A shoulder possessing an angle dissimilar to this angle of the pelvic bone is apt to produce a horse with less coordination than when these two massive features of conformation, the shoulder and the hip, are similar in their angles.

Without being terribly precise and without suggesting that there is anything significantly important regarding the exercise, I have decided to measure what I consider critical areas of three distinctly different kinds of horses. The first is a three-year-old Thoroughbred filly who I consider has quite impressive conformation. She is symmetrical and coordinated in her movements.

The next is a Quarter Horse who is thought by many to be nearly perfect in Quarter Horse conformation and who was twice judged world's champion.

The third is an exceedingly large Belgian Draft horse who verifies my earlier description by possessing this huge machine that could pull a house down while his cannon bones are as short as the other two examples.

THOROUGHBRED, FILLY, PEKEEN
Shown at 3 years old; 16.3 hands high
SHOULDER Center of withers to proximal end of humerus, 26 inches (approx. 66 cm)
QUARTERS Point of hip to proximal end of femur: 19 inches (approx. 48 cm)
FRONT LEG Elbow to back of knee: 14 inches (approx. 35 cm)
FRONT LEG Cannon bone: 7¼ inches (approx. 18 cm)
HIND LEG Stifle to posterior point of hock: 23 inches (approx. 58 cm)
LENGTH OF NECK Posterior mandible to center of withers: 33 inches (approx. 83 cm)

The knee should look flat from the front, not rounded. Roundness is a warning of potential unsoundness. The knee is the equivalent to our wrist and is a complex joint, and one that can often cause problems, especially in horses that work at speed.

The cannon bone is the only supporting metacarpal left, the splint bones being remnants of two more metacarpal bones. This is a relic of the horse's evolution from the three-toed *Protohippus* and *Hipparion*. As the horse developed into the animal we know today, these smaller toes remained the same length; the central metacarpal became elongated as

QUARTER HORSE, STALLION, QUINCY FEATURE
Shown at 3 years old; 15.3 hands high
SHOULDER Center of withers to proximal end of humerus: 26 inches (approx. 66 cm)
QUARTERS Point of hip to proximal end of femur: 19 inches (approx. 48 cm)
FRONT LEG Elbow to back of knee: 14 inches (approx. 35 cm)
FRONT LEG Cannon bone: 6 inches (approx. 15 cm)
HIND LEG Stifle to posterior point of hock: 21 inches (approx. 53 cm)
LENGTH OF NECK Posterior mandible to center of withers: 33 inches (approx. 83 cm)

survival of the fittest dictated the need for a longer stride and greater speed. The front cannon bones should, by proportion, be as short as reasonably possible. The tendons and ligaments that lie posterior to the cannon bone are some of the weakest points of the horse. In motion, they carry about 65 to 70 percent of the horse's weight. The shorter they are, the stronger they are likely to be. The collection of these tendons should present a picture that is perpendicular to the ground's surface. They should be as full at the proximal end as they are at the distal portion. I consider horses "tied in" just below the knee to have a significant con-

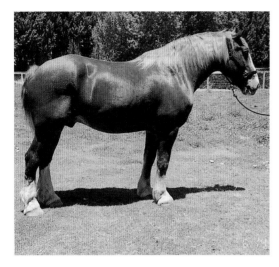

BELGIAN, GELDING, BUBBA

Aged; 18 hands high

SHOULDER Center of withers to proximal end of humerus: 32 inches (approx. 81 cm)

QUARTERS Point of hip to proximal end of femur: 21 inches (approx. 53 cm)

FRONT LEG Elbow to back of knee: 13 inches (approx. 33 cm)

FRONT LEG Cannon bone: 6 inches (approx. 15 cm)

HIND LEG Stifle to posterior point of hock: 25 inches (approx. 63 cm)

LENGTH OF NECK Posterior mandible to center of withers: 38 inches (approx. 97 cm)

formational defect. With this defect, they appear to have the tendons closer to the cannon bone just below the knee and then further from the cannon as they meet the fetlock joint.

The hoof should be generous, but not excessively large. It should have thick walls, and I prefer those of a solid color. I find walls striped in different colors will tend to crack on the margins. I prefer a wide heel and as I view the foot on the profile I want to see an angle of 52 to 56 degrees. Some improvements can be made to hoof shape by the farrier. Abnormalities can only be helped by a good farrier, but genetic defects are seldom rectified.

When I examine a horse for conformation, I will walk the horse directly away from me and then back to me. If there are significant shortcomings in the travel of the horse, I am not likely to score it high despite the aesthetic beauty it shows standing for inspection. As the horse walks away from me I would like to see all four legs traveling directly on line with the spinal column with emphasis on the front legs because of my many years with racehorses. I give about 65 percent of the importance of travel to the forelimbs and 35 percent to the rear. The feet should lift, travel through the air and strike the ground with hooves pointed straight ahead.

While I recognize that no horse is perfect, significant deviations from this condition should reduce your conformation score appreciably. When the forefeet turn dramatically outward (called the Charlie Chaplin syndrome), there is incredible stress placed upon the entire apparatus of the lower leg. The same is true with the "pigeon-toed" horse who strikes the ground with the thrust of his inertia seriously testing the tendons and ligaments that hold the leg together.

Since the hind leg is primarily a pendulum driving the body forward, it does not take the immense concussion that the front leg experiences. The rear legs, therefore, will suffer from those kinds of problems that occur during abducting or pushing off the ground. "Cow-hocked" and "bowlegged" behind are undesirable characteristics, however they are less critical than comparable defects on the forelegs.

As the horse travels toward me I have an opportunity to watch how he handles all four legs. When he stops to face me, I should be able to drop a plumb bob from the point of the shoulder to the ground and ideally the line created should pass through the center of each leg bone and joint. Again, this is more critical in front than behind. I will criticize a horse significantly for having offset or rotated knees.

As I view the horse on the profile while moving, I like to see a willing walker moving easily over the ground. I give credit to the horse who swings the hind leg well forward and places it on the ground well ahead of the track made by the front foot. This is called overstriding, and is often the measure of a good athlete.

After viewing the horse in motion, I then stand back 15 to 20 feet and get a total picture of the head, neck and body of the horse. This is when I assess his triangle most critically, and when I judge the profile of all four legs. Here, I might see the horse that is excessively "over at the knee" or that possesses what I consider the inexcusable fault of being "back at the knee." Back at the knee, a conformational defect and often called "calf-kneed," is to me the most significant fault an equine athlete can have. It places great stress on the anterior faces of the carpal bones and virtually guarantees fractures when speed or concussion is a part of the horse's discipline. I do not like sickle hocks, a condition placing the hind foot too far under the horse. This is similar to the characteristic found in the German shepherd dog, which places the foot anterior to a symmetri-

12.5 Monty shown with Barlet winning the 1962 Grand National Championship Quarter Horse Stallion class as the late Charlie Araujo looks on.

12.6 Pat Roberts on Julia's Doll winning a Championship in Western Pleasure class in 1963. Pat and Julia as a team won many championships at Halter, as well as in Western Pleasure. Julia was on the AQHA Pleasure Honor Roll in 1964 and 1965, and was awarded her AQHA championship in 1964.

cal position. However, I consider that trait far less serious than being back at the knee.

From this overall profile, it is easy to judge the angle of the pasterns. They should approximate the 52 to 56 degrees that I consider optimum for the hooves. This means that the pastern is just a continuation of the angle of the hoof as it rises from the ground through to the fetlock joint.

Excessively *sloping* pasterns will certainly add to the stress on the tendons and have your horse meeting the ground at the area of the sesamoid. Excessively *straight* pasterns will contribute greatly to injuries caused from the concussion of meeting the ground in full stride. The pasterns are the shock absorbers of the horse's undercarriage.

Judging conformation may be a subjective art. I do believe, however, that if you study what I have written here you can build a significant amount of objectivity into your examination. You should never allow emotion to take over your conformation score. A beautiful head and gorgeous neck should not overcome the negative potential of a pair of "calf knees." There are many good books written by objective people from the veterinary and equestrian professions. The better your education from books and life experiences, the more likely you are to become an objective judge of conformation.

Monty's Points

» The definition of "conformation" is the physical structure of an animal.

» Assessment hinges on the intended discipline.

» The more time you spend observing the performance of horses, the more information you will acquire about conformation.

» Study the skeletal development to learn balance and symmetry.

» There are parts that I consider critical aspects when judging the horse for a particular discipline.

» Athleticism is best accomplished when the horse's neck is parallel to the ground.

» The long, sloping shoulder is preferable to a shoulder that is upright.

» "Back at the knee" is the most serious conformational defect.

» A good horseman will take time to educate himself to the objective assessment of conformation.

Chapter 13
Questions and Answers

Q: **I had two horses at home and I brought a new one in. One horse accepted him and the other did not. Can you help with this?**

A: With a new horse, it is important to execute the introduction gradually. Horses have a social pecking order. To fail to address this issue can result in injuries to your horses. The introduction should be made only after you have created a situation where the horses can communicate over a safe fence. The process is often called "buddying up." When you can sense complete comfort, only then should you attempt to place the new horse in the new field. This can take two or three days to possibly two or three weeks.

Q: **I have a horse that is one-sided. He is perfectly fine to handle on one side, but I can do nothing with him on the other. What do I do?**

A: This one-sided condition can result from two distinctly opposite causes. One could be that the horse has been handled virtually entirely on the good side, but ignoring the opposite side, or the horse has been abused on the bad side. No matter what the situation is, the process to correct it is virtually the same. I suggest that you use Join-Up. I recommend three or four sessions on consecutive days, or until your horse is relaxed, following you and per-

fectly comfortable being with you. I would add to that two or three sessions with the Dually halter. I would then begin to work on the bad side with the artificial arm (see "Your Horse and the Farrier," p.127). I would use the artificial arm as it will allow you to effectively work with your adrenaline down. Gradually, gain the trust of your horse and this problem will go away.

Q: **Why does my dressage horse bolt suddenly for no reason?**

A: Let me start this answer by saying that no horse ever does anything for no reason. I feel confident that if I were to study the situation regarding the bolting of your horse, I would identify the cause. While the reason for your horse's behavior may come from an extremely long list, let me speculate with an educated guess. I want you to realize that without seeing your horse I could well be wrong, but I have addressed this question often in the past. Dressage horses are asked to train on a daily basis in an extremely controlled frame. Few dressage riders find value in allowing their horses to relax any time during a training session. I find that horses handled in this fashion will often reach a breaking point. Their tendency is to express themselves by forcing freedom from extreme restraint. Sometimes they rear. Sometimes they balk and run backward, and often they bolt and blast away from the training area. I suggest that you consider planning periodic segments of two to three minutes in length during the training sessions where you simply allow the horse to walk on a loose rein and not worry about strict regimentation. I further recommend that one full riding session out of ten or twelve be devoted to complete relaxation, no dressage training. Following these recommendations has resulted in the improved behavior of many dressage horses and thus their scores in competition.

Q: Does yawning have a meaning?

A: It certainly does, and it has a critical meaning when dealing with horses. The act of yawning is to take in oxygen. One element of tiring is starving the brain of oxygen. During exertion and tension we assign oxygen to muscles needed for work. Horses in their quest for survival will enter periods of extreme concern and rob the brain severely. They'll push themselves for a long time and then when they become satisfied that they are not going to die, they'll relax and yawn because their system is taking over to reoxygenate the brain. When I work with horses at starting gates, I sometimes find that it can take up to a couple of hours to achieve this state. It is a demonstrative act that means, "I'm relaxed now and I feel assured that you're not going to hurt me."

Q: What is the most important thing I should know about dealing with a two-month-old foal?

A: The most important knowledge that I can impart to you is to be safe and work with your foal without violence and force. At two months of age, probably the most important factor is leading the foal alongside his mother. I suggest the use of the Foal Handler (p. 134). I further suggest that it is important to groom and pick up feet, encouraging your foal to stand and to be comfortable with you during these procedures.

Q: What do I do with my horse who is frightened of spray? I cannot spray water on him and I cannot use insect repellant. He goes ballistic. What do you suggest?

A: This is a very common question and apparently the problem exists in great abundance. I suggest you use a box stall or small enclosure with safe, high walls or fence. It is best with a hard floor and no bedding. Place your horse in the enclosure, and with a pistol-grip sprayer attached to a garden hose, begin to spray water on the floor, well away from your animal. You can stand in a partially open door or, if possible, up high on the wall or fence. Gradually get the water closer to the horse, allowing the splash to contact the legs at first. After a short time, you generally can spray the legs. Any time you feel that the animal is acting in a way that might cause injury, you should back the water away, and reestablish calm before proceeding. It is normal that with a session or two you can direct the spray straight onto the legs and even the belly of the horse. Gradually work until it is possible to spray the horse all over, including the head and the neck. A few sessions of this, and your problem will be significantly reduced. You should not fail to use an opportunity afforded you once your horse has been thoroughly wet down. I suggest that you remove the horse from the enclosure, and with a hair dryer, allow the horse to feel the comfort of warm air on wet hair while hearing the sound of an electrical motor. Use it all over his body, neck, and head, and many problems will be addressed. Insect spray and clippers should no longer bother the horse who will stand comfortably while experiencing the outlined procedures.

Q: I am afraid of catching my horse in the field. What should I do?

A: If you are afraid to go catch a horse in the field, then do not do it. A horse can sense fear and has the potential to get you into a lot of trouble. Learn how to move around a horse and get an older, trained horse to work with before you take any chances out in the field. Once you can move around a horse well and you know where he is going, you'll be more comfortable going and catching your horse. Learn the Language of Equus (p. 11), and study Catching Horses (p. 177).

Q: Why does my horse shake her head up and down while we are out riding?

A: While I am not one who quickly recommends equipment to solve problems with horses, I suggest that the use of a black iron bit with copper inlaid in the mouthpiece is often helpful with a horse who habitually tosses her head. Once you have secured the proper mouthpiece, I then recommend a process of bitting up (pp. 33–35). I fully describe a process of bitting up that I believe will help the equestrian where head-tossing is concerned. It is critical for every rider to understand that the human hands are usually the culprit in creating a horse that tosses his head. As equestrians, we should always look inward before blaming the horse.

Q: What do you do with a horse that will only allow one person to ride it?

A: I find that a horse who tends to trust only one person generally has a good reason. Most often, it is because that one person has treated him in an acceptable manner, while others have been inappropriate in their treatment of him. I do not accept the premise to the question, however, because I believe I could deal with the horse, instruct the rider, and successfully cause anyone appropriate to ride him.

Q: Is it harder to get a very dominant horse to do Join-Up?

A: Yes, it's a bit harder, but when I say a *bit* harder I mean just that. While it may be slightly more difficult, I recommend that the horseman not dwell on the negative. The toughest Join-Up is so much easier than the best of the traditional methods that you should look forward to having fun with the process. Do Join-Up and count your blessings.

Q: How does one apply the Join-Up method without a round pen?

A: The round pen is not the critical factor in applying these concepts. It is a convenient place in which to work. Should you use a square pen, horses will tend to "stop down" their energy in the corners. If you take a square pen and panel the corners off, you effectively create an octagon. This nearly round enclosure will work very effectively. If you choose to work with horses in a wide-open space, their natural tendency will be to work in very large circles, and you must be in very good shape to go the distance with them.

Q: Do you recommend tying your horse in a trailer?

A: Sure, I recommend that you tie your horse in the trailer for several reasons. One reason is that if you have to stop very suddenly and the horse happens to have his head down between his front legs, he could be injured. Do not over-restrict your horse; the tie should be used to keep him from dropping his head down between his front legs.

Q: How does someone introduce your methods to those people who would sing the praises of traditional methods?

A: I think that the key premise in answering this question is to say that I would like my horses to do the talking for me. I believe that if I hold true to my concepts, the horses will continue to learn and perform well. There is no forcing the traditional horseman to accept my concepts. Just as I work without forcing a horse to do anything, I will never demand that another equestrian should use my techniques. I would much prefer to be a good role model advocating a nonviolent approach to training and experiencing cooperative horses for the effort.

Q: How often do you do Join-Up?

A: I do the full complement of Join-Up in my operation four, five, maybe six times and that is all. Then, you live by the concepts of Join-Up for the balance of the horse's life. This means when you go into the box stall, you do not just walk in, grab hold of him and pull him around. You walk in, and when he moves away, you look him in the eye, square-up, and move toward him. When he looks back at you, you walk away and let him catch you. I cannot teach you the Language of Equus any more than I can teach you to speak French. You have to learn it, it's a long process, and it's not something someone can teach you overnight. There is a process for learning it, and the potential is available to you now.

Q: Have you had any success with donkeys or mules?

A: Donkeys are a challenge. They are loveable creatures and I have nothing against donkeys. They're a little hard to train through the *language* because they have a lesser flight mechanism, and they're often not as responsive as horses. Mules are wonderful. They respond beautifully to these concepts. I have had many outstanding mules. They became exemplary partners for packing, trail riding, roping, racing, and reining. Mules have a long list of attributes and should not be taken lightly when it comes to performing in many disciplines. Dr. Robert Miller, the father of foal imprinting and longtime "mule man," believes that Join-Up is the most effective way to train a mule.

Q: Would you normally talk to a horse?

A: Sure. I might say, "Dually, you old man, what's up with you today?" Of course, I talk to him. But does he listen to me? Naw, probably not. What I mean is he hears my voice, but he has no idea what I am saying. You cannot go out there and tell a horse to accept his first saddle, bridle and rider, using words. Their language is silent, it's a language of gestures. I cannot be strong enough when I tell you that. I've started eight or ten horses in a day without saying a word. Should you choose to train your horse to respond to voice commands, that is fine. Voice commands are effectively used by most equestrians. You should be aware, however, that they are a habituated response. Until trained to voice commands, horses rarely respond to any of our sounds.

Q: Is it possible to do Join-Up with other horses around?

A: If there are other horses visible while doing Join-Up, it is a distraction. Wherever possible, you should strive to do Join-Up with as little confusion around as possible. Having said that, Join-Up can be accomplished even when there is significant distraction. You should remember that I do about approximately 400 Join-Ups per year with an audience present. Nearly all of them are done in a see-through round pen. My horses deal with major distractions. Since Join-Up has been 100 percent successful for more than 3,500 horses done in front of audiences, I maintain that you can overcome distractions. Because I have done more than 12,000, I am well aware of the fact that it is easier to do Join-Up without distractions.

Q: Is Join-Up effective for older horses that have been trained by traditional methods?

A: Absolutely! I have a long list of older horses formerly trained with traditional methods who then were brought to me with what seemed to be insurmountable problems. Lomitas, Prince of Darkness, Barlet, My Blue Heaven and many more were retrained using Join-Up and went on to become champions. Some horsemen maintain that my methods will eventually be better known for their effect on remedial horses than raw ones.

Q: Do you always ask horses to follow you around at the conclusion of the Join-Up session?

A: In the past few years, and with the encouragement of Crawford Hall, who has worked with me for over twenty-five years at Flag Is Up, I do it on a regular basis. Mr. Hall has come to call it "quality time," and we believe that it is quite helpful in creating a horse who is content with his work. I am certain that it does not hurt and convinced that it can be helpful.

Q: Do you recommend martingales, draw reins, tie-downs or chambons?

A: I would like you to think about this one carefully. I am being asked here for an opinion on equipment that is fully extrinsic. I believe that a horse properly trained by my methods virtually never needs any one of these. If I were asked if I have ever found them to be helpful, I would have to answer honestly that at one time or another, I have found all of them to be helpful. It is difficult ever to say never, but the need for extrinsic equipment is extremely rare when dealing with horses trained by my methods.

Q: How do you reward a horse that does not like to be touched?

A: In the Join-Up process a major reward is to walk away from the horse. Since this does not require touch, it is easy to do. Walking away, however, should be used only when the horse gives you positive responses. Properly executed, Join-Up will, in a very short period, encourage your horse to accept touching (see Chapter 4). No mustang I have ever worked with allowed touching at first, but all mustangs that I have worked with found value in it eventually.

Q: Do you treat one sex differently than another during Join-Up?

A: Where horses are concerned, we have three sex categories to deal with, the stallion, the mare, and the gelding. There are differences in their responses to Join-Up, but it is fair to say their similarities far outweigh their differences. My approach is nearly the same in all cases. The gelding is usually the most steady of the three, but only slightly so. The full male is a bit more cooperative than the female, but again to a very minor degree. Females tend to be more sensitive and thus less tolerant of "tickly" things such as saddle and girth. It is also true that the female will sometimes want you to stop in the middle of Join-Up and reserve further work for another day. Over the years, statistics will suggest that my Join-Up sessions average 27 minutes for geldings, 27½ minutes for colts, and 28 minutes for fillies. I do not feel that it serves the horseman well to worry that much about the sex of the horse.

Q: Is it ever appropriate to physically discipline a horse?

A: No, it's not. The greatest discipline a horse can endure is to be banished from the herd. Inflicting pain is not effective. They are flight animals, and they have no intention of causing harm. What good is it to whip them? It just reinforces their notion that we're predators and out to hurt them. In fact, such an action will create an adversary so negative toward the human that any hope of turning him into a partner will be greatly diminished.

Q: At home, do you begin your long lining with a bit or a halter?

A: I normally do my initial long lining with a Dually halter. When you use the Dually halter to long line or ride, it acts much as a side pull would. If you begin the training procedures bitless, the Dually can be an effective tool.

Q: Why do you touch the horse on the forehead, and why do you touch it so frequently?

A: I consistently advise that touching the horse and walking away is one of the most effective rewards an equestrian can give. The forehead happens to be a place on the equine anatomy that the horse cannot see. The horse that will allow you to touch him in a place that he cannot see is expressing great trust. When the horseman makes contact with this area, rubs and walks away, he is earning trust. These gestures are extremely effective and should be used frequently.

Q: Do you ever have a horse that does not respond to your methods?

A: No. However, I believe it is fair to say that they are not really my methods. They are methods that I have observed in nature. It is probably fairer to say that they are the methods of the horses themselves and so, properly executed, there is no way to fail. Should the horseman experience negative results, it is important to look inward. It is undoubtedly not the fault of the horse.

Q: Is there a difference between saddle horses and draft horses where your methods are concerned?

A: No. Join-Up is for equus and is effective from Shires to Shetlands. I have great respect for draft horses. We have Belgians at home that deliver the feed to the horses in the fields. Join-Up has been used effectively with virtually every breed on earth and is equally accepted by horses the world over.

Q: What is the smallest area you can use for a round pen?

A: If you are doing miniature horses, you can use a ten-footer, but if you're doing normal-sized saddle horses, about 50 feet (16 meters) is optimum. If you get into the big, heavy horses, you might want to go out to 52 to 54 feet. If you're using little Welsh ponies or the like, maybe 44 to 48 feet might be more desirable.

Q: What do you do with a horse that repeatedly runs to the gate?

A: You need to cause your horse to be uncomfortable when he is near the gate and quite comfortable when he is away from it. You can accomplish this by several means; however, I recommend cantering in small circles while near the gate. Migrate away from the gate, stop your horse, rub him and let him relax. Begin to ride again, and if he barges toward the gate, just smile and repeat the process. You should be aware of the fact that horses that tend to run to the gate are horses that have been ridden out of the gate. If a horse exhibits any tendency to display this undesirable behavior, it is a good idea to refrain from riding out of the gate from that point onward. You should do your work in the training session, dismount in the center of the enclosure, and lead the horse out.

Q: What do I do with my barrel racing horse who refuses to enter the arena?

A: This is a question that comes to me from almost every group of people I address. Barrel racing is a unique activity. It is virtually the only contest where the horse is encouraged to run out of the arena at top speed. This by itself is a technique designed to encourage undesirable behavior. Consider that the barrel horse is asked to run full out into the arena, blast through a prescribed course, complete the course and then run as fast as possible while usually being whipped. Once outside the gate,

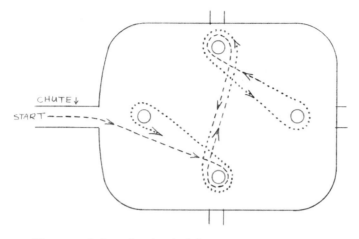

13.1 Diagram of a barrel racing training course.

I've witnessed barrel-horse riders jerking the horse's mouth with both hands to get him to stop. Then, consider that the rider will wait around for a while and ride toward the arena to ask the horse to do it again. Horses are not stupid. Why should the horse ever want to do that again? It amazes me how cooperative barrel-racing horses are under the circumstances.

For this answer, I would like the reader to understand that there are several gymkhana events that essentially fall into this category. For the gymkhana trainer and rider, I would like to recommend these same procedures. It is necessary for the gymkhana participant to tailor the course pattern appropriate to the activity in question. I recommend that training sessions for barrel racing horses should be accomplished with four barrels in the arena. I believe that the horse should be brought into the arena in a calm, cool fashion and that he should be ridden at a walk for a few minutes. Then, begin the schooling process in a constant, ongoing fashion. When the third barrel has been executed, there is another barrel course in front of the horse. You should execute the second course and then return nonstop to the first course. A schooling session might be done at the walk, trot, canter and

run. I recommend that the process then be reversed so that you end your training session at a walk.

You should allow the horse's adrenaline to fully subside. I recommend that you dismount in the center of the arena and either sit on the ground, or walk with the horse for several minutes to completely disengage the horse from the training process. Having accomplished each of these tasks, then you should lead the horse out of the arena.

If it is possible to vary the gates used in the training sessions, this is desirable. The barrel-racing trainer should pause to consider how long it takes to train a horse to run out through the arena gate. I suggest that this can be accomplished in one or two training sessions, and should in no way be a part of the daily training routine. I maintain that whipping the barrel-racing horse is highly overrated as a means to lower the total time. I have been impressed in recent years to see that many barrel racers are using a short piece of rope fixed to the saddle horn that they flick back and forth in front of them to encourage the horse to run faster. This is seldom a pain-producing maneuver, and is far more effective than a burning whip.

Q: Why does my horse refuse a jump?
A: Undoubtedly, you have overmatched him at some point. Get the fences lower, let him have fun, and rebuild his confidence. Elevate the fences gradually, attempting to discover his maximum capability.

The Sum of Me

It matters not the length of life,
But did you give your best?
The length of the road we travel
Means little when we reach our final rest.

Are you happy with the way you've lived,
And what you've made of life?
Did you maximize the good
And minimize the strife?

Was I concerned with how many loved me
And all the things I do?
Or did I work enough to give my love
To those who loved me true?

Did I realize how great it is
To give and not to get?
Or did I look to gather in
And every record set?

Did I pay enough attention to
Those who helped me through?
Did I give them what they wanted
And love and respect them too?

It matters not how long I live,
Just make my time the best!
Happiness through giving,
And true friends before I rest.

Monty Roberts, 2002

A Retrospective of the Career of Monty Roberts

Curriculum Vitae

ACTIVITIES

1940 Stunt double for Warner Brothers films until 1949: *National Velvet, My Friend Flicka, Stormy* and *Thunderhead.*

1951 Declared professional by American Horse Shows Association (AHSA).

1951 Lecturer, California Polytechnic University: Social Sciences and Horsemastership.

1979 Initiated study of wild deer habits in central California, and behavioral and naturalization study of wild fish in central California.

1986 Lecturer, Vancouver BC, on Join-Up techniques.

1987 Lecturer, New Zealand, Australia, Washington State, and Lexington KY, on Join-Up techniques.

1988 Lecturer, Lexington KY, Brazil, Argentina, and Toronto Canada, on Join-up Techniques.

1989 Lecturer, Lexington KY, and Toronto, Canada on Join-Up techniques.

1988 Demonstrated Join-Up for Her Majesty, Queen Elizabeth II of England and staff.

1996 First book published, *The Man Who Listens to Horses.*

1996 Dateline, NBC interview.

1997 The BBC QED Division of England documentary "Monty Roberts: The Real Horse Whisperer."

1998 Dateline, NBC interview.

1999 Second book published, *Shy Boy: The Horse That Came In from the Wild.*

1999 Filmed documentary, "Shy Boy: The Horse That Came In from the Wild."

2001 Third book published, *Horse Sense for People.*

2002 Lectured at the Central Intelligence Agency Annual Polygraph Division Conference.

AWARDS AND CHAMPIONSHIPS

1939 Entered first competition and became Junior Stock Horse Competition winner (ages 16 and under) at four years old.

1950 World Championship in Equitation.

1950 Supreme Champion Horsemastership Championship.

1953 National Championship in Western Equitation.

1954 National Championship Western Equitation in San Francisco.

1955 National Intercollegiate Rodeo Champion Team Roper.

1956 Three-time National Intercollegiate Rodeo West Coast All-Around Champion.

1956 National Intercollegiate Rodeo Champion Bulldogger.

1956 National Intercollegiate Rodeo All-Around Champion.

1959, 1960, 1962, 1963 World Championships in Reined Cow-Horse Events.

1964, 1965 World Championship Stallion Competition, cutting and roping.

1966 Pacific Coast Cutting Horse Championship.

1984–1998 Director of California Thoroughbred Breeder's Association (CTBA) and Founder of the California Thoroughbred Sales, an arm of CTBA.

1988 National Reined Cow-Horse Association "Stock Horse Man of the Year."

1997 Named "Man of the Year" by the American Society for the Prevention of Cruelty to Animals (ASPCA).

1997 National Horse Shows Association (NHSA) Award of Merit.

1998 ASPCA "Founders Award."

1998 Santa Barbara Wildlife Care award for "Lifetime of Dedication."

2002 Honorary Ph.D., Zurich University, Switzerland.

Monty on Ginger, June 1939, at age four, winner of the Junior Stock Horse Class 16 years and under.

Monty with Mischief winning a Hackamore Championship in 1948.

Monty with the Perpetual Trophy for the All Around Championship in junior competition. Points earned toward this trophy were accumulated through winnings in Reined Cow-Horse, Reining, Equitation, Roping, Pleasure, Trail and other competitive events. Monty won this trophy three times in succession, at which time it was retired. He still has it today.

Monty aboard Dan Tack with the Horsemastership trophy he won in 1950. The parameters of this contest were Western Stock Horse, Western Equitation, English Equitation, Show Jumping, Grooming and Handling, as well as three days of written examinations.

Monty with the saddle he won for the National Intercollegiate Rodeo Association Championship in Bulldogging in 1957.

Monty bulldogging with John W. Jones hazing, San Juan, California, 1962.

Above: Monty on Fiddle D'or in hackamore competition leading to world championships in 1961 and 1962.

Below: Alleged with jockey Lester Piggott winning the Prix de L' Arc de Triomphe in 1977. He also won it in 1978. As a yearling and two-year-old, Alleged was owned by Monty and Pat Roberts. He was started and trained as a two-year-old by Monty.

Lomitas, on his way to being named German Horse of the Year in 1991.
Monty is leading, with jockey Terry Hillier aboard.

Outstanding Performers Started by Monty Roberts

NAME	BREEDING	DESCRIPTION OF EVENT
WESTERN DIVISION		
MISCHIEF	Paycheck/Babe	Hackamore Championship, Salinas, 1948, 1949
PATRICIA	Paycheck/RO Mare	Hackamore Champion, Gilroy, 1955
FIDDLE D'OR	Bras D'Or/Fiddle Miss	World Champion Hackamore Horse, 1961, 1962
JULIA'S DOLL	Poco Rey/Spanish Springs Julia	AQHA ranked 3rd in USA, 1964
		AQHA Pleasure Honor Roll, 1964, 1965
		AQHA Champion, 1964
MR. TIV	Johnny Tivio/Night Mist	World Champion Reined Cow-Horse, Reno,1986, 1987
RACE HORSES: GERMANY		
QUEBRADA	Devil's Bag/Queen to Conquer	Champion 2- and 3-year-old, 1992, 1993
RISEN RAVEN	Risen Star/Aurania	Champion 3-year-old, 1994
CABALLO	Königsstuhl/Carmelita	Champion Stayer, 1996
MACANAL	Northern Flagship/Magnala	Champion 2-year-old, 1994
		Champion Sprinter, 1995
LAVIRCO	Königsstuhl/La Virginia	Champion 2-year-old, 1995
		German Derby winner, 1996
SURACO	Königsstuhl/Surata	International Gr. I Winner, 1994, 1995, 1996, 1997
MIDDAY GIRL	Black Tie Affair/Midnight Society	International Gr. I Stakes Winner, 1995
APIA	Cox's Ridge/Approved To Fly	International Stakes Winner, 1996
LOCO	Sadler's Wells/La Colorada	International Stakes Winner, 1998
HAMMOND	Acatenango/Happy Gini	International Gr. II Stakes Winner, 2000
DIAMANTE	Acatenango/Dawn's Side	International Gr. III Winner, 2001
HAPPY CHANGE	Surumu/Happy Gini	International Gr. Winner, rated 96.5 on Free Handicap
SILVANO	Lomitas/Spirit of Eagles	Horse of the Year in Germany, 2001 International Gr. I Stakes Winner of over $3.5 million
SABIANGO	Acatenango/Spirit of Eagles	Gr. I Stakes Winner; second-highweighted 3-year-old in Germany, 2001
RACE HORSES: USA		
GLADWIN	First Landing/Dungaree	Hawthorne Gold Cup Handicap, Amory L. Haskell Handicap
BAHROONA	Poona II/In Regards	Champion 2-year-old Hollywood Park, Graduation Stakes
SHARIVARI	Hugh Lupus/Shari	Champion 3-year-old, Champion Sprinter, New Zealand
		Horse of the Year, 1967
DORRENO	*Tirreno/Dancing Doe	Longacres Derby Handicap winner, International Gr. winner
AN ACT	Pretense/Durga	Santa Anita Derby Champion Gr. 1 Champion 3-year-old, 1976

ALLEGED	Hoist the Flag//Princess Pout	World's highest-weighted racehorse, 1977 and 1978; winner of the Prix d L'Arc de Triomphe twice
WALK IN THE SUN	Walker's/Oriental Gal	California Champion 2-year-old Filly; Hollywood Lassie Stakes Gr. II
JENNY'S BOY	Petrone/Princess Pet	Gr. Stakes winner
ENDOW	Flying Paster/Kindheartedness	California Derby Gr. II winner
SOUND OF SUMMER	Drone/Summer Mark	Ashland Stakes, International Gr. winner
BOLD SPINNER	Bold Bidder/Merry Twirl	International Stakes Champion, Japan
CURRIBOT	Little Current/Ameribot	International Stakes Winner
RIDGEWOOD HIGH	Walker's/Glass Slipper	International Gr. Stakes—placed
MEHMET	His Majesty/Soaring	International Gr. Stakes winner, syndicated for $5 million
DENA JO	Plotting/Jo Sue Lyn	Sunnyslopes Stakes Gr. II winner
MY NATIVE PRINCESS	Our Native/Marching Melody	International Gr. Stakes—placed
FIGHTING FIT	Full Pocket/Napalm	International Sprint Champion
NEPAL	Rajababa/Dumtadumtadum	International Gr. Stakes winner, Seminole H Gr. II, Canadian Turf
RARE THRILL	Nantequos/More Thrills	International Gr. Stakes—placed
JUSTONEOFTHEBOYS	Numa Pompillus/Chrissy Lou	International Gr. Stakes Winner
RAISED ON STAGE	Raise a Man/Stage Finesse	Gr. Stakes—placed
MOMENTUS	Timeless Moment/Screen Trophy	International Gr. Stakes—placed
ROLLS ALY	Ayldar/Rolling Stoner	International Gr. Stakes—placed
BALDOMERO	Pas de Seul/Clonavee	Glen Harvest H International Gr. winner
PERFECTING	Affirmed/Cornish Colleen	La Jolla H, Stakes winner
PERCEIVE ARROGANCE	Stellar Envoy/Stop the Music	Gr. Stakes winner, Oklahoma Stakes winner, Pomona Stakes winner
TIMELESS ANSWER	Timeless/Frosty Answer	Gr. Stakes winner
APPROVED TO FLY	Flying Paster/Tacit Approval	Gr. Stakes winner, Linda Vista H Gr. III, Silver Belles H Gr. II
DAYJUR	Danzig/Gold Beauty	World's Highest Rated Sprinter, 1990
SEASIDE ATTRACTION	Seattle Slew/Karma	International Gr. winner
CARSON CITY	Mr. Prospector/Blushing Princess	Sapling Stakes, International Gr. winner
PROFIT KEY	Desert Wine/Sharm a Sheik	Dwyer Stakes Gr. II, International Gr. winner
SPECIAL HAPPENING	Relaunch/Centivoc	International Gr. winner
RICHARD R	Dr. Blum/Silent Vapor	Bayshore International Gr. II Stakes winner
STAR OF COZZENE	Cozzene/Star Gem	Champion Turf Horse, International Gr. Stakes winner over $3 million
ALABAMA NANA	Fathatching/Image Intensifier	International Stakes winner
JOHNNY'S IMAGE	Stagedoor Johnny/Supreme Delight	Hollywood Turf Invitation International Gr. I winner
SKIPPIN' STONED	Majesterial/Drunkard's Dream	International Gr. Stakes—placed, 1997
AMNESTY	Fly So Free/Pasampsi	Ranked on Free handicap, 1998

SHOW RING AND JUMPING

NAPUR	Damascus/Lodge	International Champion Jumper in six countries by money won.
KING SCREEN	Screen King/Lil Jo	Champion Hunter in US, 1987
SPARRING PARTNER	Fighting Fit/Lu Qu	Champion Green Hunter in US, 1988

The 60-plus horses listed above represent only horses actually started by Monty Roberts personally. It should be noted that this list does not include the many champions produced by Monty Roberts that had been started by someone else. Each performed to a level of international importance. To achieve a position on this list they must have been a winner in competition of the highest caliber. This list does not include the winners of local competitions.

Glossary

ALPHA MARE A female horse who is psychologically equipped to lead the family group. It is an inborn tendency, which is nurtured through maturity.

ASSOCIATION SADDLE A saddle designed by the Professional Rodeo Cowboy's Association to be used in competition on bucking horses.

BELLY OVER A procedure by which a handler legs a rider onto the back of a horse, leaving both legs on one side of the horse and the rider's head on the other side, so that the rider's belt buckle is on top of the saddle.

BLINKERS A hood-like arrangement that restricts the vision of the horse.

BREASTCOLLAR A strap (generally leather) which attaches to and passes from the right side of the saddle to the left side while traversing the chest of the horse. It's used to keep the saddle from sliding back.

BUCK STOPPER A piece of quarter-inch cord (generally nylon) that is tied so it passes just under the upper lip of the horse and circles the head. It usually has a browband and a length of cord that travels the crest of the neck and attaches to the saddle. It causes discomfort when the horse bucks.

CASLICK A procedure that partially closes the vulvic labia of the female horse to reduce air intake.

CHARGEY Used to describe a horse that is anxious to go forward at a more rapid rate of speed than is wanted by the rider.

CUTTING The sorting of cattle. It generally refers to separating one animal at a time from the herd while on horseback.

DORSAL Areas on or near the back.

DUALLY™ HALTER The trademarked name of a particular halter invented by the author.

DUMMY or **MANNEQUIN** A term used for an inanimate human form, for example stuffed human clothing used to simulate a rider.

FLANK An area of a horse's anatomy considered transitional—that area between shoulder and rib cage, or hip and belly.

FLANK CINCH A belt-like object generally fixed to the Western saddle and back from the normal cinch. It's used to anchor the rear portion of a Western saddle.

FOAL HANDLER The name of a piece of equipment designed by the author, used to control untrained foals.

GANGLION Spider-web shaped group of nerves generally associated with the more sensitive areas of the horse's anatomy.

GASKIN Refers to the area of the hind leg between the stifle and hock. The tibia and fibula are the bones of the gaskin.

GIDDY-UP ROPE A braided, cotton-fiber rope with a tassel on one end and loop to fit over wrist on the other. It is used as an aid to create forward motion while riding.

GOGGLES An apparatus similar to blinkers, but with a see-through structure that completely covers the horse's eye.

HARROW An agricultural farm tool often used to prepare the soil of riding areas.

PACIFIER The pacifier is a type of goggle made of see-through wire mesh. It is designed in a dome shape to cover the eye of the horse.

PREDATORY or **"PREDATORIAL"** A word to describe the aggressive actions of a flesh-eating animal.

PRESSURE ZONE That distance from the horse where it is likely that he will decide to press into pressure rather than flee from it.

SACKING OUT The action of tossing a frightening object at a horse with the intent to desensitize.

SAFETY ZONE Used in this context to describe a place where the flight animal feels comfortable to go.

SIDE REINS Belt-like straps of leather with a section of elastic. These are attached to a saddle or surcingle on one end and attached to the horse's bit on the other. When attached, they position themselves approximately where the rider's knees would be.

SURCINGLE Often called a belly band, a surcingle is a belt-like object. It is to be placed around the circumference of the horse's body, most often termed the heart girth. It is generally from 4 to 6 inches (10 to 15 cm) in width, and has an English-style girth on the bottom portion. It may or may not have a breastcollar.

TWITCH A mechanism of restraint most often made by placing a loop of cord at one end of a wooden pole approximately 1 yard (1 meter) in length. The loop of cord is generally about 8 inches (20 cm) in length, and is used to encircle the nose of the horse and twisted in such a fashion that it causes so much discomfort the horse is immobilized.

For More Information

My life's goal is to leave the world a better place than I found it, for horses and for people, too.

In that effort, I invite you to call for further information regarding the Monty Roberts International Learning Center, clinics, conferences, educational videos or other educational material, including my three previously published books:

The Man Who Listens To Horses

Shy Boy: The Horse That Came In from the Wild

Horse Sense for People

USA toll-free
1-888-U2-MONTY
1-888-826-6689

Outside the United States
1-805-688-6288 or 1-805-688-4382
Fax: 1-805-688-2242 or 1-805-688-9709

On line: www.montyroberts.com
E-mail: admin@montyroberts.com

Thank you,

Monty Roberts